I0093207

Understanding Landscape Values: A Scottish Highland Case Study

Camilla Priede

BAR British Series 502
2009

Published in 2016 by
BAR Publishing, Oxford

BAR British Series 502

Understanding Landscape Values: A Scottish Highland Case Study

ISBN 978 1 4073 0628 5

© C Priede and the Publisher 2009

The author's moral rights under the 1988 UK Copyright,
Designs and Patents Act are hereby expressly asserted.

All rights reserved. No part of this work may be copied, reproduced, stored,
sold, distributed, scanned, saved in any form of digital format or transmitted
in any form digitally, without the written permission of the Publisher.

BAR Publishing is the trading name of British Archaeological Reports (Oxford) Ltd.
British Archaeological Reports was first incorporated in 1974 to publish the BAR
Series, International and British. In 1992 Hadrian Books Ltd became part of the BAR
group. This volume was originally published by Archaeopress in conjunction with
British Archaeological Reports (Oxford) Ltd / Hadrian Books Ltd, the Series principal
publisher, in 2009. This present volume is published by BAR Publishing, 2016.

Printed in England

BAR
PUBLISHING

BAR titles are available from:

        BAR Publishing
        122 Banbury Rd, Oxford, OX2 7BP, UK
EMAIL   info@barpublishing.com
PHONE   +44 (0)1865 310431
  FAX   +44 (0)1865 316916
        www.barpublishing.com

Table of Contents

Preface

This work takes an inductive approach to understanding the values that people hold for the landscapes of the Scottish Highlands. In addition to describing these values, the influences on them are also discussed. This is undertaken with reference to fieldwork in the Central Scottish Highlands in two case study areas: Lochtayside and Lochlomondside.

A novel methodology was utilised in this work in order to elicit the opinions of a broad cross-section of the population, from primary school children to adults. This involved both quantitative and qualitative techniques, to understand the influences on landscape perceptions. The strengths and weaknesses of this approach are examined, in particular the use of visual prompts and proxies for the landscape in landscape research. The research finds that the way that people value landscape is a product of their identity and the temporal and cultural contexts of their encounters with the land. It is suggested that similarities in landscape values are caused by similarities in identity, rather than any ideas of the land having a 'materiality' which influences values. Ideas of the Highlands first constructed in the Romantic Movement of the nineteenth century appear to still influence how people view these landscapes today. However, whilst affected by these cultural trends, people's landscape values and the influences thereon are found to be unique to the individual. This has implications for how archaeologists study past landscapes. A phenomenological approach to understanding the past relies on there being an essential sameness to landscape experiences. However, the rethinking of the influences on landscape perceptions in this work shows that there is no way that a researcher in the present can think the same thoughts and understand a landscape in the same way as a person in the past.

This research was funded by an ESRC Case studentship, and the National Trust for Scotland was the partner organisation in this work. As such the research is intended to have practical uses. Recommendations are made for ways of integrating the findings of this research into the landscape designation and planning process. These focus upon the integration of the public's landscape values into landscape planning and designations, the broadening of participation in the planning process and the use of visual proxies in landscape research.

Acknowledgements

Firstly thanks must go to my supervisors Lorna Philip, Douglas Macmillan and Robin Turner (Head of Archaeology for the National Trust for Scotland) for all of their advice and support over the course of this project. As an ESRC Case studentship, this work was supported by the NTS and Loch Lomond and the Trossachs National Park, my thanks to both of these organisations for their financial and practical support. The studentship was also a component of the Ben Lawers Historic Landscape Project, and I am very grateful to all the project partners for their advice and support. In particular thanks go to John Atkinson, for allowing me to hijack his excavation volunteers, and Derek Alexander for introducing me to the project. Images used in this work were provided by Steve Boyle from RCAHMS and I am very grateful for this. Special thanks go to Debbie Jackson, for all of her help and advice with the schools element of this research, without her guidance this would not have worked so well.

This research would not have been possible without the participation of volunteers. I am extremely grateful to staff and pupils at Killin, Kenmore and Luss Primary Schools, participants on NTS Ben Lawers Thistle Camps and residents of Killin, for giving up their time to undertake an exercise, the purpose of which could not be described fully before their participation. Thanks also to NTS staff at Lynedoch, Killin and to the LLTNP ranger service at Luss for allowing me to use their premises, and helping with the recruitment of volunteers.

Thanks are also due to the postgraduate communities at both Aberdeen and Kent Universities, for their friendship and support (both academic and emotional!). Thanks also go to friends and family, in particular my dad, Monty for his continued support and belief in me. Special thanks must go to my husband Tim Allen, who through the course of this research has fulfilled the roles of IT helpdesk, agony aunt, proof reader, sounding-board and friend.

Any errors that remain in this work are very much my own.

1

Understanding Landscape Values:
A Scottish Highland Case Study

1.1. Introduction

This work examines the values that people hold for the landscapes of the Scottish Highlands. The Scottish Highlands are famous globally for their spectacular scenery and are a popular tourist destination. Although often thought of as 'wild' and 'unspoiled' these landscapes are the product of millennia of human activity and face considerable pressures from tourism, agriculture, and other developments including wind farms and associated infrastructure. There is no one 'best' way to manage these landscapes, and all management decisions involve making value judgements.

The central premise of this work is that to make decisions about the best way to curate landscapes it is necessary to understand the values that people have for landscape, and what are the main influences on these values. Currently landscape designations tend to be based on material qualities, and largely on the opinion of expert 'landscape professionals'. Landscape planning decisions take account of these material designations, with 'public opinion' often taking a backseat. This is something which is changing in Scotland, with the most recent planning legislation (The Planning etc (Scotland) Act 2006) calling for increased public participation in the planning process.

It is argued within this work that the values that 'the general public' have for landscape should be fully incorporated within landscape planning and policy. As such it is necessary to develop a greater understanding of the way that people relate to and value landscapes. Coupled with this, there is a need to widen participation within the planning system, to include communities who are traditionally excluded from the planning process.

1.2. A Highland Case Study

The doctoral research reported in this book was funded as an ESRC CASE studentship with the National Trust for Scotland (NTS) being the collaborative partner. Two key research questions were identified at the outset:

• How can qualitative preferences and values for landscape best be captured and measured in a repeatable and reliable manner?

• To what extent and in what ways does an increased knowledge of landscape history affect people's landscape preferences and values?

The first research question refers to the fact that landscape is a public good: it is something experienced by everyone. Therefore organisations charged with caring for the environment should consult on how to best manage the landscape in a way which the public wants. Decisions can no longer just be based on professional/academic opinions, and there is a need to determine what public values for landscape are. This is important as currently there is no understanding as to whether aspects of landscape that are valued by experts are the same aspects that are valued by people more generally.

There is no consensus on the best way to examine landscape values, with various different methodologies having been used in previous research. No standard methods exist for assessing both preferences for landscape and the influences on these values that are repeatable with a large cross section of the population. Many studies into human-landscape interaction in the social sciences and humanities take the form of embedded qualitative research, which is not readily repeatable, or quantitative research using economic measures which records the strength of these preferences without understanding where these preferences and values are rooted. Bearing all of these issues in mind, the first research question was reworded to:

Revised Question 1: What methods can be utilised to understand qualitative preferences for landscapes, which work with a large cross section of the population, and can be used in a repeatable and reliable manner?

It was realised early on in the research that it was not possible to examine knowledge of landscape history without looking at ideas of knowledge in general and how what you know affects what aspects of a landscape you value and what these values actually are. It was also realised that there is currently a poor understanding of what the main influences are on people's landscape values. It is argued here that understanding the influences on people's values is instrumental to understanding the values themselves, and as such the second research question was revised to:

Revised Question 2: What are the main influences on peoples' landscape perceptions and values?

This book works with the definition of landscape set out in the European Landscape Convention (2003); that landscape *means an area, as perceived by people whose character is the result of action and interaction of natural and/or human factors*. This is the idea that landscape is not the physical surroundings themselves, but instead the individual's landscape is based on their interpretation of these surroundings. It is therefore necessary to understand what this landscape is, what it contains, and what it is of the landscape that people care about.

1.3. Structure of the PhD Research

This research was funded by an Economic and Social Research Council CASE studentship. The collaborative partner was the National Trust for Scotland, who received money to fund their contribution to the studentship from the Loch Lomond and the Trossachs National Park (LLTNP) who subsequently had limited formal involvement in the PhD. CASE studentships were developed by the Research Councils to foster collaboration between academia and industry, and for research projects to be undertaken on real life 'problems'. In this case, the problem involved was finding new ways to understand landscape values.

Because of the nature of this research, the case study areas (Lochtayside and a comparative study area within LLTNP) and sample population were predetermined at the start of the study. The fact that the research had to provide information that was of relevance to the partner organisation also set parameters to the type of study that could be undertaken. These constraints are further discussed in the methodology chapter.

1.3.1. A Personal Note

My background is in archaeology. As an archaeologist I am used to working with a limited body of material evidence in order to reconstruct past lifeways. Archaeological research necessitates an inductive approach where the material is worked with primarily, and theories are based on the material evidence. Working as an archaeologist has led me to develop an understanding of the importance of context: when material is excavated it can only be understood in relation to other material found on the site, and on other similar sites. Without context this material cannot be understood fully: it can be understood typologically, or valued for its beauty, or rarity, or other reasons, but it cannot be related in any way to its original use. I was therefore surprised when I first approached literature about landscape values to find that most studies worked with the premise that value and meaning was inherent within the landscape, rather than being guided by the contexts in which landscape is experienced. It is this background which led me to be almost more interested in the influences on a person's perceptions of landscape than the perceptions themselves, and to realise the importance of understanding the context of people's landscape perceptions when

forming landscape policies.

1.4. Outline

This work commences with a literature review (Chapter 2), in which the concepts of 'landscape' and 'value' will be unpackaged. Both are complex constructs which can be understood in a number of ways. The main schools of thought in determining the values that people hold for landscape are introduced, in terms of what academic discourses they are situated within. This will include some central tenants of this work including the concept of materiality, which is often used as a way of explaining why certain landscape features are valued by many, whereas others are commonly disliked. This work refutes materiality as a causal mechanism for landscape values, as when landscape values through time are examined it is clear that the same physical spaces and features have been understood and values in different ways at different periods. Instead it is suggested that the issue of context is key to the understanding of how people perceive landscapes. Context can be summarised as the circumstances in which a person encounters and builds relationships with a landscape. This idea of context is separated into three different aspects, those of time, culture and identity, and aspects of these will be introduced within the literature review. As a CASE studentship this research had to have relevance in the 'real world' as well as academic relevance, and as such it was decided to examine how methods used and information gathered in the course of this research could inform landuse and landscape policy decisions. In order to situate this work an overview of landscape policies and methods of landscape assessment currently used in Scotland is included in the literature review.

The third chapter is an introduction to the two case study areas chosen for fieldwork, Loch Tay and Loch Lomond. The rationale for the selection of these areas is discussed and their physical properties and history, as well as profiles of the case study communities, are presented. In this chapter the role of the NTS and the LLTNP in supporting this research is also discussed further, along with the Ben Lawers Historic Landscape Project which this research is a component of.

Chapter four outlines the methods used in this research. An inductive approach was taken, insofar as instead of any one hypothesis being tested, the premise that 'people have values for landscape and it is necessary to understand what these values are' was worked with. This is instead of any one specific hypothesis such as 'this research will investigate the premise that people from urban areas value different qualities of the landscape than those from rural areas'. It was also decided that it was necessary to work with sectors of the community other than those commonly consulted in landscape research. To this end primary school children participated in research as an example of a community generally excluded from research. The process of finding a method which would be accessible to participants of all ages is introduced and the rationale of this methodology is discussed, alongside the process of recruiting participants. This is important, as if only a sample of the population drawn from a certain demographic group (e.g. those on the electoral roll who have ticked the box to allow their details to be made public) are worked with then it is likely that only a small subset of the spectrum of values that people hold for landscapes will be discovered.

Chapter five briefly presents the information collected for this study, in terms of a profile of the research participants, and what aspects they value of the landscape and why. One of the exercises used in this research to used photographs as visual proxies for the landscape, and findings from this section of the research highlighted problems with this method, these issues are discussed here.

Chapter six presents an in-depth discussion of the information collected, in terms of understanding what influences individual's landscape values. These will be situated within the different contexts that affect people's relationships with the land, and in turn their landscape values. After this the second discussion chapter examines the way that landscapes and heritage features are currently managed. Whether these current designations and polices reflect the values that the public hold for landscapes will

be discussed, and recommendations will be made for ways of changing these designations to reflect public values. In particular methods for the assessment of people's landscape values within a planning and policy context will be discussed. Issues surrounding using a purely people lead approach to landscape and heritage legislation will also be discussed, in terms of the need to overcome a 'now bias' where features that are currently not valued may be valued by future generations. This work presented in this book also has implications for the way that past ideas of landscape are studied, and this chapter will contain a critique of current methods in landscape archaeology. These methods currently rely on an idea that there is an essential same-ness that is inherent within experiences of landscape, which thus allow the researcher to understand past ideas of landscape by recreating these experiences in the present. This idea will be deconstructed here.

This work concludes with an overview of and reflection on the work undertaken and conclusions which can be drawn from this. New avenues of research which could be investigated as a result of this work are suggested and wider academic, policy and practical implications of the research are considered.

2
Literature Review

2.1. Introduction

This chapter will review the main strands of literature drawn upon in this book. The research contains two complex concepts, landscape and value. These terms are used in a variety of ways within the academic community, and the first section of this review will focus on defining landscape and then value as they are used in this work. Landscape as it is understood in relation to the Picturesque and Romantic movements will be examined. This will be undertaken within the context of the history of the term landscape, and will be discussed further with particular reference to the history of Scotland. Later in this work, it will be argued that the central tenets of the Romantic Movement remain an important influence on how the landscapes of the Scottish Highlands are understood by people. There are very specific reasons that make this the case (Edmonds 2006, Prentice & Guerin 1998). Later cultural trends which were borne out of these movements, including nationalism and anti modernity will also be discussed, both generally and within a specific Scottish context.

The different meanings of value will be discussed. It is a term that can be understood in a number of different ways, and is used in these different ways by the various academic disciplines that examine 'landscape value'. This leads onto an examination of what different schools of thought consider to be the influences on landscape values. The second research question investigated within this work focuses on the understanding of these influences. The idea of materiality (the land having inherent material properties which act as an anchor for meaning and value) will be discussed, alongside an alternative idea, and one which is favoured by this research, that an understanding of the context of individuals' landscape values is the key to understanding them. In the discussion (chapter 6) the different contexts of people's landscape values will be examined, and it will be argued that the temporal context of encounter with the landscape is a key influence on landscape values. Therefore in this chapter the different ideas of time that will be examined later in this work will be outlined.

As a CASE project it was always intended that this work would have practical uses. Recommendations will be made in chapter 7 about how results from this study may be used to inform methodologies used for examining landscape perceptions which are used for the creation of landscape policies. Therefore this review will finish with an overview of landscape policies and designations as they pertain to the Scottish landscape.

2.2. Defining Landscape

This section will discuss the various ways that the term 'landscape' has been understood.

2.2.1. The first 'Landscape'

The word 'landscape' reached English from the German term *landschaft* which simply means 'a bounded area of land'. However, the term 'landscape' or *landscap*, as it is now understood as a cultural construct first emerged as a way of seeing in the 15th and 16th centuries in renaissance Italy and the Netherlands (Olwig 2005, Winchester et.al. 2003, Bender 2006). It was founded upon scientific theories and knowledge and involved the use of visual tools such as perspective to map the world in a rational way with 'everything in its proper place'. This was of great importance in the emergence of a Colonial age, as tools of mapping born from this movement were used to legitimise claims to lands discovered in the New World. This same process is evident at a smaller scale in the British Isles as at this time some of the first scale representations of large estates were created (Bendall 1992). Many of these representations were created in order to plan wholesale remodelling of the land, allow reallocation of land to tenants in demarcated and regulated plots, and create designed parkland landscapes for the enjoyment of the aristocracy (Hoskins 1955, Shaw-Taylor 2001, Williamson 2002). This first idea of landscape was synonymous with 'prospect', insofar as early understandings focus on a landscape which you look 'out on' rather than 'exist within' (Cosgrove 1985). Ideas of mapping and landscape in this early usage were all about control, to map a place was to own it and all the people and resources which existed within.

"I'M *'Picturesque'—I suppose* YOU'RE *'Wind-tossed-Celtic-mystery'* . . . . . ?"

Figure 2-1 The Picturesque and Romantic Movements, as viewed by Emmet of 'Punch' Magazine (1948)

2.2.2. Landscape in the Picturesque and Romantic movements & beyond

For centuries after the invention of the term, landscape was used solely and largely uncritically as a term referring to the aesthetic qualities of scenery (Schama 1996). The aesthetic landscape is particularly linked to the Picturesque and Romantic movements in which artists such as Constable and Landseer created paintings of 'ideal' landscapes and designers such as Humphrey Repton, and Lancelot 'Capability' Brown created 'ideal' landscape parks (Smout 2005, Williamson 1995). In the Picturesque, a whole series of conventions were created to advise artists and people venturing out into the countryside of the best way to 'see' and to reproduce scenic beauty (e.g. Gilpin 1789).

The Romantic Movement can be seen to develop as a reaction against the rational theories of the Enlightenment (Hunt 1993, Duncan et al 2004). Enlightenment philosophers, including Smith and Hume embraced the humanist ideas of the Renaissance and attempted to order the world through structured, objective thought. In the Enlightenment mode of thinking '*man* (sic) *was valued for*

his rational intellect and ability to comprehend the laws of nature' [In contrast the Romantics] '*valued man rather for his imaginative and spiritual aspirations, his emotional depths, his artistic creativity*' (Tarmas 1991:367). Both movements can be seen to have humanist roots, but they celebrated drastically different traits in humanity. Within the Romantic movement the irrational was celebrated, with particular emphasis on scenic beauty and sublime 'horror' of landscape (Edmonds 2006). The Picturesque movement can be seen almost as a stepping stone between the two philosophies; it celebrates sublime beauty, but in a very ordered way, with a vast number of rules set out by 'experts' to guide the uneducated gaze in the best way to 'see' a landscape. The Picturesque sensibility also involved the alteration of the land and of built structures to make them conform to these rules (the polite parklands of Capability Brown are part of this tradition) (Williamson 1995). The idea of a movement which is supposedly celebrating the natural advocating the 'improvement' of nature is mocked by William Combe in his (1809) *Tour of Dr Syntax in Search of the Picturesque* which also highlights the fact that the Picturesque view was one which excluded seeing the real hardships faced by the everyday rural population. A similar accusation can also be levied at the Romantic movement, for their portrayal of everyday people as 'noble savages', who live happily, and timelessly at one with nature (Womack 1989, Whyte & Whyte 1991). There is something of a continuum of these ideas evident in the Nationalist philosophies of the early twentieth century, these are discussed more fully below.

The Scottish Highlands feature large in the Romantic movement from when James Macpherson claimed to 'rediscover' the works of Ossian in the 1760's (Duncan et al. 2004) through the literary work and tartanry of Walter Scott (Muir 1936, Reed 1980), and Queen Victoria's attachment to Royal Deeside (Withers 1993). The Highlands were not celebrated within the Picturesque, mainly because the political situation in the mid eighteenth century meant that the area was unsafe for outsiders to visit and were thus seldom visited (Fry 2005, Prebble 1971). The shift in attitudes from the Picturesque to the Romantic movement can be seen to be precipitated by a shift in the political relations between Britain and the idea of the Scottish Highlands which altered its perception from being a place of real danger, to a place imbued with scenery and a history which can be celebrated for its sublime 'horror' and noble savagery (Glendening 1997). This is part of a wider trend evident at this time of empire building where the removal of perceived (and real) threats leads to nostalgic imaginings of places and landscapes, which are now celebrated for their 'irrational' anti-modernity (Tilley 2006, Schama 1995).

2.2.3. 20th Century Landscapes – Nationalism to Postmodernism

Cosgrove (1985) suggests that the humanist renaissance in geography of the 1970's and 80's brought the idea of landscape back to the forefront of social science research. The idea of landscape as a social, cultural construct was developed. This was first purported by Carl Sauer, of the Berkeley School of geography in the first half of the twentieth century. Sauer talked about cultures fashioning a landscape from the physical surroundings they inhabited, suggesting that *'culture is the agent, the natural area is the medium, the cultural landscape is the result'* (Sauer 1925:343). He suggested that this landscape is created both through physical manipulation, and the mental constructs and memories of the culture inhabiting the area (Ashmore & Knapp 1999). The work of the Berkeley School was a reaction against the environmental determinist school of geography (Crang 1998). The central tenet of the environmental determinist idea is that *'man* [sic] *is a product of the earth's surface'* (Semple, E 1911:1), and as such all lives are controlled by the physical environment. The ability of societies to progress was governed by the physical geography of their surroundings, and as such certain 'primitive' societies were unable to progress from their present 'uncivilised' state (Crang 1998). Ideas of environmental determinism were heavily influential in the Nationalist philosophies of the early twentieth

century. The ideas of certain cultures having ancestral homelands, which could be traced by the identification of certain 'cultural complexes' was purported by several archaeologists including Vere Gordon Childe in his 1929 work 'the Aryans'. It was believed that nations' homelands could be traced through the distribution of key artefact and building types. These ideas were used by researchers such as Gustaf Cossina to rationalise National Socialism, by suggesting that the Nazis were just working to reclaim the ancestral homelands of the Aryans who now inhabited Germany (Preucel & Hodder 1996, Halle 2005).

One of the first researchers to react against the strict environmental deterministic ideas of people-landscape interactions was Martin Heidegger (1870 – 1976) (Seamon & Mugerauer 1989). Heidegger, working in the early twentieth century, reacted against Cartesian philosophy with its distinctions between Nature, Culture, Mind and Body, dismissing them as a modern creation, and one which should not be treated as 'a given'. Instead people and place should be seen as parts of the same entity (Thomas 1999). In other words landscape shapes people at the same time as they shape their landscape, indeed people and place cannot be studied as separate entities. This is similar to environmental determinism but, in this case humans are seen as forging a cultural landscape, instead of being created by their physical surroundings. Heidegger developed his theories of 'dwelling' in an era where there had been a rapid expansion in long distance travel, exploration, anthropology and ethnography. Suddenly a vast corpus of information about people from far off places was available, places where peoples' cosmologies and epistemologies were completely opposite to western rationalism (Milton 2002). Society in these places existed in opposition to the industrial philosophies of Northern Europe, which saw man (sic) conquering and commanding nature (Schama 1996). Instead, accounts were coming of communities which had intimate connections with their place, to the extent that they are ultimately inseparable as is the case with aboriginal Australians (Chatwin 1989). Heidegger suggested that these people were living 'authentic' lives, in harmony with nature, and advocated that Europeans should strive for a simpler, more authentic life that was connected to their own environment and 'ancestral homeland'. It was out of this that the first ideas of landscape as a cultural construct were born however these theories fell out of fashion for several decades, mainly because Heidegger had been a member of the Nazi party and his theories of 'dwelling' and 'authenticity' had been used to legitimise the actions of the Third Reich, by providing a rationale for the 'cleansing' of Europe (Thomas 1999, Eickhoff 2005).

After World War II theories of cultural landscape were tainted by this brush with extremism, and as such both Archaeology and Geography shifted to a 'new' paradigm which was characterised by rigid quasi-scientific research undertaken into people – environment interactions (Trigger 1990; Barnes 2001). Within Geography there was a 'quantitative revolution' in thinking, as disciplinary paradigms shifted from being merely descriptive to quasi-

Value (Oxford English Dictionary 2006)

1. *That amount of some commodity, medium of exchange, etc., which is considered to be an equivalent for something else; a fair or adequate equivalent or return. Phr. value for money (freq. attrib.).*

2. *The material or monetary worth of a thing; the amount at which it may be estimated in terms of some medium of exchange or other standard of a similar nature.*

3. *of value, valuable. of. value, possessed of (a specified) material or monetary worth.*

4. *The equivalent (in material worth) of a specified sum or amount.*

5. *Worth or worthiness (of persons) in respect of rank or personal qualities. Obs.*

6. *The relative status of a thing, or the estimate in which it is held, according to its real or supposed worth, usefulness, or importance. In Philos. and Social Sciences, regarded esp. in relation to an individual or group; gen. in pl., the principles or standards of a person or society, the personal or societal judgment of what is valuable and important in life.*

Figure 2-2. Definitions of value, as given in the Oxford English Dictionary

scientific, as observances of human interactions were shaped into theoretical models such as those created by Weber and Christaller (e.g. Berry & Marble 1968). Archaeologists borrowed from this 'new' geography and a processual archaeology was born. Mathematical models were used to predict settlement patterns, and social interactions (e.g. Clark 1968, Binford & Binford 1968), and the reconstruction of scientifically provable 'atheoretical' elements of the archaeological record such as environmental histories and subsistence patterns were the key subjects studied. Revolutions in computer science meant that increasingly complex models and patterns could be computed (Barnes 2001). There was, however, an understanding that this reversion to environmental possiblistic geographies and archaeologies meant any understanding of how individuals and cultures interact with and create landscapes was being lost (Trigger 1990 Hodder 1982). It was realised that computer models of 'human-environment' interactions avoided any meaningful discussion of social relations. For example, research in to the Mesolithic period was characterised as *'hunter-gatherers have*[ing] *ecological relationships with hazelnuts'* rather than social relations with each other, or the land around them (Bradley 1984:11). This dissatisfaction was coupled with a renewed social acceptability in the late 1970s and early 1980s for social scientists to deal with concepts as 'cultural landscapes' as theories such as Heidegger's became destigmatised (Crang 1998).

The term landscape is now in common usage within the academy as a social construct, created by the actions, memories, and identities of the society that inhabits an area, and this is the sense in which it will be utilised in this work. Within a heritage and environment management context, decisions are increasingly made at a landscape scale, this is discussed further in section 2.7 of this chapter.

The postmodernist school of thought suggests that there is no environment, only landscape (Ucko 1999). It has been argued that a place with no human experience (and therefore no history) does not exist and is merely blank space, regardless of its physical appearance (Tuan 1977). Places

and landscapes emerge through their use and understanding by humans. They are produced by 'dwelling' a concept derived from Heidegger, and revisited in this resurgence of landscape study (Thomas 1999). Ingold defines a dwelling perspective as *'a perspective that treats the immersion of the organism-person in an environment or lifeworld as an inescapable condition of existence'* (2000: 153). It is the idea that people create meaning of the environment by dwelling or inhabiting within it (something exemplified by Tuan 1977:6 *'What begins as undifferentiated space becomes place as we get to know it better and endow it with value'*.). This inhabitation is not necessarily physical, indeed Ingold argues that by the time a person visits a place first hand they already have a mental construct of it; one which is created solely from second hand information so it is already part of their landscape biography. Ingold (pers comm.) also argues that it is impossible to think of separate fixed 'places', and that instead life operates at the scale of the landscape, with certain 'nodes' accruing meaning through repeated use.

This research uses the definition that *'Landscape means an area, as perceived by people, whose character is the result of the action and interaction of natural and/or human factors'* (as defined in the European Landscape Convention 2006). It will explore the tenets that people create their own landscapes through exploring, imagining and learning about and discussing the world, and examine what influences the landscapes that people create. This definition was selected as it is one that has been agreed upon and adopted across Europe, and allows for the idea that as well as being a physical entity, landscapes are conceived within the minds of people.

2.3. Defining Value

The previous section of this review explored the concept of landscape, and how it has been used, and refined through time. This work deals with a second problematic concept, that of value. Value is a term which has multiple definitions and is used in a variety of ways within the sphere of the social sciences (Reser & Bentrupperbäumer 2005). The following section will review the different definitions of value, demonstrate how they have been used, and how the term value will be used within this work. The different value types ascribed to the cultural landscape will be addressed.

The above figure shows just some of the multiple meanings of 'value'. In a strict economic sense the 'value' of a commodity equates to the monetary worth that a person will place upon that commodity. In other social sciences, 'value' takes on a more complicated meaning. In the social sciences values are understood as the 'worth' of an item in moral terms (Graber 2001). What both of these definitions of value (and the many definitions in between these two poles) have in common is that there is a realisation that value only exists within the minds, or the society of the people who are placing the value (ibid), nothing has an inherent material worth. When trying to define values in the 1940's and 1950's Clyde Kluckhorn said that values are *'conceptions of the desirable'* (Graber 2001:3). They are ideas of what people want, and ought to like in life but not the meaning of it; in other words all values are culturally constructed. The difference between the two disciplines, and therefore the way that they understand value is that *'Economics is about predicting individual behaviour; anthropology is about understanding collective differences'* (Graber 2001: 8). Economists are interested in gaining a general idea of the value that people give to a place, in order to predict how the individual will think about this. Anthropology, and other social sciences are interested in understanding the differences in what different individuals and societies value of the world, and why these differences occur (ibid.). This book will examine the influences on people's values as well as examining simply what people's values are. It will work with the idea that landscape values are individual and shared community or societal beliefs about the significance, importance and meaning of the landscape. These values are *'within human individuals, and find expression and representation across all human activities, relationships and cultural products'* (Reser & Bentrupperbäumer 2005:141). Therefore, by studying people's relationships with the land, you can uncover the values that they hold for the landscape, and the underlying reasons for these.

2.3.1. Investigating Landscape Values

When investigating the concept of landscape values, a multitude of definitions have been invoked, which have at their hearts the different disciplines which they are rooted within (Reser & Bentrupperbäumer 2005). In this section some of the different types of landscape value will be discussed. In previous studies (from within both the academic and policy communities) a variety of schemes have been used to describe the different types of values that landscapes and heritage features can have (e.g. Carver 1996, Darvill 1995, Garrod & Willis 1999, Hewison & Holden 2006). Many attempts to create schemes of value end up oversimplifying this complex topic, or rely overly on 'intrinsic' value which is linked to the idea of there

being a material fact of landscape to which values are attached. Issues with this will be discussed further within this section and throughout this work.

Landscape is a public good, in that its *'consumption by one person in no way detracts from its availability to others'* (Garrod & Willis 1999:9) and it not possible for the owner of a public good to prevent people from using it. It is possible to place restrictions in the form of this use; for example anyone can look out on a hillside, but certain areas may be fenced off to access (Brown and Taylor 2000, Darvill 1995). Public goods can be seen to have both 'use' and 'non use' values; values that come from the use of the resource, and values that come from their very existence in people's minds.

Use values for landscape include (Garrod & Willis 1999)

• Informational Value: The information that can be gained from studying a resource, and the value of its use as an educational tool.

• Option Value: The option to use the resource for economic gain in the future.

• Economic Value: The monetary value that can be attached to the use of a resource, for example.

Non-use values include (Garrod & Willis 1999)

• Altruistic Value: The value that comes from the realisation others may benefit from this good.

• Bequest Value: The desire to conserve a resource for future generations

• Existence Value: The value that people give to a good (a building/landscape); which results simply from it 'just being there'.

The idea of features or landscapes having an intrinsic value is one which is dominant within the heritage community (Hewison & Holden 2006). It is one which is problematic as it assumes that a good has an inherent worth. Whilst landscapes may have a worth outside economic systems this worth is not something which exists within the physical landscape. Instead it is cultural value created by the society valuing the land (Bourdieu 1984, Thompson 1979). Thompson's (1979) *'Rubbish Theory'* describes the process by which an object moves from having a market value, to having no value (it is in essence rubbish), to having cultural value where it is valued not for its original use or original reasons. Thompson uses the antiques market to demonstrate how an item which once had value for its potential use (e.g. a toy car) goes through a process of becoming 'rubbish' (i.e. not valued for any purpose and perhaps having negative value) to becoming an 'antique' where it is values for cultural reasons including rarity, sentimentality and desirability, but not necessarily as a toy. Cultural values are the values which reflect a society's or an individual's relationships with that item, they are driven by desires or beliefs which are separate from the original worth of an item and change as society changes. Landscapes do not have a market value in the first place, being a public good, and not spatially bounded since they exist within the mind, but Rubbish Theory acts as a demonstration of how items accrue 'cultural values'; and how these cultural values are not intrinsic, but instead reflect how a society *at that time* values an object (Carman 2002, Reser & Bentrupperbäumer 2005).

In 1992 the concept of 'cultural landscape' was adopted by UNESCO World Heritage Committee (Jones 2003). This category was developed to provide protection, not just for landscapes which have been fashioned by humans, but also landscapes which have significant value because of their cultural associations. These associative values are about attachments people have to a place, not necessarily about the physical environment, about experiences and memories of a place (Alexandra & Riddington 2006, Proshansky et al 1993, Simmons 1993). Cultural values for landscape also include literary and artistic associations of a place, for example the Trossachs of Walter Scott, or Hardy's Wessex (Schama 1995, Muir 1935). There is no consensus as to the best approach to studying cultural or other values for landscape. The rationale behind different approaches is outlined below.

2.3.2. Determining Values: An Economic Approach

Economic valuation of the environment operates under the premise that there are multiple values that can be ascribed to landscape, including aesthetic, emotional and cultural values. However, environmental economists suggest that all of these values can be seen as influential in terms of the monetary value a person will put on a landscape (Garrod & Willis 1999). As such, it is assumed that these values can be represented by a monetary figure (EFTEC 2005). It is suggested that landscapes and heritage assets (Getty Institute 1999) can be seen as non-market commodities with both use and non-use values, which can be calculated and used to determine a landscape's overall 'worth'.

Use values of heritage sites or landscapes might include visits made to a site by people or the use of premises such as a listed building for a business enterprise (Garrod & Willis 1999). Use values can be modelled by simple economic tools, one of which is the 'travel cost' method whereby the total cost to a person visiting a site is taken into account (including transport costs, admission costs, food and gift-shop purchases). In this model the 'travel cost' is seen as a direct expression of how much a person 'values' the use of the site. When a site is free to access, a 'payment card' approach, involving individuals' Willingness To Pay (WTP) to visit a site, is considered. WTP methodologies involve asking individuals to state the greatest amount of money that they would be willing to pay as an entrance fee for accessing a site or area.

Contingent Valuation methodologies and Non-use values

Non-use values can be measured by contingent valuation (cv) techniques, which are part of a suite of economic techniques known as 'stated preference techniques' in which individuals make choices about how much the presence of a thing means to them (Willis & Garrod 1993 Venkatachalam 2004). People have to decide how much a resource means to them in relation to other (generally financial) choices. Sample questions in a cv study might be:

'Tax payers would have to cover some of the cost of conserving this landscape feature. How much extra would you be willing to pay on your quarterly council tax bill?'

Or

'If the stone circle was removed, local residents would be compensated for this loss. What is the minimum amount of compensation you would be willing to accept?'

The sum of all these different use and non-use values for a site is the 'Total Economic Value' of its existence, and this can be measured against the costs of managing a site or landscape and the money which is lost by not commercially developing an area (Macmillan et. al 2002). Using these techniques, it is possible to determine what way makes 'economic good sense' to develop and interpret a landscape.

Problems with the Economic valuation of landscapes

On some levels, there is much to recommend an economic approach to the valuation of landscapes. Such studies can be undertaken in a short timeframe and produce relatively 'clear cut' results that can be proven accurate by a variety of statistical means. As such, they are very popular in the short timeframe of land-use policy studies, where there are limited funds, and specific policy decisions are being evaluated (e.g. Colombo et al 2006, Macmillan et al 2002, Willis et.al 1996). There are, however, several shortcomings to a purely economic approach to the valuation of landscape and some of these will be outlined here.

One of the central problems in economic landscape valuation is that the results exist only in the 'present' in which the survey is undertaken. This leads to significant problems when the data are used outside of this time-limited context. By situating a study in the present, economic evaluations of landscape do not take into account future potential changes to the landscape. It may be that in the future a particular feature becomes increasingly rare, and therefore is of increasing value. The longhouse of the Scottish Highlands is one of a multitude of possible examples of a type of structure which was until recently ubiquitous but is now very rare. This type of building, dating from the late eighteenth century was once the typical vernacular form of the area but through time the majority of these houses were either modified into larger structures or abandoned and left to decay (Soulsby 1993, Harrison 2005). The remaining standing unmodified examples are now seen as culturally significant as mnemonic devices used to recall past life-ways, and are thus conserved, with people paying large amounts to visit examples in remote areas of the Highlands. Had a contingent valuation of longhouses sites been undertaken in the early twentieth century, they would undoubtedly have been seen as worthless, rather than 'priceless' as they are now widely perceived. They have gone through the value cycle from economic to cultural value as outlined in Thompson's 'Rubbish Theory' (1979).

In order to counter this 'present moment' effect economic studies often include expert witness reports about what is, and what may become 'culturally significant' within a landscape. However, not all landscape users are 'experts'. Landscape laypeople also have perceptions and values for landscape which must be taken into account when undertaking examinations of a landscape's worth (Strang 1999, Moore-Coyler & Scott 2005, O'Rourke 2005). This is one of a variety of ethical considerations which have been highlighted pertaining to valuation of the environment, (Azqueta & Delacamara 2006). Other issues are problems of defining a community for landscape research (O'Rourke 2005), and the fact that landscape decisions made today will affect how the landscape is shaped in the future. The issue of defining a community for landscape research is particularly pertinent to the Scottish Highlands, as they are an iconic area valued globally for their scenic and associative qualities (Paterson 2002, McCrone et al 1995). This will be discussed in more detail in section 4.5.1.1 of the methodology chapter.

Another issue with economic valuations of the environment is that the product of the research is a single monetary figure, or a number of figures given by a certain individuals. In many studies (e.g. Willis & Garrod 1993) there is little emphasis on understanding how this figure is reached. This delivers no understanding of what elements of the landscape people care about (although a guess can be made when the study involves choice experiments). Without an understanding of the context of landscape perceptions (as will be discussed further below) the results of economic studies are just figures which cannot be understood in relation to any actions, motivations and interests in a person's life. This is by far the main issue in classic economic studies of the environment, although more recent studies, and critiques of these studies (e.g. Becker 2006, Faber 2008, Schlapfer 2008) are attempting to address this by integrating these quantitative studies with qualitative information. The use of mixed methods in landscape research will be discussed more fully in section 4.4 of the methodology chapter.

2.3.3. Understanding values for landscape. A qualitative approach

Social sciences working in the qualitative tradition of research often adhere to a post-modern idea of cultural landscape as discussed in section 2.2.3 above. This idea of landscape can be summated as 'there is still no answer to what landscape is; it is still very much a case of what it can be' (Johnson 1998: 58). Individuals create a personal landscape from their interpretation of the surrounding world, and this landscape is imbued with 'cultural values'.

Qualitative research into perceptions and values for landscape often involves discovering an understanding of what people's values for landscape are and discovering the influences on these values (Bryman 2001, Cloke et al 2004). Methodologies for these studies commonly involve the 'embedding' of a researcher within a society to understand how people's value systems work (e.g. Layton 1999, Lee 2007). These studies produce very rich data which are not easily reduced to answer the specific questions of some policy-lead research projects. The relatively long timeframe for research such as this also makes it unsuitable for policy driven research. As a result of this a variety of methods have been developed to produce 'rich' qualitative data that can be processed in a shorter time frame (e.g. McCormack 2002, Robertson et al 2003, Young & Barrett 2001) and contain elements of quantitative data. The methodology employed in this research draws from this body of work which will be discussed more fully in chapter 3 of this work.

Materiality and the Landscape Idea

In the qualitative tradition of research, emphasis is placed upon discovering the roots of cultural values for landscape. Often this involves the search for a 'big theory' to explain these influences, and the similarities between people's perceptions as well as cultural differences. Anthropologists such as Barbara Bender have long argued that landscapes are subject to multivocality, that there are multiple ways of viewing and understanding a landscape, and that no two people will experience a landscape in the same way (Bender 1993, 1998, 1999, Allison 1999, Derby 2000, Hirsch & O'Hanlon 1996). Bender (2006:303) argues that *'The same place at the same moment will be experienced differently by different people; the same place at different moments will be experienced differently by the same person: the same person may even, at a given moment, hold conflicting feelings about a place'*. She suggests that, although there are a huge number of permutations for people-place interactions landscape possesses a 'materiality' which sets up restraints and constraints which make it impossible to act in certain ways, or to experience certain things. Materiality can be defined as substance, of something comprised of physical elements or constituents. It has been described as *'the tangible, existing or concrete, the substantial, the worldly and real as opposed to imaginary, ideal and value laden aspects of human existence'* (Tilley et al 2006:3). It therefore supposes that landscapes have essential characteristics which act as guidelines to people's perceptions, that they have a guiding 'agency' which places the human 'actor' in certain mindsets (Jones 2006), and means that they will think in certain ways.

Stedman (2003) concurs with this view, suggesting two models to explain the constraints on perception that humans have. In his 'meaning mediated model' he suggests that certain settings lend themselves to certain meanings or interpretations. For example an area with a low population density is far more likely to be viewed as a 'wilderness' than a busy urban centre. He expands upon this, and avoids being overly environmentally deterministic by forwarding an 'experiential model' wherein he suggests that *'previous behaviours or experiences of landscape may create lenses through which humans attribute meanings to landscape'* (Stedman 2003:674). He suggests that whilst an area such as a field can only be viewed in certain ways, the way that individuals think about this is governed by factors linked to their identity. Therefore a field will be viewed in very different ways by a farmer, a hunter, or a property developer.

Stedman's research in Lakeland Wisconsin reveals that, to the people who visit, 'wild' lakes have very different meanings to ones which are more developed. Less developed lakes tend to inspire more feelings of 'escape' and 'freedom' than ones with more buildings. He also demonstrates that these feelings of 'escape' are only associated with visitors to the areas, whereas local residents will talk about them being 'at home'. Williams and Vaske (2003) agree with this analysis suggesting that 'place attachment' is embedded in the physical characteristics of a landscape, and as the physical appearance of the landscape changes, peoples' relationships are affected. It is therefore vital to understand which aspects of the physical landscape are integral to people's place attachment, to ensure that these relationships are conserved, promoted and fostered. From a management and tourism perspective this is also important, so that decisions can be made as to which aspects of a landscape should be marketed to different sectors of the population.

Again focussing on the material elements of landscape, Prentice and Guerin (1998) have suggested that techniques of landscape evaluation have focussed too strongly on people's responses to landscape, rather than what aspects of landscape they are responding to. Their study of visitors to Loch Lomond and Ben Lomond therefore focussed heavily upon people's landscape experiences as well as their reactions to it.

This work argues that whilst it is essential to examine which elements of the material landscape people value, the influences on these values are not material facts of the land. Instead the main influences on peoples' values for landscape are their knowledge; in terms of their identity, experiences and social situation. They are influenced by the social norms of the time, and their position within society (Schama 1996). This becomes increasingly evident when evidence of people's landscape values through time is discussed.

In the discussion chapter (chapter 6) ideas of landscapes and time will be considered more fully. This book argues that there is a social hegemony, which is separate from the physical properties of the land, and which guides people's perceptions of the landscape. The way that then Central Highlands of Scotland has been imagined and valued

through time is discussed, with reference to how social forces (at the time) have guided people's perceptions of the land. Peoples' biographies are essential in examining perceptions of landscape, more so than the physicality of the land itself.

2.4. Context, an alternative mediator of meaning.

This work examines the influences on people's landscape values, and seeks alternatives to the idea of the land itself being the key influence on people's landscape values. The idea of context is central to this way of thinking. The following section will review the meaning of context, and some of the various contexts in which people exist and how these may influence landscape values.

This research works with the idea of context as the 'anchor' of meaning rather than it being the material. For me, this way of thinking is rooted in my background in archaeological research where the understanding of context is key to the understanding of the past. Context can be defined as the place of deposition and the cultural environment of an artefact or remains (Shaw & Jameson 2002). In terms of archaeological excavation in Britain the standard system of recording was developed by the Museum of London Archaeology Service, MoLAS, in the 1970s (Chadwick 1998). Within the MoLAS system each individual deposit, cut (of a pit), fill, or built element has its own individual context. This is assigned a unique number and matrixes are created to link these contexts together so that the stratigraphy of the site can be understood. Artefacts found on sites can be understood within their contexts of deposition, and without the surrounding context, artefacts are regarded as essentially meaningless (Barker 1993). As well as a physical context for remains, archaeologists examine cultural contexts. These cultural contexts are often hard for archaeologists to understand, as the material that they are working with is fragmentary, and often (always in the case of prehistory) outside of any narrative account of usage. The wider cultural context of an archaeological site, artefact or landscape includes the temporal context and the social (both identity based (surrounding the individual) and cultural) context.

Within the social sciences context is a useful term to discuss the different aspects which comprise a person's situation and in terms of understanding people's relationships with the landscape, context is crucial. This book argues that the context of the encounter with landscape is ultimately more important than the landscape itself in terms of what governs a person's landscape perceptions.

In this work three different types of context will be examined, identity; culture; and time. Identity can be a complex construct, and is one which has numerous different meanings within the social sciences (Cloke et al 2004). In this case it is taken to mean the different circumstances particular to the self, and may be seen as synonymous with subjectivities. Elements of identity which provide a context for the formation of perceptions may include age (Haartsen et al 2003), personal biography (in terms of knowledge experiences, and beliefs), place of residence and other elements of a landscape biography (what landscape people have experience of).

Culture is an enormously complex idea, about which much has been written in the social sciences and is one of the other types of context which will be discussed in this work (Barnard & Spencer 1996). Culture can be defined in a number of ways, and both as something that one aspires to having (such as becoming a 'cultured' person who is knowledgeable about arts, classical music and literature etc.) and something which grows organically through shared beliefs and practices (Eliot 1948). Eliot suggests that culture can be seen as *'a product of a variety of more or less harmonious activities, each pursued for its own sake'* (Eliot 1948:19) and operates at the levels of individual, small group and society. In this work culture is understood in the second, more organic, sense. It is taken to mean shared knowledge and beliefs that people have, and the influence that this has on their thoughts and actions within society. Through time there are certain cultural trends which become hegemonies, or dominant discourses, and these may influence people's landscape perceptions, as certain viewpoints become a 'cultural norm'. Cultural trends which have been influential in people's values for the Scottish Highlands include Romanticism, Nationalism and Anti-Modernity (it will be argued in the discussion chapter, section 6.2.1). These themes have already been introduced in this chapter, and will be addressed within a Scottish context in section 2.6.1.

The third context which will be examined is time, and the temporal context of people's landscape perceptions. Both identity and culture are situated in time. There are a number of different types of time which can affect the context of individuals' encounters with landscape. These will be addressed in the following section.

2.5. Landscapes, Values and Time

Perceptions and values for landscape are affected by time (Ingold 1993). This is not just the linear 'clock' time of historical eras. Perceptions also occur in cyclical times such as through seasons and lifecycles (Barrett 1999). The following section will outline different types of time, and examine how these affect landscape experiences in turn affect people's landscape values. Time as envisaged by different societies is an extremely complex topic, and many *other* types of time such as 'dreamings' exist (Gell 1992). This section focuses on the types of time that provide a context for individual's encounters with landscape as articulated by participants in this research (see section 4.6.2 for an outline of the participants in this research) and as such discussion will focus upon specific types of linear and cyclical times. Linear and cyclical time are dynamic in nature, and a person's encounter with landscape will be affected by both of these types of time. They are discussed separately here not because they happen separately but purely for ease of discussion.

2.5.1. Linear Time

The first type of time that will be discussed is linear time. This is the time of 'timelines' in which things happen, and cannot be returned to.

Calendar Time

Calendar time is a type of linear time and is the time in which history 'happens'. It is the passing of days, years, decades and centuries as recorded by society. The social and political landscapes change within calendar time, as do social relationships.

These changes in society can precipitate alterations to the physical surroundings (such as the wholesale reorganisation of the Loch Tay landscape in the late eighteenth century (Harrison 2005). This leads to alterations to the context within which people experience landscape, and the appearance of the physical landscape itself which may in turn affect individual's landscape values. Movements such as Romanticism happen in calendar time. In other time periods, when there were different cultural norms the landscape was viewed differently. It is not possible to know, in any singular or absolute sense, how people in the past viewed the landscape but there is much material evidence to demonstrate that people in the past, particularly in the prehistoric period, thought of the land in very different ways to how we do today.

The examination of 'non-western' perceptions of landscape is a useful tool in demonstrating quite how different people's views of landscape are to those held by many in our post-enlightenment society. In many non-western societies the landscape is interpreted through a series of mythologies, such as the dreamings of Aboriginal Australia (Strang 2005). Through these mythologies values for the landscape are developed, certain places have taboos, others are sacred and others home. Natural phenomena have agency and values in these belief systems. For example, the Q'eqchi of Guatemala have gods who are anthropomorphised natural phenomena and certain mountains are gods who talk to each other through thunder and lightning (Gonzalo 1999). There is archaeological and folklore evidence to suggest that the pre-Christian societies in Britain also had cosmologies based on relationships with natural phenomena, e.g. the kelpies, or water horses, of Scottish folklore (Cope 1998). The creation of these cosmologies is a way of understanding the world, and developing a value system around certain places and phenomena. The 'difference' that is evident in these alternative views of landscape serves to demonstrate how the passing of linear (calendar) time allows the forgetting of once dominant ways of understanding landscape.

Through the passing of calendar time, and changes in society there has been a collective forgetting of these past ideas of landscape. In the Scottish Highlands this has been exacerbated by the loss of Gaelic (which in Perthshire happened in the late nineteenth century (Withers 1982)), which has led to place names which once had specific

Figure 2-3 cup marked boulder at Tombreck, Lochtayside. (H. Corley) cup marked stones are common in Bronze Age upland landscapes, and there is a particular concentration of these in Lochtayside. They represent an understanding of the landscape very different to one we have today, one which has been forgotten in the passing of time, and in later events. This particular boulder has been removed from its original context, and is now situated in a (now disused) nineteenth century field boundary.

meanings loosing these meanings for most individuals, and becoming simply contextless sounds. These particular interpretations of the world have lost resonance through time, and historians and archaeologists can only attempt to reconstruct past value systems through examination of material evidence and fragments of remembering which have been preserved (albeit often in a much altered state) within folklore. Throughout calendar time several areas (including both Loch Tay and Loch Lomond) have had the same 'bones' materially (neither have changed shape significantly since the last ice age) but people's interpretations of the landscape have changed markedly through these times suggesting that it is not the material form of the landscape that is the driver of people's values, and that they are instead contextually influenced.

2.5.2. Cyclical Times

As well as happening in a linear way, there are cycles of time. There are various scales of cycle ranging from those which occupy a long timescale (such as geological time, in which, for example tectonic processes occur), to those which are experienced within human lives (such as seasons and days). How these cycles situate people's relationships with land is explored in the Annales school

of French philosophy and history, where exponents wrote about history within the different temporal cycles that people experienced life (e.g. Braudel 1949).

Landscape is experienced within cycles of time. The experience of landscape is altered by the changing seasons and time of day. In upland areas the effect of the seasons is particularly noticeable (Palang et al 2005). Both study areas for this research are 'marginal' agricultural landscapes and routines within these landscapes have fitted into a seasonal round (Coles & Mills 1998). This has been particularly evident in the past when the sheiling system meant that certain areas of the land were only inhabited at certain times of year. In the winter months, the hills would have been places which were only visited sporadically, with life mainly taking place in the lower ground by the lochside. In the spring and summer certain members of the community would move to the high pastures with their stock and the Highlands would become a lived place once more (Olwig 2005). In modern times, both areas have 'tourist' seasons, times when the majority of visitors come to the area (Tourism in Scotland 2006). Therefore a number of visitors only experience the Highlands in certain seasons, meaning that the landscape is only 'known' in certain weather conditions, rather than the full seasonal cycle (Brassley

1998). Lochlomondside is often very crowded during traditional holiday times, and many tourists only know this landscape as a place full of visitors. As almost any local will tell you, there is a vast difference between living in the Highlands in season and out of season, in terms of climate and also in terms of ease of living in and moving around the landscape. Weather is a time based factor which also affects the context of people's encounters with landscape: it is partially affected by seasonality, but in the Highlands there is no guarantee of fair weather at any time of the year.

Another cycle which requires consideration is the time of the day, as this also affects context of encounter with the landscape. The experience of a lit landscape is completely difference to one in darkness. Different qualities of light can alter the landscape considerably, making certain aspects more or less visible through the passage of the day. Certain areas may be in shade for part of the day and light in others, altering the physical experience of the landscape. A person's mood changes throughout the day. Being alert or tired, hungry, fed up or enthusiastic will all alter people's attitudes to landscape.

Life operates in cycles. There is the human lifecycle, and that of animal species and vegetation. As individuals move through the human lifecycle, their landscape experience changes (McCormack 2002) in terms of an individuals' mobility (how they are able to experience landscape), agency (what of landscape they are at liberty to experience, the extent to which they are making their own choices about their landscape experience) and wants (what they wish to experience of the landscape)

How people experience landscape may be influenced by these times, be it the physical experience which alters through daily and seasonal cycles, or the social context which alters through historical time. However, as temporal cycles alter the material world, like the material world, time does not have an essentialist role in determining how people view landscape.

All of these temporal contexts combine to create what psychologists term a 'now bias' in terms of landscape perceptions (Fay 1996). Perceptions of landscape are grounded in a present. The present is an amalgam of the place in 'calendar time' and the position of that present on the multitude of different cycles. In other words what stage the individual is at in their lifecycle, the time of day where the 'present' is, when the season is etc. will influence landscape perceptions. Any research into landscape values can only investigate a single 'moment' or a short period of time, but these changing perceptions in time should not be ignored. Instead ways should be found to determine how fixed or transient perceptions are.

When an individual is asked to comment on their preferences and values for an area of landscape their responses will be affected by both embedded and transient influences. These produce two different types of landscape value which have been categorised by Stevenson (2005) as 'surface

values' and 'embedded values'. Surface values are those developed on the day' and are associated with the physical appearance of the surroundings at the time and as such are more susceptible to change, whereas embedded values are can be seen as deeply rooted in histories of place and affected mainly by more knowledge based influences. It is important to understand the context of people's landscape perceptions so that these two types of value are separated. When future land-use and interpretation decisions are made people's embedded values for landscape will provide a better guide to their long-term thoughts and desires for a landscape's future. Many methods of landscape valuation, particularly those within the quantitative school of research do not take this division of values into account, and as such may be misleading due to the 'clouding' of embedded values by transient elements.

By the examination of influences on value it is possible to determine whether values that are being recorded are likely to remain with a person through time, or change rapidly. This is important when making decisions about future land use based upon research which takes place in one 'present'.

2.6. Cultural Contexts and landscape values

In this research culture is taken to mean shared elements of human thought and practice, practiced by many, as opposed to similarities in identity, such as age, gender or personal biography as discussed above. Cultural movements affect how people have viewed the landscapes of the Scottish Highlands, and some ideas still prevalent today have their roots in the political and cultural upheaval, and associated artistic movements of the eighteenth century (Makdisi 1998). These themes of Nationalism and Imperialism, the Sublime and Romanticism will be discussed below, with reference to how they still affect how people see the Highlands today. The growth of the Highlands as a tourist destination from the late eighteenth century onwards is also central to this discussion.

2.6.1. Cultural influences- Romanticism, Nationalism and Imperialism

As introduced earlier in this chapter (section2.2.2) the Scottish Highlands were a key area within the Romantic Movement. It differed from earlier artistic and cultural movements, which celebrated more 'polite' landscapes which had been designed by man. (Williamson 1999). The concept of 'wilderness' was borne out of Romanticism and continues to be influential in the present day. Cronon (1996) discusses how wilderness is a human creation, and a reflection on society rather than a 'fact'. He introduces the idea that the concept of wilderness is inextricably linked to 'progress' and to 'urbanisation' within an North American context, where the 'wild' only becomes valorised when the frontier is conquered. American national parks were developed specifically to celebrate the 'wild' and all traces of 'man' were removed from the landscape at the time of their demarcation (Olwig 1996). The same is true of Romanticism. It is only after the alteration of the landscape, and the removal of all genuine threats (such as hostile natives, lions, tigers and bears etc.), that wilderness is truly celebrated.

The Highlands, as portrayed by the Romantics was a wild beautiful landscape, populated by noble Gaels, highland cattle and lonely stags, which can be seen as a reflection of how that certain sphere of society viewed the Highland landscape. (Yarwood 2005). The emergent British middle class was engaged in the rhetoric of nation and latterly empire building (Glendening 1997), after the Act of Union (1707) enhanced the sense of a unified British Nation. In the early years of the Union the Highlands fitted uneasily into Britain, as numerous clans supported the Jacobite claim to the throne, and were known to many mainly for their cattle raiding exploits, and vast debts. As a result the area was seen as too dangerous to be visited by outsiders from lowland areas, until the quashing of the final Jacobite rebellion in 1746. William Gilpin visited Lochtayside in the early 1770's and was unimpressed with the countryside surrounding Loch Tay as it did not conform to his picturesque ideal, developed in the Cumbrian Lake district. *'They* [the surroundings] *exhibit no bold shores, broken promontories, not other forms of beauty, but are rather tame hills than picturesque mountains. Nor are they furnished with wood or other pleasing appendages'* (Gilpin 1776: 167). He suggests that the 'greatest glory' of Lochtayside is the village of Kenmore, which was planned by the third earl of Breadalbane, and would have been the area of the landscape most similar to the Cumbrian lakelands. Killin itself was also favoured by Gilpin, as it was purported to have been the last resting pace of Fingal (the giant) and it could therefore be celebrated as part of a mythical Arcadian landscape. In opposition to these manufactured horrors of the Picturesque, Romanticism is linked to an idea of 'authenticity' and a development of 'real' places (Glendening 1997). The Romantics favoured the authentic experience of the wild countryside (and this section will examine how this was itself manufactured within a Scottish context).

The Romantic movement is very much about nostalgia, which is a pseudo-Greek term, developed in the late eighteenth century that *Combines the sense of bodily pain (algia) and returning home (nostos)* (Cosgrove 2006:3). It is about mourning a 'lost' past, which may not have been there in the first place. Much of what is now valorised as the Highland ideal was quashed in the 18th century, most notable the wearing of the kilt and tartan, which were banned to all but the military between 1746 and 1782 (Fry 2005). As well as this, agricultural developments of this 'Age of Improvement' resulted in a landscape becoming more similar to estates in upland England and lowland Scotland, when large tracts of hitherto open landscapes are subdivided into large regular fields similar to those resulting from Parliamentary enclosure in England (Devine 1994). Throughout the eighteenth century, the Highlands were opened up to outsiders by a programme of military (and latterly toll) road building commenced in the 1720s by General Wade (Fry 2005). Towards the

end of the eighteenth century there was a steady increase in the number of people visiting this region for pleasure, which continued through the nineteenth century to the present day (Glendening 1997) It can be suggested that at this time the Highlands of Scotland were fitted into the Romantic heroic wilderness born out of the Imperialism of the British Empire, which included such disparate noble savages as the Eskimos of the 'polar wastes' and the pygmies of 'Darkest Africa'. (Knight 2004). The Highlander was one more specimen of otherness who had been 'tamed' for the amusement of polite society. The start of the nineteenth century in Scotland is portrayed in the popular imagination as *'a Romantic haze of tartans, bagpipes and bonnie princes and obscures the reality of a traditional and conservative society under stress and on the brink of extensive and far-reaching changes'* (Whyte & Whyte 1991) At this time the rural population was facing disease and poverty, and overpopulation worse than ever seen before. The ethos behind the paintings of Landseer and his contemporary Hamish McCulloch have been described as *'Much like today considering Africa as a destination for wildlife tourism and not dwelling on its disease and poverty'* (Smout 2005:13). This story of the development of the Romantic Movement ignores this two tier Highlands, at the time of the clearances the 'Gael' was seen by some as being a more primitive race of human than the lowland Scot (Fenyo 2000), with popular newspapers suggesting that the Highlanders were an inferior race best removed, and that the Highland famine was a result of their incompetence rather than any other factors. This behaviour (although not the clearances themselves) has been largely forgotten in popular accounts of Highland history, and in the minds of those who visit the Highlands, and as such is outwith the cultural context in which many individuals view today's Highland landscape.

Nationalism

Romanticism is closely linked to Nationalism. Scottish Nationalism, in its current form[1] can be seen to have its rooted in the work of Walter Scott who was one of the main creators of the 'tartanry' tradition in the early nineteenth century. Members of Edinburgh Society such as Scott were trying to redefine Scottish identity, after it became clear that the Union was going to be permanent, and Scotland faced becoming a faceless province of 'North Britain'. The quashing of the final Jacobite rebellions also meant that for the first time Scotland could be seen as a single entity, rather than as a country divided by its topography. As a boy Scott had read, and been intrigued by the poems of Ossian which had recently been 'rediscovered' by James Macpherson (for a discussion of their authenticity or otherwise please refer to Stafford 1988), and saw them as proof that the Highlands had a thriving cultural tradition which should be celebrated rather than repressed. Scott took certain elements of the past, and used them to form a new collective identity for Scotland, one which existed in his ideas of how he wished to see the past in the present (Olivier 2004). This can be seen as part of a wider

---

[1] By this I mean cultural, rather than political nationalism.

Nationalist movement which emerged across Europe in the eighteenth and nineteenth centuries (Olwig 2002). Hobsbaum and Ranger (1983), discussed the idea of the 'invention of tradition' and attempts to establish continuity with a suitable historic past. (Hobsbaum 1983). He suggests that there are three different types of invented tradition: *'a) those establishing or symbolising social cohesion or the membership of groups real or artificial communities, b) those establishing or legitimising institutions, status or relations of authority, and c) those whose main purpose was socialisation, the inculcation of beliefs, value systems and conventions of behaviour'* (Hobsbaum 1983: 9). The Nationalism of Scotland can be seen to involve all three of these types of tradition invention, through re-establishing a 'Scottish' nation and encouraging people to participate in this new found national pride. It has been theorised that individuals' sense of national identity is enhanced by visiting nationally significant monuments (Palmer 2005, Wallwork & Dixon 2004). Participating in heritage tourism, by visiting specific places which can be seen to be significant in a shared past (such as 'The Highlands') is a way of constructing a national identity for a united Scotland, and the development of specific tours of Scotland can be seen as part of this nation building.

Mass tourism developed from mid Victorian times to the present day, and the construction of an image of the Highlands which still has currency today was developed alongside this (Durie 2003). Travel to the Highlands developed organically at first with early tourists taking advantage of political stability in the Highlands, and finding the grand tour of Europe closed because of war on the continent. These tourists mapped out routes and published journals of their travels which led to the creation of more formalised tours that encompassed key sites such as Fingal's Cave, Fort William, Inverness etc. Tours also took in places with literary links such as Loch Katrine (Lady of the Lake) and Loch Coruisk (The Lord of the Isles). Photography was also key to the democratisation of the Highland landscape. Photographs taken of the area (such as those taken by George Washington Wilson and others from the late nineteenth century onward) were of ideal views, were easily and cheaply reproduced, and brought the Romantic vision to the masses (Withers 1993). Through the later nineteenth and twentieth century 'package' tours were developed which would take people to these ideal places (Durie 2003). This change in the way the Highland landscape was understood was associated with the movement away from the land associated with clearances or depopulation which began in the early eighteenth century. An area which was once a living social landscape of occupation was reduced to an landscape only occasionally visited, and used for completely different purposes than only a few decades prior to that time, and became managed, and valued for different purposes (Jedrej and Nutall 1996). Largely, this was no longer a landscape for agricultural production, but instead one that existed to be 'consumed' by sportspeople and tourists. The shift from 'production to consumption' has led to a change in the way that landscapes are managed, which has continued to the present day. Highland landscapes are now largely managed to preserve and conserve the landscape for field sports, in a way that gives a 'natural' appearance which attracts tourists to the area (Butler et al 1999, Jenkins et al 1999).

Nationalism from Industrialisation onwards

As the population of Scotland became increasingly based in major urban centres and employment moved away from the land to heavy industries, the Highland landscape was no longer part of people's everyday experience. From the early eighteenth century the population of the Highlands decreased greatly as individuals and families moved from the land to central belt towns, and rural populations were moved from farm towns to planned villages built by large estates to centralise their workforce. For a large section of the population people's everyday was now an urban existence with men often working 6 day weeks in mining or manufacturing industries (Kay 1996). With these long weeks the majority of excursions to the Highlands were restricted to those areas easily accessible by bus or train from the central belt *'every mountain within 2 and 6 of Glasgow'* (Kay 1996). These included such areas as the Campsie Fells, Loch Lomond and 'the pipe run' where walkers could follow the route of Glasgow's main water supply to Loch Katrine in the Trossachs. The only time that further forays into the Highlands could be made was the annual 'trades fortnight' when excursions were organised to places such as the Cullins of Skye or the central Cairngorms. This tradition was disrupted by industrial decline and depression in the inter-war years with mass unemployment in the 1930s reshaping traditional gender roles from the household.

In Scotland industrial decline started post WW1, when the whole of the UK was sliding into depression. At this time men were returning home having fought for nation and empire to find no reward, and no work. There was an increasing sense that people had fought for nothing, a Scotland, and a Britain which was not theirs. In England, mass trespasses were undertaken on sporting estates in areas such as Kinder in the Peak District, in order to try and force open the landscape for the public (Bunce 1994). Ultimately after WW2 this lead to the National Parks Act in 1949 and the first National Park (the Peak District) designation in 1951.

In Scotland after 1918 there was a marked decline in the traditional shooting estates in the Highlands which provided holidays for the privileged few, as economic downturn and the loss of a generation of young men meant that families no longer had the resources to run these estates. Instead a new generation of landlords took over, who were mainly interested in making money from the land, and mass tourism was one of the main ways of increasing revenue. This was coupled with the wider availability of the motor car and the opening up of motor touring and coach tours. Publications such as H.V. Morton's *'In search of Scotland'* encouraged visitors to the area, and like earlier travel volumes created specific sites that people were keen to visit (Morton 1933). This trend of the Highlands as a tourist destination which offers an escape from modernity has continued until the present day, and the associated trends of Anti-Modernity and the 'rural idyll' will be discussed further below.

2.6.2. Current Ideas of Romanticism – Anti-Modernity and the Rural Idyll

Trends evident in Romantic discourses in terms of the 'noble savage' and simplicity of rural life are still present in imaginings of the rural, and specifically ideas of the rural idyll (Jedrej & Nutall 1996, Wallwork & Dixon 2004). The rural idyll is a term coined to describe constructions of the 'rural' as an 'authentic' place of peace which exists in opposition to urban modernity (Matless 1998). This is especially true of ideas of mountains, and the Scottish Highlands are seen as an otherworld, place of freedom and an escape from modern 'real life' (Prentice & Guerin 1998, Halfacree 1994). There is a current trend of 'counter urbanisation', where people move towards rural areas from larger towns and cities for a change in lifestyle, which is linked to the anti-modernity ideas of Ruskin, Tolkein and others (Bunce 1994, Hoskins 1955). Rural areas have been seen to some as a 'golden land of opportunities for children' (Giddings et al 2005), where parents can raise families safely without any of the dangers' of urban life. The Highlands are seen as an 'authentic' place, away from the stress of urban life and Highlanders are seen by some as living 'simple' lives in a quaint, stress free place to live. There is an idea that tourists visit the Highland landscape to 'actualise a dream' (Prentice & Guerin 1998), whereby individuals seek to experience the ideal, mythologised Highlands. It is a position which entails the need for a physical landscape which is 'wild', insofar as it is lacking in noticeably 'modern' features, but also allows for people to engage with the Romantic Highlands. Whatever the truths or otherwise of these ideas these are the notions that provide a context for perceptions of landscape which are within common currency today.

As there are a multitude of constructions of the Highlands, there are also a large number of constructions of 'the rural' and research in recent years has focussed on this plurality of discourses (e.g. Rye 1996, Yarwood 2005, Pratt 1996, Cloke & Little 1997). This will be expanded upon later in the work in both chapter 4, where methods for working with different population sub groups are investigated, and chapter 6 where respondents' values for landscape are discussed.

This section has described some of the different contexts in which people's encounters with landscape are situated and which can influence people's landscape perceptions. In chapter 6 attitudes to landscape examined in this research will be discussed with reference to these contexts and the influences that these have on landscape perceptions and values.

2.7. Landscape and Policy

As noted in the introduction, this research was funded by a collaborative CASE studentship. CASE studentships were established in order to foster collaboration between academic research and industry, with the aim being that the research they supported would have practical implications. In this case the research was designed to further investigate people's landscape values, and make recommendations as to how these could be integrated into the management of the Scottish landscape. It is therefore necessary to introduce the ways in which Scotland's landscape is currently curated. There are currently a number of different policies that exist for the protection of Scotland's landscapes and heritage features. The following section will review these, and examine some of the decision making tools which are used when land management decisions are made. These different policies will be addressed in order of scale, from world heritage inscription, to regional designations which are specific to Scotland. These will be discussed with particular reference to the values that the nebulous group of individuals known as 'the general public' have for landscape rather than designations which are made on material grounds, involving intrinsic value (such as particular heritage features, or rare habitats, or 'outstanding natural value') by landscape professionals.

2.7.1. Landscapes for the World

On a global scale landscapes can be granted World Heritage status. In 1972 the first UNESCO Convention concerning the protection of the World Cultural and Natural Heritage was held and as of 2003 one hundred and seventy five nations had ratified the treaty. At first sites could be inscribed on the World Heritage List because of their cultural or natural significance. It was not until 1992 that the category of 'cultural landscape' was added to the list of categories that could attain World Heritage status, and in 1993 Tongariro National Park in New Zealand was the first site afforded this status (Fowler 2003). This site had been a Natural World Heritage Site since 1990, but it was realised that the 'natural' features had great cultural significance, and had indeed been subject to millennia of human manipulation (Fowler 2004). This served to demonstrate that the dichotomy created by proclaiming sites to be either of 'cultural' or 'natural' heritage was false. It was decided, however, that this dichotomy was one too enshrined in the World Heritage literature, and as such could not be dropped. Therefore sites can have world heritage status conferred on them for both cultural and natural reasons, but only twenty four sites hold this accolade globally, including St Kilda, UK (2005) and Uluru-Kata Tjuta National Park, Australia (1994) (UNESCO.org 2006).

In order to attain world heritage status, monuments and landscapes must be of 'outstanding universal value', which is defined by a number of criteria, which stress the need for sites and landscapes to be outstanding examples or rare and exceptional natural and cultural traditions. Originally, landscapes and monuments were only included on material/ structural grounds, but now they may be inscribed if the site can be seen to *'be directly or tangibly associated with events or living traditions, with ideas, or with beliefs, with artistic and literary works of outstanding universal significance'* (UNESCO.org 2005). In 2003 UNESCO presented the convention for the safeguarding of the intangible cultural heritage. This *'expressions, knowledge, skills – as well as the instruments, objects, artefacts and cultural spaces associated therewith – that communities, groups and in some cases, individuals recognize as part of their cultural heritage. This intangible cultural heritage, transmitted from generation to generation is constantly recreated by communities and groups in response to their environment, their interaction with nature and their history, and provides them with a sense of identity and continuity, thus promoting respect for cultural diversity.'* (UNESCO 2003).

They suggest that this is manifest within:

• Oral traditions and expressions, including language as a vehicle of the intangible cultural heritage.

• Performing arts.

• Social practices, rituals and festive events.

• Knowledge and practices concerning nature and the universe.

• Traditional craftsmanship.

These are all formal expressions of traditions, and belong to wider cultural phenomena rather than individual values for landscape. These may, and do, overlap with people's attachments to landscape, but do not encompass the whole spectrum of attachments that people have to landscapes, which are not linked to any particular traditions or indigenous knowledges.

Decisions on what sites, monuments and landscapes merit world heritage status are made annually by the World Heritage Committee, which is comprised of an international group of impartial experts who assess the relative merits of different proposed sites. As part of their proposal, community values for the site or landscape can be presented, but this is as far as community involvement in the world heritage process reaches.

2.7.2. The European Landscape Convention

The European Landscape Convention was adopted in 2000, and ratified by the United Kingdom in February 2006. It operates alongside numerous other international treaties which touch upon, but do not expressly include landscape including: the European Convention on the Protection of the Archaeological Heritage (Valetta 1992); the Convention on the Conservation of European Wildlife and Natural Habitats (Bern 1979); the Convention for the Protection of the Architectural Heritage of Europe (Granada 1985); and the Convention on Biological Diversity (Rio 1992).

The aims of the Convention are given as:

• Providing a means for landscape to become a mainstream political concern, as it is the concern of all, not just managers or specialists.

• Giving people an active role in decision making on landscape, and a way of influencing their surroundings, and through this valuing their surroundings more.

• To encourage public authorities to adopt policies and measures at local, regional, national and international level for protecting, managing and planning landscapes throughout Europe.

• To provide a framework for protection of landscape values.

The Convention starts with a definition of landscape as *'an area, as perceived by people, whose character is the result of natural and/or human factors'* (this is the definition used in this work, as outlined above in section 2.2.). This definition works with the idea that landscape is a mental creation, about how people think of the physical properties rather than the properties themselves. This is an important departure from traditional material based definitions of landscapes. The text goes on to assert that that landscape is everywhere; it is not just exceptional areas and includes both urban and rural areas.

The Convention sets out both national and international measures which must be undertaken to promote European co-operation on landscape issues. These include legal measures to recognise landscapes as an essential component of people's surroundings, and as such encourage public participation in the planning and management process. Nations also have to establish policies for landscape protection, management and planning, through a set of specific measures, including a full characterisation of the nation's landscape types and the undertaking of public and expert consultations about landscape meanings and futures. On a pan-European level countries have to co-operate in terms of skills and knowledge exchange between landscape professionals. It is also recognises that landscapes, and physical landscape features are not bounded by national boundaries, and as such there must be international cooperation to manage these 'transfrontier landscapes'. Whilst making it clear that legal measures must be taken to promote landscapes, the Convention places emphasis on the role of the general public in the consumption and management of landscape. The document, however, gives scant advice as to how countries should implement the convention aims within their national context, as such there are vast discrepancies between different European countries' landscape policies (Dower 2001).

Landscape Policies Across Europe

Until recently, landscape designation and policies focussed on preserving the 'exceptional'. This was implemented in a variety of ways across Europe. Dower (2001) undertook a comparative study of seven European countries' landscape policies and found marked differences in the ways in which they undertook landscape management. The landscapes studied were: Denmark; Austria; Czech

Republic; the Netherlands; Norway; England; and Italy. Landscape policy choices ranged from Denmark which had no specific protected landscapes, instead relying on the appliance of countrywide land-use planning and nature conservation, to Austria which has a large number of protected landscapes, designated at a provincial level, but no overarching landscape policy. Other countries such as England and Norway have a number of areas of landscape protected by specific designations as well as nationwide programmes of landscape characterisation and management. The Czech Republic and the Netherlands have similar approaches to landscape conservation; both having a variety of protected/designated areas which are interlinked by a national ecological network. Italy has a system of protected landscape areas as well as regional landscape plans designed to protect specific landscape types designated by law in 1939 (Dower 2001). As well as having different policy strategies and landscape designations, the motivation behind their formation differs between nations. In some countries (e.g. Austria and Denmark) nature conservation was the main impetus behind landscape protection, and in others, (e.g. the Netherlands) the cultural heritage has been the main motivating factor. In England, scenic beauty was the main driver of landscape designation.

Despite these national differences in implementation there is evidence of a movement towards nationwide schemes of landscape characterisation and protection in many countries is testament to the growing realisation that landscape is the everyday as well as the extraordinary. Also, all countries are moving away from the original motivations for landscape protection towards designation of landscapes in general, something which is intertwined with a realisation that there is no separation between natural and cultural landscapes (Fowler 2001). It has been recognised (Phillips 2001) that, on a physical level, few, if any areas of landscape can be said to be 'untouched' by humans and on a mental level, all landscapes are conceived through human experience (SNH 2003).

Having briefly outlined the international and European context the following section will examine in greater detail landscape policies and management in Scotland.

2.7.3. Landscape Policy and Management in Scotland

Scottish Natural Heritage is the government body charged with curating and managing Scotland's landscape. They are assisted in this role by their historic environment equivalent, Historic Scotland. The following section outlines some of the legal designations and policies for landscape conservation and management which are currently in force in Scotland.

National Designations

National Scenic Areas

The National Scenic Area (NSA) designation was established by the government in 1980, after a survey

undertaken by the Countryside Commission for Scotland identified forty areas *'of unsurpassed attractiveness which must be conserved as part of our national heritage'* (SNH 2000). They are designated as being sites of 'at least national importance', and partially replaced a number of different local designations. In 1999, SNH published advice to government on NSA's suggesting that there should be more public participation in the promotion and management of them, and that local authorities should be increasingly responsible for their management. SNH also expressed concern that there was no official legislation protecting these areas from habitat destruction and unsympathetic development.

Sites of Special Scientific Interest (SSSIs) & Scheduled Monuments (SMs)

The SSSI designation was developed in England in 1949, and was first applied to Scotland after the enactment of the Wildlife and Countryside Act (1981) (English Nature 2006). SSSIs 'represent the best of Scotland's natural heritage. They are 'special' for their plants, animals or habitats, their rocks or landforms, or a combination of such natural features.' (SNH online 2006). Their cultural equivalent is the scheduled monument designation. SM protection is given by Historic Scotland using the Ancient Monuments and Archaeological Areas Act (1979) to archaeological and historical sites which are seen as being of national importance.

In practice both of these designations are a legal protection given to areas of land, to provide limits to what activities can be carried out in these areas, preserve them for the nation and to protect them from development.

National Parks

National Parks in Scotland have a short history compared to the rest of the UK. In 1997 that the Government asked SNH to provide advice on how National Parks for Scotland[2] should best operate, which in turn lead to the National Parks Act (2000). This act defines the four purposes of National Parks as to:

• Conserve and enhance the natural and cultural heritage of the National Park.

• Promote sustainable usage of the area's natural resources.

• Enhance the social wellbeing and economic prosperity of its local communities.

• Promote the enjoyment and understanding of the area's special values.

In the first instance two areas were suggested for National Park status, Loch Lomond and the Trossachs and the Cairngorms. These were selected not only because of their outstanding landscapes, flora and fauna but also because the areas face considerable pressure from visitors and

---

[2] Although they have been considered on a number of prior occasions.

landuse changes, meaning that there is a need for greater management to maintain the area's character. One of the case study areas used in this research, Luss, is within the Loch Lomond and the Trossachs National Park (LLTNP) boundary, as is the village of Killin where many of the Lochtayside participants come from. LLTNP Authority also provided part of the funding for this research, to aid them in their landscape management work, and it is therefore important to examine the set up of this park in more detail.

LLTNP was the first National Park in Scotland, formally receiving its designation in 2002. The area was selected for the following reasons (LLTNP 2005 SNH 1999):

• The area is a very accessible, and valued recreational space for the population of West central Scotland, with the A82 and A84/5 trunk roads running through it. There are therefore heavy recreational pressures on the hills, loch and footpaths meaning that the area needs intense management to cater for the needs of visitors at the same time as preserving the natural environment.

• The area has scenery which 'has a special place in the affections of the people of Scotland'.

• The area has some unique habitats and species, and a unique cultural heritage. All of these require conservation, management, research and interpretation.

• The area is a 'working countryside' and there are many management conflicts between the various economic uses of the landscape, and the need to conserve the resource.

• The economy of the National Park area is dominated by the provision of visitor services, and as such local communities are being eroded by pressures such as increasing numbers of houses belonging to second home owners, and resources and facilities being used by visitors rather than local residents. There is therefore a need for planning to service community needs, to maintain and strengthen their character, and to help diversify their economy in ways which are appropriate to their National Park status.

A consultation exercise carried out both nationwide and in the proposed park area revealed that there was a large amount of support for the establishment of a National Park in that area. After this exercise the remit of the Park Authority was defined. The Park Authority has powers over:

• **Conservation and Environmental Protection** including managing land on behalf of SNH, H.S. and the Forestry Commission, coordination of water catchment and fisheries research and the undertaking of environmental improvement works.

• **Recreation and Visitor Management** including having a park-wide ranger service on both land and water (including regulation of water-borne activities), making park bylaws and providing interpretation facilities at key

areas within the park.

• **Town and Country Planning**, especially controlling the development conflicts present in the areas, and promoting sustainable development. Consultation also revealed that a number of respondents were in favour of the National Park Authority being the principle partner in the development of structure plans for the area, ensuring that the plans adhere to the main aims for National Parks.

• **Traffic Management**; the resolution of congestion problems linked to the large numbers of visitors to the area, including the provision of integrated public transport services for the area.

• **Agriculture and Forestry** are integral to both the economy and the character of the National Park area. It is important, however, to ensure that both of these are developed in a sustainable way, which maintains their economic viability without being detrimental to the environment.

• **Social and Economic development**. The idea that the Park Board is involved in the social and economic development of the area was supported by the consultation area. It was proposed that the board would work closely with Local Enterprise Companies and Tourist Boards to ensure a sustainable future for the park area.

It was also agreed that the National Park body should be mainly comprised of residents of the area, to ensure that local interests are truly represented within this national designation.

There are now two National Parks in Scotland, LLTNP and Cairngorms National Park (which was granted National Park status in 2003). The two parks have different operating practices, with CNPA not having as extensive planning powers as LLTNP. A third, marine National Park is proposed and the consultation process for this is underway at the time of writing.

2.7.4. Local Landscape Designations

Landscape designations are made at a local level as well as a national one. In the past, these designations were commonly made in the form of Environmentally Sensitive Areas (ESAs), which are specific areas of land deemed to be of special environmental significance. ESA regulations were used as a policy tool to encourage agriculture as a curation of landscape rather than a process of food production (Gourlay and Slee 1998, Halfacree 1997). Within ESA policy farmers were rewarded financially for the maintenance of specific landscape features such as hedgerows or drystone walls and increasing/maintaining biodiversity by using environmentally sensitive farming techniques. ESA schemes were replaced by Rural Stewardship Scheme Agreements (RSSA) which have now been replaced by Single Farm Payments. The SFPs are now the sole subsidy payment that farms receive, and they include measures to encourage farmers to use environmentally friendly practices, and to maintain and enhance certain landscape features and habitats (Scottish Executive 2005). Although in some respect similar to ESA agreements the conservation measures outlined in SFPs are more wide ranging, encompassing the protection of SMs (scheduled monuments), historic gardens and designed landscapes.

Instead of ESA's, SNH is encouraging local authorities to earmark areas as Special Landscape Areas (SLAs) and in 2005 SNH produced a guidance note on these local landscape designations. In reality there are a number of different names given to these areas including for example: Regional Scenic Areas (Dumfries and Galloway); Areas of Great Landscape Value (AsGLVs) (Moray, Clackmannanshire, West Lothian and others); and Sites of Special Landscape Importance (SSLI) (Glasgow). These are non statutory, and as such do not need to be taken into account in the landscape planning process.

2.7.5. Informing landscape planning

Until recently, 'expert' evidence informing landscape designation existed in a fragmented state. Local authorities would have to examine lists of SSSIs, SMs etc. to discover which areas of landscape were the most worthy of designation. However, two schemes of whole landscape characterisation are being undertaken which can be used to inform the designation process, namely Landscape Character Assessment (LCA) and Historic Landuse Assessment (HLA) (a similar scheme exists in England and Wales where is referred to as Historic Landscape Characterisation(HLC) (Clark et al 2004)). Historic Landuse Assessment investigates past and present landuse, and provides data on when the basic character of today's landscape dates from (e.g. at what time the field boundaries in the area were created) (Kirkpatrick et al 2006).

HLA involves an examination of the processes that have led to the formation of the current landscape, and the time depth fossilised within it. Different types of landuse are assigned (there are 52 different types e.g. planned village, drained managed moorland), which fall under 14 different categories (e.g. fields and farming, woodland and forestry) (RCAHMS & HS 2000). The relict period of the feature is also noted (CC Network 2006). All three variables are combined to produce a searchable GIS database, which can be used alongside the National Monuments Record (NMR) when researching the history of an area and making decisions about its landscape future. In the English version of this scheme it is suggested (Clark et al 2004) that all types of values for landscape can be incorporated into the HLC process, but in reality these are mainly 'institutional' or 'informational' values as designated by heritage professionals.

Landscape Character Assessment is a UK-wide programme of research (SNH 2005). The eventual aim of the exercise is to produce a GIS database of the entirety of the British isles with information on both natural and cultural aspects of the landscape (see tables below), which can be viewed as a series of overlays on Ordinance Survey maps. Information

is gathered from a variety of sources including: previous landscape designations; geological and topographic maps; regional development plans; and countryside, forestry and tourism strategies of areas. Aerial photographs and site visits are also used to gather evidence of the landscape's present character.

Natural Factors	Cultural/Social factors
Geology	Landuse (including farm types)
Landform	Settlement pattern
River and drainage systems	Patterns of field enclosure
Land cover (including semi-natural vegetation)	Time depth – the historic dimension of landscape (in less detail than HLC/A)
Soils	

Figure 2-4 Factors covered by LCA in the UK

Once a characterisation of the landscape has been undertaken, it is then the responsibility of local authorities to identify places which are worth formal designation. SNH (2005:17) state that *'while this process should be structured and informed by professional advice, such judgements require wider public debate, both to inform decisions about the character and qualities of their landscapes which local people agree to be particularly important, and also to help identify the specific places which possess these attributes'.* Authorities are asked to judge landscapes according to their significance (within the context of the local authority area), representativeness (of the local area's distinctiveness) and relative merit (their significance in comparison to other parts of the local area).

As well as this 'top down' designation of landscapes, local authorities are encouraged to carry out consultations with communities. SNH (2005) suggests that the public's views are solicited throughout the process of designation, from initial surveys and public meetings, through to production of consultation documents and liaison with landowners in the latter stages of the process. However, there is no guidance as to what form consultation should take, who should be consulted, and how much sway any consultation should have in affecting plans made for landscapes.

In chapter 7 the role of public opinion in forming landscape policy will be discussed, in terms of whether current legislation for landscape represents people's landscape values as investigated within this research and how this legislation may be changed to better account for these values in places where it does not. This will be accompanied by a discussion as to whether the idea of designating certain landscapes or heritage features as being special actually helps in any long term land management strategy.

2.8. Summary

This chapter has provided an overview of the main themes in literature associated with the valuation of landscapes. The terms of 'landscape' and 'value' have been discussed, and working definitions for this research have been stated. This may be dismissed as a semantic issue which has little relevance to research into this area, but given the interdisciplinary nature of landscape research, and the plurality of meanings for terms used, such definitions are essential (Tress et al 2005, Reser & Bentrupperbäumer 2005). The rationale behind different approaches to the assessment of values that people attach to landscape has been discussed, and will be addressed further within the methodology section of this book.

The ideas of the Romantic Movement have been introduced, and I have suggested that ideas and values developed in this period are still central to how the Scottish Highlands are imagined by many people today. This idea will be expanded upon in the discussion section (chapter 6) where influences on perceptions and values of landscape evident in the research carried out will be discussed. This discussion will also focus more fully on the idea of materiality and landscape and it will be argued that social hegemony is the dominant force guiding people's perceptions of landscape, and the creation of cultural values rather than the material, physical 'fact' of the land. The idea of context being the main mediator of landscape perceptions and values has been introduced, alongside the three main types of context that will be discussed in this work; identity, culture and time.

Current policies and legislation for landscape management in Scotland have also been introduced, starting with protection at a global level, and working through to local landscape designations. Some of the processes by which these designations are made have also been discussed, including LCA and HLC/HLA and the paucity of consultation with landscape stakeholders in this decision making process outlined.

The following chapter will present a background to the areas selected as case studies for this research, commenting on the reasons for their selection, physical characteristics and history.

3
Case Study Background

3.1. Introduction

This chapter contains a description of the areas selected as case studies for this study; Lochtayside and Lochlomondside. Both of these areas are on the southern fringe of the Scottish Highlands. They have occupied an uneasy position on the edge of both the Highland and Lowland worlds, and their shifting allegiances through time attest to this. Their location, close to the Central Belt has meant that they are popular tourist destinations for day and weekend trips- Loch Lomond, in particular has been described as 'Glasgow's Playground' (Kay 1996).

The chapter will commence with an explanation of why Lochtayside and Lochlomondside were selected for study. The collaborative nature of the work undertaken guided the choice of areas, as mentioned in the introductory chapter and this will be fully outlined below. This work examines how the properties (physical and intangible characteristics) of a landscape and an individual's knowledge of that particular landscape and the wider world affects how they think about and act within the landscapes. Some background is useful with which to approach these properties of the study area (including history, geomorphology, vegetation, land use) so that the reader is aware of knowledge people are drawing upon when perceiving. A review of present day representations of the study areas in popular culture will also be presented. The areas have certain similar properties and where these occur they will be discussed together and when there are significant differences between the study areas they will be treated separately. After the landscapes of the area have been discussed, the communities in which the study took place will be introduced. Finally, the characteristics of the actual study sites and their immediate surroundings will be presented.

3.2. Selection of Case Study Areas

The Ben Lawers estate was purchased by the NTS in 1950 with the aim of preserving the rare alpine flora found toward the summit of the mountain range. The purchase was made using money from the Mountainous Country Fund, initiated by the mountaineer and philanthropist Percy Unna, whose conservation principles the Trust still largely adhere to. Land adjacent to the core of the property was subsequently purchased to safeguard other upland areas (Tarmachan Ridge purchased in 1996) and to gain control of the grazing rights to the hillside (Mardon, pers. comm.). The Lawers Range is extremely popular with walkers. It is reputed to be Scotland's easiest Munro as the car park is located almost halfway up the hillside and this has led to severe footpath erosion on the mountain. Until the mid 1990s all research and management of the site focussed on preserving the biodiversity of the estate. However, a survey of the area that was undertaken by the Royal Commission on the Ancient and Historical Monuments of Scotland (RCAHMS) revealed a complex multi-period archaeological landscape of which very little was known. The BLHLP was initiated to further investigate the landuse history of this area. The Heritage Lottery Fund (HLF) was one of the main funders of the project and one of the conditions of their funding (as it is of all their archaeological research projects) was that opportunities for volunteer and local community involvement were provided. This fitted in with the NTS's own aim of educating people about the properties in their care. An extensive outreach and education programme was initiated including travelling exhibitions, an annual project conference and an education programme for the local primary schools.

Participants in the Loch Tay part of the research mainly came from the village of Killin at the west end of Loch Tay. Killin today is home to c.600 people, and is a service centre to a large geographical area, encompassing much of Lochtayside, Tyndrum and Glen Lochay (MacLennan 2002). In common with most of the inland Scottish Highlands, the main industries are tourism, agriculture and public services, and over 30% of the population are aged over 60. The village has a primary school, with a stable roll of c.70 pupils. In 1947 the population of the village swelled to over 5000 people, as people migrated to the area to work on the construction of the Luberoch Dam hydroelectricity scheme (Miller 2002). This is remembered by many of the older residents as being a golden age for Killin, with several of the local women marrying 'hydro-boys' (West, pers.comm). Since this time the village has reduced considerably in size, but because of its geographical remoteness from other centres, has managed to maintain many of the services which would be expected of a much larger settlement, such as a bank, doctor's surgery, post

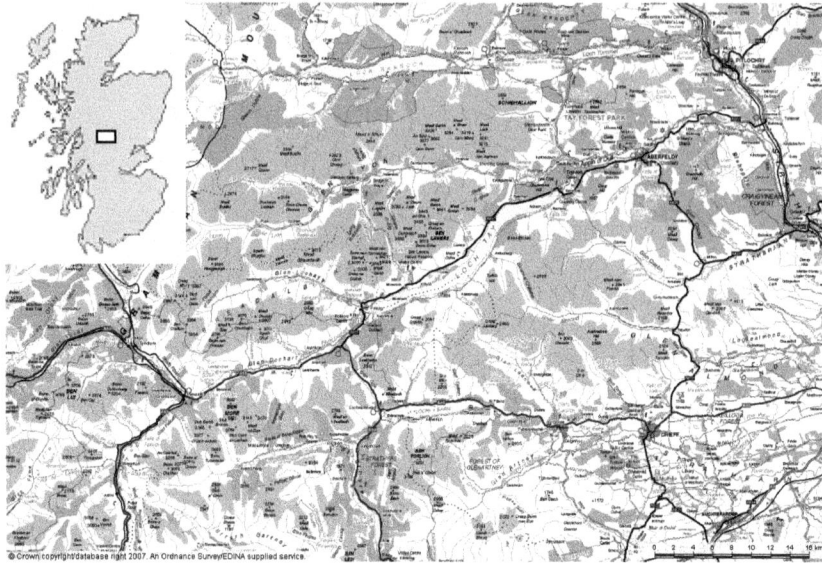

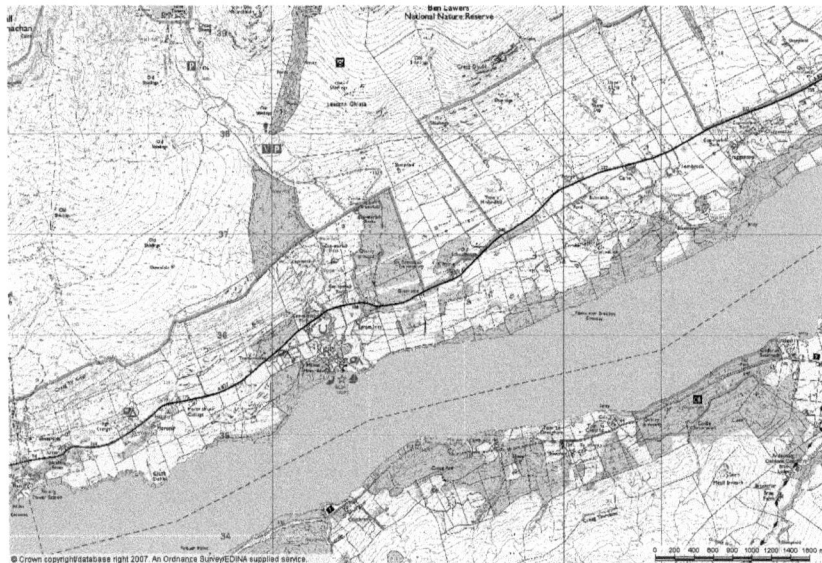

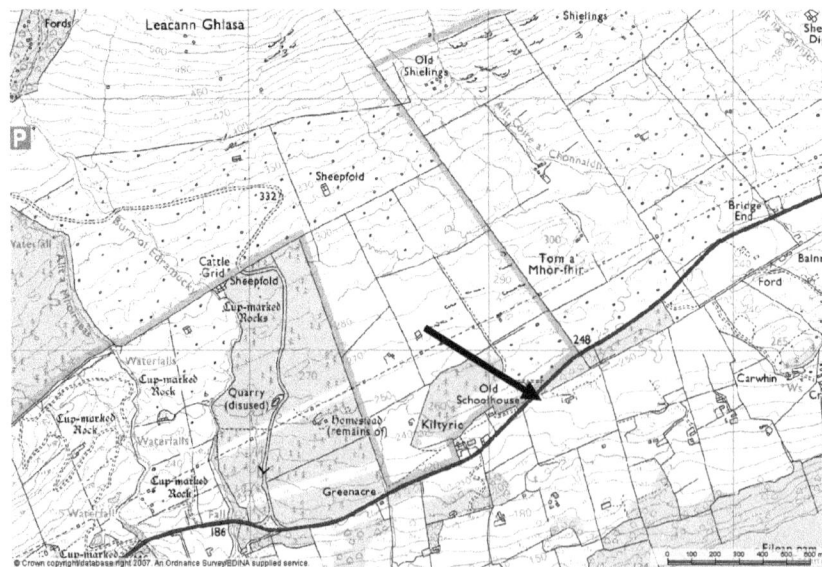

3-1 Location of Kiltyrie (Lochtayside) study site © Crown copyright Ordnance Survey. All rights reserved. 2009.

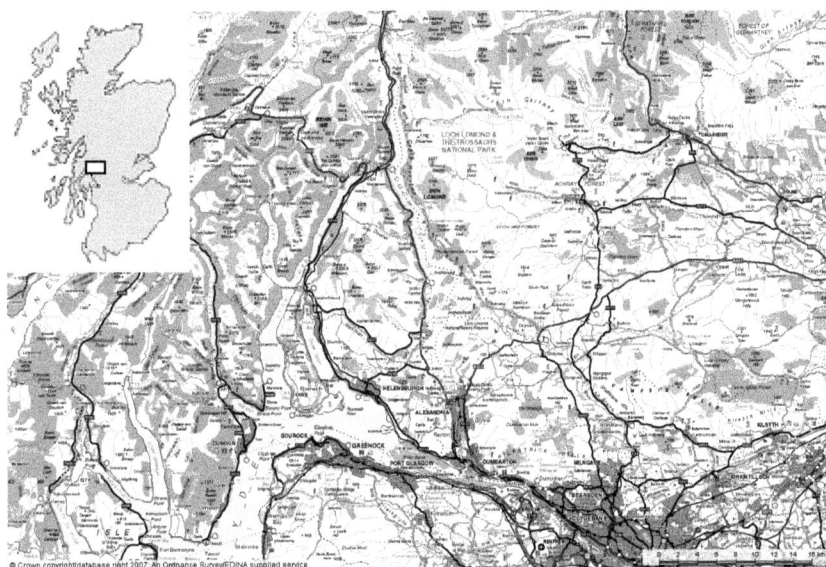

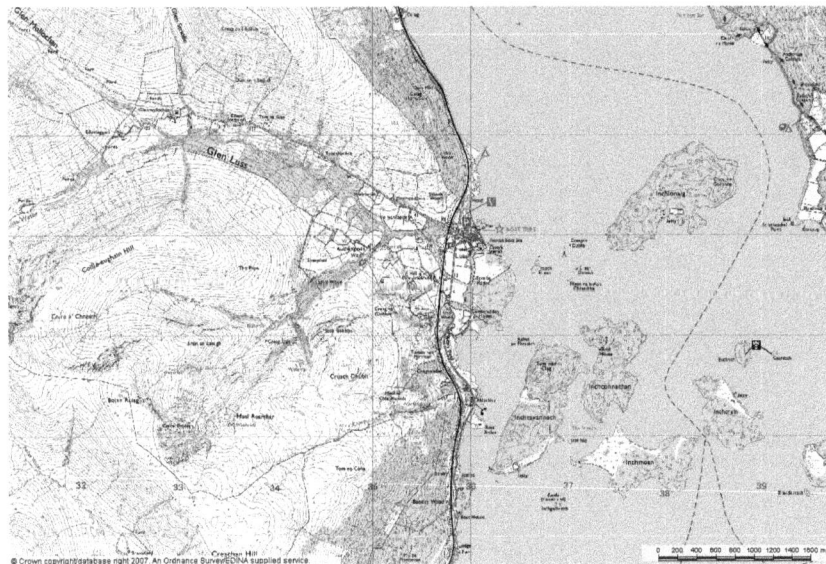

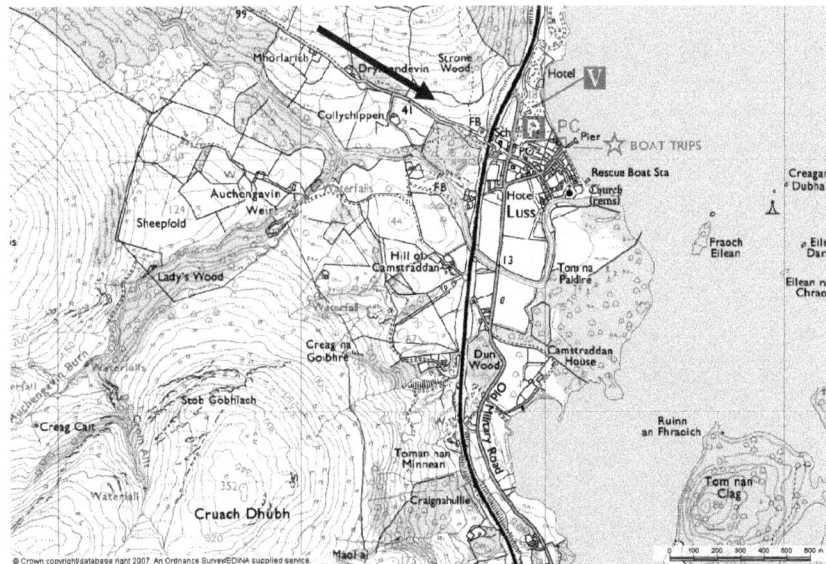

Figure 3-2. Location of Luss (Lochlomondside) study site © Crown copyright Ordnance Survey. All rights reserved. 2009.

office and several shops. The community also has a busy web site (www.Killin.com),and a quarterly Killin Newspaper. It was possible to use these networks to recruit adult volunteers.

It was necessary to select a second study area, in order to gain a comparative dimension to the research. In particular it was important to work with schools and communities which may not know as much of the history of their area as the communities of Lochtayside might do. This community had to be drawn from the area of Loch Lomond and Trossachs National Park, as the Park had a role in funding this research. Various sites and areas were considered for study, with reference being made to a series of community profiles created by the National Park in 2002 (e.g. Davidson-Kinghorn 2002). A series of criteria were chosen which were seen as being important in the selection of a comparative study area. These were: being of a similar size to Killin, the primary study village; being a nucleated settlement with a community and having a primary school. It was also important that the study site itself occupied a similar topographic position to the Lochtayside field site, and as such a loch-side community was sought.

After a review of National Park reports, Community Futures reports and discussion with National Park personnel it was decided that the community of Luss on Lochlomondside would be the most appropriate comparative area. Luss is a small, nucleated village located about halfway up the west bank of the loch with a small primary school. Luss school has pupils from similar backgrounds to Killin and when approached, the teachers were very enthusiastic about the idea of participating in the research. The location of Luss also had practical advantages. The study site was within walking distance of the village, and the National Park has a visitor centre in the village, which they were allowed to use for the indoor component of the exercise. Luss Estates, the main landowner, were also amenable to having the fieldwork undertaken on their land.

Luss parish has a population of c.520, with 209 of these living in the village itself (Davidson-Kinghorn 2002) and, like Killin, 30% of the entire population is of retirement age, a substantially higher proportion than the national average. There is a primary school with a roll of c.18 pupils, which is set to decrease in the next few years unless more families move to the area leading to concerns about its long term viability (King pers. comm.). The main industries in Luss are tourism and agriculture, with many 'retired' individuals operating bed and breakfast accommodation, with many of these individuals coming from the greater Glasgow area. Many of the younger adults who live in Luss commute to Glasgow daily for work.

Luss was chosen as the site for a visitor centre (which is open seasonally) for the Loch Lomond and the Trossachs National Park and a large car park was built to the north of the village centre to accommodate visitors. Within the local community there are mixed views about this development, with some embracing the economic opportunities that

National Park status and the visitor centre potentially bring, whist others suggest it contributes further to the overcrowding of the small village centre by tourists (Travis pers. comm.). In particular, many of the children feel that 'their' play facilities in the village are overrun by visiting families during weekends and holidays. The uneasy relationship between community and Park will be discussed further in section 4.6.2.

The remaining sections of this chapter will present an outline of the 'personality' of Lochtayside and Lochlomondside, looking at their physical characteristics and history. There will also be a short introduction to how the areas have been portrayed recently in tourist literature, particularly through pictures, as this is as likely to affect an individual's perception of landscape as the actuality of the land itself.

3.3. Physical Characteristics of Study Areas

The Highlands of Scotland are a large and diverse area, stretching from the Highland Boundary Fault in the south (which runs from Stonehaven in the northeast to Helensburgh in the southwest) to Caithness and Sutherland in the north. The hills and mountains were formed during the Caledonian Orogeny, an episode of tectonic uplift which also formed the Appalachians in North America (McKerrow et al 2000, McKirdy & Crofts 1999). There have been other episodes of tectonic activity in the area, leading to the formation of its complex geology which is comprised mainly of igneous and metamorphic rocks. The present day topography of the area can mainly be ascribed to the actions of successive ice sheets which covered the area during the Pleistocene. The case study areas are both in the southernmost portion of the Highlands (which, confusingly, is often referred to as the 'central highlands'), indeed the Highland Boundary fault runs through Loch Lomond itself, meaning that the village of Luss holds the title of 'the first village in the Highlands'.

3.3.1. Lochtayside

In common with most of the Scottish Highlands, Lochtayside has a very complex geology. The Loch Tay faultline runs along the loch bed, meaning that rocks from many different periods are present in the hillsides, including metamorphic schists and a band of limestone (Treagus 2003). The loch is a classic 'ribbon lake', in that it is long (23km), narrow (c.2km at widest point) and deep (150m) with steep sided banks. The loch is bordered to the north by the Munros of the Lawers range, and by the gentler Breadalbane Hills in the south.

Much of the area's distinctive geological character comes from a band of metamorphosed calciated-silicate hornfels, found at c. 760 m OD (Tipping et al. 1993). Hornfels are fine-grained metamorphosed sedimentary rocks, and are formed under great heat. This rock type is scarce in upland Britain and as such there are very rare alpine plants associated with this. The fine grained nature of the rock means that it fractures concoidally (like glass). It was exploited in the Neolithic period for stone tool manufacture, at a site on Creag na Calliach; the westernmost peak on the Tarmachan Ridge.

3.3.2. Lochlomondside

Loch Lomond is comprised of two distinct basins, the broad, shallow southern basin, with many 'inches' (islands) and the long, narrow and deep northern basin, which is more similar to other Highland ribbon lakes such as Loch Tay. The Highland boundary fault runs across its two basins, and is broadly responsible for their distinct characters. Most of the rocks in this area date from the Cambrian period, about 570 million years ago (Mitchell 2001). These rocks were thrust up and metamorphosed in the Caledonian Orogeny, and include the Luss-Aberfoyle slates which were mined on the lochside in the eighteenth and nineteenth centuries. There were further episodes of uplift in the Silurian period, followed by episodes of deposition of Old Red Sandstone in the Devonian. As the area straddles a faultline, it has been the focus for a large amount of volcanic activity, especially in the Carboniferous period. Some of the many inches in Loch Lomond are volcanic plugs surviving from this time (ibid).

Geologically speaking Loch Lomond is a very young loch: study of mollusc shells has demonstrated that after the final Loch Lomond Stadial, the loch was an inlet of the sea (Ballantyne & Dawson 1997). It is only at about 4300 BP that isostatic rebound created the Vale of Leven through the final separation of the loch from the sea. This is reflected in the presence of a unique fish species in the loch; the powan, which is related to the salmon, but is commonly known as 'freshwater herring' (Adams 1994).

3.3.3. Vegetation & Wildlife

Both Loch Tay and Loch Lomond have similar vegetation histories. (Tipping et al 1993, Edwards and Whittington 1997) After the final glacial period woodland spread across the landscape, with birch, hazel and oak being the dominant species in this area. This woodland starts to be cleared c.4000 BC (ibid), and (through anthropogenic clearance and changing soil conditions caused by changes in climate and landuse) it is thought that the hillsides would have been broadly open by c.1000 BC, although there would have been a further episode of woodland removal when large numbers of sheep were introduced to the areas in the eighteenth century.

The majority of the woodland in the areas today is the result of modern plantation. One exception to this is the west side of Loch Lomond which has ancient oak woods designated as being of national importance (LLTNP 2006), as they represent one of the few surviving tracts of semi-natural broadleaf woodland in Scotland. They are designated as a Site of Special Scientific Interest (SSSI). This woodland and the surrounding loch-side are home to many rare birds and mammals including capercaillie, black grouse, otters and several bat species. In Lochtayside, areas of hillside have been fenced as exclosures from grazing to allow the

regeneration of natural woodland and grassland features away from grazing herbivores. As well as the semi-natural woodland there are also several conifer plantations on the west bank of the loch. The National Park authority sees these as detrimental to the 'special qualities' of the area (LLTNP 2005) and is developing a long term strategy for their removal from Lochlomondside and replacement with native species.

Both lochs have extensive areas of upland moorland and grassland although these are threatened by the spread of bracken in the area, as changes in farming practices see the reduction of grazing. The open moors and upland grassland are home to numerous rare plant and animal species, including alpine saxifrage, alpine gentian and moss campion as well as black grouse, mountain hares and golden eagles. The alkali rocks of Ben Lawers mean that it is home to species of moss and lichen found nowhere else in Britain. The presence of these rare flora led to Ben Lawers being designated a National Nature Reserve (NNR), as well as a SSSI.

3.4. History

This section will present a brief account of the history of the study areas. Both Lochlomondside and Lochtayside have a variety of landscape features which originate from different events in their past. Therefore material remains found in the area will be discussed at the same time as historical events.

3.4.1. Prehistory

The material remains found in Lochlomondside and Lochtayside are very similar, and as such the narratives of their prehistory may be dealt with together.

Early Prehistory

During the Mesolithic period (McGregor 2002, Finlayson & Edwards 1997), (from about 8500 – 4500 BC in Scotland) people used both Lochtayside and Lochlomondside sporadically as part of a seasonal pattern of movement through the landscape. Mesolithic people would have been hunter-gatherers, although there are some suggestions that they would have exerted control over the landscape via 'fire ecology' to create clearings in forests to attract grazing prey (ibid). The evidence of Mesolithic occupation in upland areas tends to be fairly ephemeral, taking the form of small hearths (often containing burnt hazelnut shells), stake holes, or isolated stone tools of characteristic 'long blade' technology. The distribution of this material suggests that the glens of Tay and Lomond were used as routeways through the Highlands, something that continues in subsequent periods in these areas' history.

From about 4500 BC in Scotland there was a gradual transition in society. Material evidence demonstrates that more permanent ritual and domestic structures were created in this time, which coincides with the introduction of arable cultivation and animal husbandry. Over the next two millennia society became increasingly sedentary and many of the classic monument types of British Prehistory were constructed including the first stone circles (of which there are examples in Lochtayside), Chambered tombs (of which examples of the 'Clyde' type are found in both areas (Ashmore 1996)), and cup and ring rock art. A recent (2004-5) survey revealed over three hundred sites on Lochtayside with rock art and several sites are known also in Loch Lomond. The purpose of these markings is unknown, but it has been recognised that there are large concentrations of them on the boundaries between cultivatable land and what would have been open hillside.

The start of the Neolithic is also marked by a change in material culture, when the first ceramics were introduced to the areas. Stone tool technology also changed at this time, and polished stone implements were introduced. Stone axes are the most common implement type found from this period, and particular rock types were sought out, leading to the creation of 'axe factories' in specific places. These tool manufacture sites are mainly in places that are hard to access, such as mountain summits and cliff edges, and the axe manufacture site at Creag na Caillich at the west end of the Tarmachan Ridge on Lochtayside is no exception (Edmonds et al 1992). This site would have been visited by people coming to the area, perhaps from as far away as continental Europe (Edmonds 1999).

Later Prehistory

In c.2000 BC bronze was introduced to Scotland. This is commonly held to herald the start of the 'later prehistoric period'. Bronze Age axes have been found in both areas, and Crannogs, man-made islands, have been identified in both Loch Lomond and Loch Tay (RCAHMS 2006). Little research has been undertaken on the Loch Lomond crannogs, but the crannogs of Loch Tay have recently been surveyed and radiocarbon dated by the Scottish Crannog Survey. It has been found that crannogs have a very long history of use in Scotland – the earliest known dating from 5000 BC (from a crannog in the Outer Hebrides) and one Loch Tay example is mentioned as being still used in the seventeenth century AD (Dixon pers. comm.). On the basis of the radiocarbon dates the crannogs of Loch Tay appear to date from two distinct periods, around 500 BC and a later episode around 0 BC/AD (Dixon 2004). Other evidence from the later prehistoric period exists in the form of ring forts (large roundhouses) and hillforts such as one located at an island at the mouth of Loch Tay, which is also the burial ground of the Clan MacNab (RCAHMS 2005). Despite the combative names, there is no evidence that these structures were ever used for warfare in the area, and instead can be seen as defended sites, which perhaps acted as local centres of power for a wider community (Collis 1981). The relationship between these sites and crannogs has not been investigated. In Lochlomondside, ringfort sites are sometimes known as 'Duns'; a class of small defended sites across the west of Scotland.

Both Lochtayside and Lochlomondside were very much

on the edge of the Roman world (Despite local legends speaking of Pontius Pilate being born at Fortingall, near Loch Tay) (Firstoff 1954). This is true for of Scotland to the north of the Forth – Clyde isthmus (the site of the Antonine Wall). Both study areas contain Roman marching camps, temporary structures used for a couple of nights by an army on the move, and it is likely that there would have been some interaction between the local population and the Roman army.

3.4.2. The Historic Period

Early Christianity.

After the Romans 'left Britain' traditional accounts suggest that Britain regressed into a 'Dark Age'. To a certain extent this may be argued for southern Britain, but in the non-Romanised Highlands, domestic life appears to have continued in a largely unaltered state. Belief systems in the area appear to change, however, when Christianity when introduced to the Highlands from St Columba's monastery in Iona in the mid fifth century AD (Bradley, 1999). At first Celtic Christianity can be seen as little more that a small cult, being moved across the landscape by saints on missions (Cavill & Jackson 2000). Both areas have evidence for early cult sites: Luss being traditionally associated with St Kessog and Lochtayside with St Fillain. What we know of the movements of these saints comes from *vitae* or lives of saints, which are written accounts often produced by monasteries for specific political purposes centuries after the event occurred (Bradley 1999). There is, however a large amount of material evidence for early Christianity in the study areas, including carved cross slabs, which are found in both areas, and a number of early handbells which have been found in Lochtayside. There are also place names in both areas, which suggest that they may have been early monastic settlements.

The above section has discussed the pre-and protohistory of the case study areas. At that time the areas were at the edge of many different worlds. They were influenced by several cultures, but appear to have acted as a centre for none. In the later periods of history, their position on the boundary of the Highlands put them in a unique position between the increasingly separate worlds of the Scottish Highlands and Lowlands. The following section will discuss the historic period in the area, and in particular how both areas have material remains pertaining to both Highland and Lowland ways of life.

Medieval to Improvement Periods

The medieval period in Scotland is often termed 'the age of the clans', where certain families accrued power and status. Clans are based on a kinship system so theoretically all members of a clan are related by blood or marriage ties (Prebble 1971). There is little documentation for the period up to c.1500 AD in either of the study areas (Harrison 2005), and as such any ideas of the formation of clans in Lochtayside and Lochlomondside come from much later mythologies. It appears that many structures from this time were built of turf, and have been erased by later agriculture, the only ones which survive in Lochtayside are located above the late eighteenth century head dyke on land which has not since been cultivated.

Both areas are part of the droving system of agriculture which emerges in the late sixteenth century (Haldane 1997) when cattle were a major element of the highland economy. Remains of shielings (small turf structures) associated with seasonal grazing of stock in areas of high pastures are found beside burns on the hill slopes of both areas.

From c.1600 – 1800 there are great changes in the economy and the 'personality' of the Scottish Highlands. Through this time, including the Union of Crowns in 1603, the 1707 Act of Union and the Jacobite Rebellions of 1715, and 1745, Highland Scotland becomes increasingly part of a 'British' economy. Laws created after the final Jacobite rebellion forbade the wearing of tartan and the speaking of Gaelic was actively discouraged in many areas. The lairds of both Lochtayside and Lochlomondside, in common with many at the time became increasingly active in Edinburgh society and were broadly sympathetic to the Hanoverian cause (with some cautionary forays into Jacobitism) (Fry 2005). Participation in Edinburgh and London society necessitated monetary wealth, and as such the estates of Breadalbane and Luss were run as commercial concerns rather than through clan based kinship ties. In the eighteenth century both families embarked on ambitious 'Improvement' schemes to make the estate lands profitable, introducing new farming techniques, crops and land organisation. The majority of features extant in the areas' landscapes today date from this time, as the period is characterised by the construction of large regular fields, with linear boundaries that pay little or no heed to existing topographic or structural features. A number of present day farms, and visible ruined farmsteads also date from this period.

Through the nineteenth century both areas became tourist centres influenced by the Picturesque and Romantic traditions and the Tartanry of Sir Walter Scott, Landseer and others (Durie 2003). The construction of railways to both Killin and Lochlomondside during the Victorian era, made the areas accessible to all, not just the upper and middle class tourists of the early nineteenth century.

Historic period in Lochtayside

From around 1550 AD Lochtayside has been the land of the Campbells of Glen Orchy (latterly called the Campbells of Breadalbane). Through the eighteenth century the Campbells commenced wholesale remodelling of the Bredalbane estates. In 1769 John Farquharson was employed to map the entire area as it looked at the time, and lay out new field boundaries, in regular rectilinear form, and associated settlements (Stewart 2000). This new layout included settlement of areas which were hitherto in 'outfield' cultivation. The remains of this reorganisation form the basis for the organisation of land in the area

today. This Improvement continued through the 18th and early 19th centuries. In 1792 the 4th Campbell earl, asked the agronomist William Marshall to Lochtayside (Soulsby 1993) to make a report on the best ways of improving the region. Marshall made recommendations on the best ways to improve the landscape and brought black faced sheep and Cheviots experimentally to the area in the 1790s, and suggested new cropping regimes to increase revenue from the land. It appears that many of the outfield farms had failed and were abandoned by the mid nineteenth century. This is part of a trend of population decrease in north Lochtayside which has continued to this day. Many long term residents of the area mention structures that are now ruins being inhabited, and there being a number of small hamlets along the lochside which are now single homes.

Historic Period in Lochlomondside

Through history sections of Lochlomondside have been governed by many different clans. The purpose of this chapter is not to discuss the entire history of the area, but instead to examine how and when the material remains found in an area were created, as well as presenting some of the histories which have been attached to them. Therefore this section will focus on the area surrounding Luss which has been controlled by the Colquhoun family since 1368.

Glen Luss is the first place in Scotland where the Black Face sheep was introduced, in 1747 by John Campbell of Lagwyne (Forsyth 1806). This event is commemorated by the Tup Bridge, commissioned by Sir Ivor Colquhoun and built in 1777 and is part of a wider programme of Improvement in the area. This included the movement of people away from the Glen and into the planned village at Luss which replaced an earlier settlement at the site (RCAHMS 2006). In the late eighteenth and nineteenth centuries several new industries were started by the estate including a saw mill, a cotton mill and slate quarries. Prior to the introduction of black-faced sheep the glen was an important droving route for cattle being brought across from Argyll (Mitchell 2000).

In earlier times the Glen is supposed to have been one of the seats of early Christianity in Scotland, and has a long association with St Kessog. There are local tales of Edentaggart Farm, about halfway along the glen being a former monastic settlement with its name deriving from *Eudann t'sagairt* meaning 'the face of the hill of the priest' (Bray 2001). It is also suggested that one group of shielings are actually the remains of monastic cells dating to c.700 AD. More concrete evidence for Early Christian settlement in the area comes from the graveyard in Luss Church itself where there are several carved stones, including a 'hogsback' grave slab, a style typical of tenth century Norse graves, and two carved cross slabs from the late seventh century (RCAHMS 2006). Further up the Glen there are the ruins of the fifteenth century St Michael's chapel (RCAHMS 2006), this fell out of use when Luss church was built by the Colquhoun family in 1875 which replaced an earlier church built on the site in 1771.

From the late eighteenth century Luss has been an important stopping off place for travellers and tourists to the Scottish Highlands: 200 years ago it was a day's travel away from Glasgow. Luss was a key destination for Picturesque and Romantic tourists as it afforded fine views of Ben Lomond, and 'the Cobbler', near Arrocher was nearby (Bowman 1986). The inn at Luss was visited in 1803 by Dorothy Wordsworth (sister of William), who described it as overcrowded and squalid, and the landlady as being *'the most cruel and hateful looking woman I ever saw'* (Campbell 1999). From this time until the present day the village has been an important tourist centre, along with all of Lochlomondside. The building of a railway to Balloch in 1850 meant that the loch was easily accessible for day or weekend trippers from Clydeside, and the erection of a steamer pier at Luss ensured that the village received a steady stream of visitors.

In the 1980s the planned centre of the village gained televised fame as 'Glendarroch', the fictional village in 'Take the Highroad', and filming was carried out there until the series ended in 2003. The village is still a tourist destination for coach parties of a certain age, keen to see Glendarroch for themselves.

3.5. Present Landuse

3.5.1. Lochlomondside

Although the current landscape of Loch Lomond has been shaped by agriculture and forestry, tourism is the major economic activity around Loch Lomond. In 1993 there were 2 million recreational visits to the Loch Lomond area, with over 90% of these happening at weekends (Dawson et. al. 1993). This has led to increased visitor load on footpaths, and the narrow area of flat land surrounding the loch. The loch itself is facing pressure from water pollution and overcrowding due to pleasure craft, and since its formation the National Park has been developing a series of bylaws to combat this.

3.5.2. Lochtayside

There is no longer any arable cultivation carried out on Lochtayside. Instead, much of the low lying land is rough pasture, which is becoming increasingly covered in bracken as stocking levels on the hillside are reduced. The high hill slopes are covered in a combination of heath and moorland, although on NTS estates there is a programme to reintroduce native woodland species such as dwarf willow. Much of the land is also given over to recreation, particularly at the two ends of the loch where there are large holiday park developments. The other major landuse in the area is commercial forestry: on both the north and the south shores there are extensive areas of sitka spruce monoculture. In addition to this there are mixed woodlands, which were planted by the Breadalbane estates. There are still an unusually large number of ruined buildings and field boundaries extant in the landscape, many of which are a testament to the failed agricultural expansion of the eighteenth century.

3.6. Study Sites

The previous sections have dealt with the characteristics of the entire areas of Loch Tay and Loch Lomond. This section will deal with two specific field sites. Specific field sites were selected for the landscape workbook section of the study (see section 4.7.1 of methods chapter for details). Participants were taken out into the countryside and asked to comment on their surroundings in a number of different ways. These sites were selected because of their accessibility, the fact that they had features typical of the area, and open views of the surroundings. The following section will describe these two sites.

3.6.1. Kiltyrie, Lochtayside and Environs.

The site selected for the Lochtayside part of the study is located at Kiltyrie farm (NN 628 375), near to the centre of the north side of the loch. A field was selected with a large number of archaeological and geological features and vegetation typical of the area. This site is part of the Ben Lawers land owned by the NTS and as such it was easy to negotiate access. The site is only a short walk from the main road so is accessible even to individuals with limited mobility. The field also (weather permitting) has open views of a large area of Lochtayside, including Bein Ghlas, one of the Munros in the Lawers Range, the Tarmachan ridge and the loch itself.

The field at Kiltyrie occupies an area of around four hectares and is currently used for mixed grazing, by cattle and sheep. Grazing rights are rented from the NTS. Although the field is predominantly covered by grass, there are extensive areas of bracken present at certain times of year, as well as several waterlogged patches of ground with abundant sedges. In common with many upland areas, soil cover is very thin, and in several areas of the field limestone bedrock is visible. The geology of the area is mixed in character with bands of quartz-mica-schist, limestones and diorite running east-west along the hillside (BGS 2005). In addition to a large limestone ridge, the topography contains palaeo-channels and limestone mounds, giving the field a hummocky appearance. Several glacial erratics are present in the field, the largest of these being over two metres high, and as such were not removed in a wider programme of field clearance associated with agricultural improvements in the area. The surrounding area is home to a large number of red deer, who are mainly found on the upper hillsides, and only graze the lower hillsides in winter. Birds found in the area include golden eagles, buzzards, ospreys, ptarmigan, ring ousels and several smaller birds (Angus pers. comm.).

There are a variety of archaeological features present in the Kiltyrie field, dating from prehistory to the nineteenth century. In the northern half of the field, one of a line of mounds running east - west across the site is described in the National Monuments Record (NMR) as a possible round barrow, a type of funerary monument which usually dates to the Bronze Age; however no records pertaining to investigation of this site exist. No features associated with landuse from the Iron Age (c. 500 BC) to medieval periods exist within the site, any such features have probably been erased by the wholesale land reorganisation of the late eighteenth century (see above for details) although shieling grounds and lazy beds associated with medieval settlement are evident on the higher slopes of the hillside. Prior to the land reorganisation, the field at Kiltyrie was part of the outfield system of cultivation, and would have been used for grazing and occasional crop cultivation. Within the field there is a longhouse which was constructed some time after 1790, when the estate was reorganised. This site is shown as abandoned on the 1864 Ordnance Survey map of the area. A similar structure in the next field was excavated by the BLHLP in 2003 and was found to have only one phase of construction and occupation, suggesting that ultimately this attempt at upland living had failed.

There are two limekilns in the field, associated with bands of limestone which run through the area. These are also linked to the Improvement period settlement, and the new 'scientific' farming methods of the time. Lime was used to neutralise the highly acidic peaty soils, in an attempt to make this upper land viable for arable cultivation. Remains of quarries associated with this extraction of lime and the construction of field walls are still visible in the field. The boundaries of the field, although now consolidated with barbed wire, still follow the alignments laid out by Farquharson in his 1769 plans of the area. The study site also contains features from the recent past, including structures associated with the current farming regime such as metal sheep pens, feeding troughs and tracks from the farmer's Landrover. By far the largest extant modern structures in the fields are the row of electricity pylons which were built in the glen to link the Luberoch Hydro Electric scheme to the National Grid as part of the 1959 'Power from the Glens' scheme (Scottish Southern Energy 2005). About 500 metres to the west of the field there is a large, rectangular, densely planted conifer plantation. This stands in contrast to an area to the south of the field which has had all grazing excluded by the NTS in order to allow for native woodland regeneration. This area now has a mixture of young hazel, oak, rowan and willow trees growing.

3.6.2. Site at Glen Luss and immediate environs

The field selected (NS 354 952) in Glen Luss is very similar to that at Kiltyrie in terms of topography, landuse and vegetation but is only about one hectare in extent. It is close to the mouth of the glen and as such has a clear view over the southern half of Loch Lomond, and the village of Luss itself. It is grazed by sheep, and the vegetation is a mixture of grasses, sedges and bracken, as well as some small trees, and bluebells in the springtime. It is owned by Luss Estates, the major landowner in the area and is leased to a tenant farmer. It is close to the village, and was approached by crossing a wooden foot bridge over the busy A82, the main trunk road for the west coast of Scotland, running from Glasgow to Inverness via Crianlarich. The field itself has no visible historical or archaeological features, save

for relict stone and earthen field boundaries. However, the ruined nineteenth century farmstead of Collychippen is in a neighbouring field on the other side of the single track road which runs to the upper reaches of Glen Luss. This neighbouring field could not be used for the exercise since at the time fieldwork was being conducted the farmer was using it for lambing. The extant field boundaries date from the nineteenth century reorganisation of Glen Luss by Luss estates. The field also contains modern landuse features, including sheep farming paraphernalia and a row of electricity poles which provide power to the farms and houses further up Glen Luss.

3.7. The study areas as known by visitors

The previous sections have outlined 'factual' information about the study areas and the specific field sites used in this research. The main characteristics of the landscape have been described, along with the specific case study areas. This information given is not, however, the type of information that most visitors to the area access before their visit. Instead, visitors are more likely to have an impression of the area which is gained from promotional tourism literature, or portrayals of the area in popular culture. The use of Luss as the location for 'High Road' and the tourism associated with this has already been mentioned, but within popular culture there is a very clear characterisation of the areas as scenically beautiful places that can be used as an escape from everyday life (McCrone 1995). The areas are also popular locations for outdoor activities, and are marketed as destinations for hill walking and watersports in particular. Visitors may have also had exposure to friends and families experiences of the areas which will be part of their particular background of the area. Obviously all of these cannot be discussed here, but these may include recollections (and pictures) of visits spent in the areas, or stories of when people lived in the area. These recollections may be positive or negative, and may dwell mainly on certain characteristics of the area, perhaps even characteristics that are no longer readily apparent, but may still form people's dominant impressions of the area.

3.8. Illustrations

With the exception of location maps this chapter is unillustrated. When determining how to illustrate this chapter I first thought it best to use a number of pictures that I had taken myself of the area to illustrate different aspects of the landscape. This however would only give an impression of the area as I saw it, including certain aspects which I saw as being important, which others may not notice, and avoiding other features which were not of interest to me, but may be central to others' ideas of the area. Instead I would suggest that the reader carries out an internet search for images of 'Loch Tay', 'Killin' and 'Loch Lomond'. They will be confronted by promotional images taken in sunlight and portray typical aspects of the Highland scenery, including the lochs themselves, surrounding mountains, waterfalls and Happy Highlanders. Modern landscape features and poor weather are noticeable for their absence. This approach offers a particular window on how the two lochs are 'seen' by people who are yet to visit them.

3.9. Conclusions

This chapter has presented an overview of the topography and history of Lochtayside and Lochlomondside. The areas have been discussed at three different scales, that of 'the Highlands', Lochtayside and Lochlomondside, and the individual field sites. The village communities worked with in the study have also been introduced.

I have sought to give an 'objective' account of various events in the area's past that have given the landscape its present character. I have tried to describe the bare bones of a landscape that can be drawn upon by people to form their perceptions. However, no history of an area can be 'objective' and dispassionate, coloured as it is by the author's knowledge, personal preferences and beliefs. The description that I have given of the area is clouded in the belief system of the present day: where geological processes have rational explanations, history is presented in a politically correct, non-biased way, and management of land in both areas is based on a conservation rhetoric (in the case of Lochlomondside, it is within a National Park, and the study area in Lochtayside is owned by the NTS). In the past people would not have seen landscape in this way, something which was introduced in the literature review (chapter 2) and will be dealt with further in chapter 6 of this work. The next chapter will focus upon the methods used for understanding people's landscape perceptions and the rationale behind them.

4
Methodology

4.1. Introduction

The literature review (chapter 2) outlined the main strands of academic research into landscape values which have informed this research. This chapter will take these ideas, and demonstrate how they have been used to develop a methodology for this study. Research questions addressed by the work will be presented, followed by the concepts which these questions necessitated investigating, including theories of landscape perceptions and preferences, and who the research should focus upon. After reviewing other studies on landscape perceptions it was realised that there were a number of strands of information that the methods used would need to generate in order to explore not only people's perceptions for landscape, but the influences on these perceptions. Following this, the methods used for information gathering and analysis will be outlined.

Some of the methods used in this research are novel (such as the landscape workbook and image workbooks outlined in sections 4.7.1 & 4.7.2) and other data collection and interpretation techniques have not been combined in this way before, and were chosen for a very specific subset of reasons. These include the need to find out what people value of their landscapes and why people hold these viewpoints. The need to work with a broad cross section of the population, which included adults and children, and visitors to and residents of the area informed the choice of data collection and analysis techniques. In this chapter these reasons will be outlined and placed within the context of the theoretical and practical constraints and opportunities presented by the research project.

4.2. Research Questions

The broad research questions to be addressed were established in the studentship application. These were:

Research Question 1 How can qualitative preferences and values for landscape best be captured and measured in a repeatable and reliable manner?

Research Question 2 To what extent and in what ways does an increased knowledge of landscape history affect people's landscape preferences and values?

These research questions can be addressed in a number of different ways. The theoretical stance informing this research has been introduced in the literature review and will be further outlined within this chapter, and has shaped the way that the methodology for this study has developed. The inductive approach taken within this study required that the methods used had to allow for open ended questions to be used which would identify different types of attitudes and behaviours, rather than questions which investigated a specific hypothesis. This approach is supported and guided by the understandings of both 'landscape' and 'value' outlined in the literature review (sections 2.2 & 2.3). The study area was determined by the project brief: as outlined in the previous chapter research took place in Lochtayside and Lochlomondside in the Central Highlands.

An examination of literature surrounding the ideas of the different values people hold for landscape led to the refinement of the initial research questions. The wording of the first research question was not changed markedly, but the changes that were made are important. Firstly the word capture was replaced with 'understand'. Capture suggests permanence in landscape values, and the idea that once they are captured they will not change. 'Understand' takes into account the dynamic nature of people's landscapes and therefore the values that they hold for them. Landscape values are not a single entity that can be captured, instead they are part of person's complex identity and their relations with the world surrounding them and as such, interpretation and understanding is required rather than just capturing.

To understand the multiple and complex values that people hold for landscapes it is necessary to look at a wide cross-section of the population, and any methods used should be able to do this. This is something that is not accounted for in many existing methodologies for examining people's landscape values (e.g. methods which contain concepts which are too complex and/or time consuming for certain population groups, c.f. Jacobs 1997, Kaltenborn& Bjerke 2002) and as such it was specifically added to this research question:

Revised Question 1: What methods can be utilised to understand qualitative preferences for landscapes which work with a large cross section of the population, and can be used in a repeatable and reliable manner?

The second research question was altered considerably. It was realised that to examine the effect of knowledge of landscape history on people's landscape preferences and values it was necessary to examine what factors influence people's landscape perceptions. It is impossible to examine one strand of influence in detail without an understanding of how people's landscape perceptions are formed more generally. The examination of influences on landscape values has often been neglected in previous research, and as such there was little information available on ways of understanding this. Research which has been undertaken nto this has tended to be part of the qualitative tradition and has been investigated by ethnographic approaches, where an individual spends an extended period in a community examining their attachments to landscape (e.g. Layton 1999, Strang 1999). As such few methods exist to examine the influences on landscape values that work in a repeatable and reliable manner, and there is no clear theory as to why people's attachments exist. Within this broad research question it was still possible to examine the influence that knowledge of landscape history had on an individual's landscape perceptions. The altered second research question read:

Revised Question 2: What are the main influences on people's landscape perceptions and values?

4.3. Key issues in landscape values research

When the methodology for this research was developed several key issues in landscape research were examined. This section will review these issues, including why it is important to examine the values that people hold for landscapes, and why it is necessary to understand why people value certain elements of the landscape.

4.3.1. Why is it important to examine landscape values?

Why it is important to examine why people value landscapes? A landscape, whilst it can be used, thought of and valued in multiple ways, can only have one physical form. This is unlike other commodities which can exist in several different forms in parallel to satisfy the need of all users. For example, different types of housing can be built to satisfy different needs, or there can be different art forms and musical genres to satisfy all tastes. People interact with the physical landscape in a multitude of different ways and if the character of the landscape is altered then it may damage these interactions, and therefore the values that they hold for these features. Therefore it is necessary to find out how people use, think and value a particular landscape before policies are made which will affect future landscapes. *'The necessity to include local people and other stakeholders to achieve just and sustainable solutions and to utilise local knowledge is generally acknowledged'* (Soliva et al. 2008:57), and in recent years there have been numerous studies where stakeholders have been involved in landscape planning (e.g. Lange &

Schmidt 2003, MacKay 1995, O' Rourke 2005, Sang & Birnie 2005).

In a 2002 report for the Getty Institute, Mason outlines some of the difficulties which are faced when trying to examine the values that people hold for heritage. Heritage and landscape are similarly slippery issues, they do not have clear boundaries, and are imagined differently by everyone. He suggests that there is a diverse range of values that people hold for heritage and that these values change through time, and as such cannot be captured: they need to be understood in their wider social context. These values often conflict, so it is not possible to come up with a single model of value for these, instead he suggests that there has to be a *'deliberate, systematic and transparent process of analysing and assessing all the values of heritage'* (Mason 2002:5) which understands the contexts of individual's values as well as the values. I agree with this statement, and this study will attempt to address these values. The focus will be on individual's values, that are personal rather than any economic, institutional and informational values that may also be held for landscapes.

A further reason why it is important to look at landscape values is that there is no baseline knowledge about how people think about the landscape of the Scottish Highlands. Consultations about landscape perceptions tend to be undertaken when a landscape is going to be subject to change, such as the consultations which are currently ongoing at the sites of numerous proposed wind farm developments. There is need for non event-based consultations on landscape perceptions. It is necessary to know what people think about land when there is no immediate threat to its appearance or character so that it is possible to ascertain how much of a person's perceptions gauged at the time of a potential change are constructed in direct relation to that threat of change. In threat scenarios responses are likely to be unduly focussed upon this single issue, they are affected by a 'now bias' There is also a need for discovering the perceptions of people excluded by standard public enquiry based consultations. Public enquiries tend to operate in a fixed discourse, with a small cross section of the population (adults on the electoral roll who live in the area concerned) and valorise rational attitudes to developments in landscape, such as objections on environmental, economic or community wellbeing grounds (Jacobs 1997, Scott & Shannon 2007). This study seeks to redress this, by discovering something of individuals' landscape perceptions and the main influences on them, in a context which does not include any threat to the landscape. This will be undertaken in such a way that allows people to voice all of their opinions of landscape, rather than those which can be seen to be relevant in landscape policy terms.

Destigmatising 'NIMBY'

Arguments based on irrational attachments to landscape are too often dismissed as Nimbyism (Not In My Back Yard) when these emotional reasons are just as 'real' and valid as more rational attitudes. They are just more complicated and harder to understand, measure and justify in policy terms. There is a need to celebrate and promote 'irrational' responses to landscape, as much of how people value landscapes comes from these responses (something which this work examines in particular detail). In recent years, in planning debates, especially those with much media coverage (e.g. debates into the siting of nuclear power stations, or waste plants, or major road projects) there has been a reaction against 'Nimbyism' with connotations of parochialism. However, your neighbourhood is the everyday place that you live in. You have attachments to the area not for rational reasons, but if these arise in the planning process then they are often attacked as being small minded and local. There are current arguments about the validity of the NIMBY concept. Hubbard (2005, 2006) talks about the problems of Nimbyism in terms of environmental racism, where rich, empowered (normally white middle class) individuals are able to use campaigning savvy to ensure undesirable developments do not happen in their neighbourhood. However Wolsink (2006) suggests that NIMBY is a confused concept and bundles together too many thoughts, emotions and practices. He argues against the concept of Nimbyism being purely negative. It is described in the OED as '*an attitude ascribed to persons who object to the siting of something they regard as detrimental or hazardous in their own neighbourhood while by implication raising no objections to similar developments elsewhere*' (OED online 2007). However Wolsink argues that in reality many people are opposed to the development being anywhere (NIABY), rather than just being in their 'back yard'. Also, it is uncertain what is intrinsically wrong with wanting to protect your local area. Often it appears that anyone who objects to something on purely locational grounds runs the risk of being called a NIMBY, even if they would object to the development being sited at any location. There is an idea that irrational reasons for opposing a development are invalid and borne of the selfishness of the opposition. So, for example, when Hubbard (2005) talks about Nimbyism and prostitution, he validates arguments about the safety of prostitutes above those which talk about how 'they don't want hookers on their street'. These he appears to see as NIMBY arguments and therefore invalid. This is also true of landscape planning decisions, where it appears that opposition to developments, which are based on irrational grounds, are less valid than rational arguments about habitat loss, the presence of 'nationally important' species or damage to designated historic environment features (Abram et al 1996, Jay 2007).

I believe that local arguments (those which often fall under the banner of NIMBY) are valid, and are made to appear less valid by the pejorative sense that NIMBY carries. These do not need to be rational arguments, and can be seen to be quite selfish, but should still be taken into account, and people should not feel ashamed to express them. Instead it is important to understand these complex irrational relationships with land and celebrate them, and ensure that they are given the same weight as more rational arguments

(those based on quantifiable 'facts') in landscape planning and designation processes.

These intangible, irrational attachments to landscapes and heritage have been examined previously within a Scottish context by two researchers from Manchester university Sian Jones examined the broad range of values that the local community attached to the Hilton of Cadboll Pictish symbol stone. Jones used excavations at the site of the stone in Easter Ross as a focus for debate on belonging, ownership and repatriation of artefacts. The cross slab itself is currently located in the Museum of Scotland, in Edinburgh which is a bone of contention to many of the local population. A combination of workshops and interviews was used to examine these contentions, and to give a voice to a local community which had previously been ignored by heritage managers (Jones 2005)

In her PhD research Angela McClanahan Examined the uses and meanings of the monuments in the Heart of Neolithic Orkney World Heritage Site. Perceptions and values for both the sites and the World Heritage legislation itself were examined, and both residents of and visitors to the area were worked with. This work produced interesting data on peoples uses and perceptions of the monuments within the WHS including the Ring of Brodgar and Stones of Stenness.

Both of these studies focussed solely on archaeology, in the form of monuments (The Orkney sites) and artefacts (the Hilton of Cadboll stone). With both of these studies the landscape context, or setting of these features was crucial to people's understanding of them. Rather than examining specific monuments, this study looks at the landscape in its entirety, and examines people's values for the entire landscape and the historical features that exist therein.

Why you need to examine 'the Why' in landscape values?

As already stated in the literature review (2.2) people's landscapes are a product of their identity. How you think about landscape is governed by who you are, what you do, what you have done, what you believe and what you are interested in. This kind of information is needed to make informed policy decisions about long term landscape futures, rather than just reactionary studies which answer a specific question. Therefore in order to examine perceptions and values for landscape it is necessary to find out what the perceptions are, what physical elements of the landscape people are drawing on when they show these perceptions and what has lead people to hold these views. Although it is argued in this book, people's experience of landscape is primarily governed by identity based and personal reasons, they are also reacting to the physical properties of the surroundings [3].

[3] For example there may be an open hillside which is valued by someone as a 'wild' open space which is altered by the placing of a row of pylons on it. Because people exist within a 'now' that sees pylons as a bad thing, then they see the hillside as being spoiled. The pylon is not 'telling' the person that the land is spoiled, rather the landscape is 'spoiled' for the person because of their ideas of land, Highlands and pylons.

To research the complex relationships that people have with landscapes it is possible to do a 'deep' ethnographic study and embed yourself within a society in order to discover, though a process of interviews and participant observation how people think about the world. This was impractical to implement with a large number of people within the scope of PhD research, and studies which do not examine a large spectrum of the population are often seen as being of little use to policy studies, as a small sample cannot represent the population as a whole. The alternative approach to these is quantitative methodologies. These provide a specific answer to specific questions and give a broad brushstroke approach to landscape perceptions. However, these questions do not allow the understanding of the myriad factors that affect people's landscape values. This instead requires information that people have volunteered and a method which allows people time to think about their responses, and offer up information that they would perhaps not have thought about in the first place. For this study it was therefore necessary to examine methodologies which bridge this quantitative/qualitative divide. The following section will briefly examine the differences between qualitative and quantitative research.

4.4. Bridging the Quantitative/Qualitative divide in landscape research

Until recently studies into landscape perceptions and values could be subdivided into two main groups: short term quantitative studies with large sample populations and those which employed qualitative, ethnographic techniques, which take place over a longer time frame and are more 'in depth' with a small sample population. Land use policy studies often relied on quantitative methodologies, and examined people's attitudes to changes to the physical landscape. In certain cases qualitative interview data were included, but it sometimes appeared to be something of an afterthought in the research, inserted into an appendix to enrich the 'core product of the report' (e.g. English Heritage 2005). This was true of policy related research more generally, it has only been in the past decade or so that qualitative approaches have become accepted across the policy field. In opposition to this there are anthropological studies where researchers take at least a year to embed themselves in a local community where they attempt to understand how a population inhabits its environment (e.g. Layton 1999, Lee 2007, Strang 1999). There has, however, been a recent trend towards methodologies which bridge this gap (e.g. Stedman 2002, 2003, Herzog 2002) which has been lead by a realisation that in depth studies into people-landscape interactions do not need to be long term, and therefore policy inaccessible. This is part of a wider adoption of mixed method approaches to social science research (Brannen 1992, Onwuegbuzie & Leech 2005).

4.4.1. The Quantitative and Qualitative research traditions

Quantitative research can be defined as a quasi-scientific approach to social research (Brannen 2004). This type of research strives for objectivity, and the influence of the researcher is removed as much as possible from the research process. Quantitative research project design is based upon deductive principles, initially developed in the natural sciences, whereby a hypothesis is created through an analysis of current literature and relevant theoretical models. This hypothesis is tested on a sample population which should be representative of the larger population as a whole. Methods are used which isolate the causes and effects of phenomena and allow these to be quantified, as the sample is representative these findings can be generalised and general laws and theories created. Quantitative research has been attacked as no research can be seen to be entirely objective and instead all research involves subjectivities. Flick (2005:4) suggests that *'Despite all the methodological controls the* [quantitative] *research and its findings are unavoidably influenced by the interests and the social and cultural backgrounds of all those involved. These factors influence the formulation of research questions and hypotheses as well as the interpretation of data and relations'*. Therefore there can be seen to be no such thing as completely objective research and there need to be methods which account for these subjectivities.

Qualitative research operates with the premise that there are no universal truths, or underlying rules of behaviour which can be uncovered by empirical research, therefore methods focus on understanding behaviours and relationships, rather than quantifying the results of these behaviours (Seale et al. 2004). There is a realisation that no research is without subjectivities, and that the subjectivities of the researcher are part of the research approach. Instead qualitative research is about the understanding of phenomena within their temporal and cultural context. Qualitative methodologies work with ideas of holism, that humans cannot be understood outside the context of their life world. It is about the study of social relationships, and the mechanisms by which these relations operate. In qualitative studies the object under study is the determining factor of the methodology (rather than a hypothesis which is tested with reference to a specific sample population). Therefore the field of study in a true qualitative research project is not an artificial situation set up in a quasi-scientific way, but instead an observation of (and interaction with) subjects in their everyday lives. It is realised, however that any research process interferes with 'normal' behaviour, and creates artificial situations, as under normal circumstances the researcher would either not be within the community they are studying, or playing a different role within this community. It is the task of the qualitative researcher to recognise the biases which are created by this interference, and account for them when writing the findings of research.

Quantitative research is still dominant within practice, particularly within research with an expected policy relevant outcome (rather than just an academic exercise) (Hammersly 2000). Qualitative data are still seen to be irrelevant by some, on the grounds that it is too subjective, and can never be seen to be representative of the larger population, whereas others counteract by suggesting that quantitative research is only a poor man's relation of the richness of qualitative data (Flick 2002). In reality, the two different types of technique lend themselves to different types of research questions. When a particular phenomena is being examined in detail then qualitative techniques may be of the most use, whereas when causal relationships are sought (and frequencies and distributions which can be used to predict from findings is required) then quantitative methodologies are required. This is not to say that the two types of technique should always be used in isolation, instead methods which use both qualitative and quantitative techniques can produce a far richer dataset. Information from the two types of method can be triangulated so that the qualitative information can inform quantitative research, and qualitative data can be transformed into quantitative data, by means of coding, meaning that the two types of techniques can be used in parallel. Coding is a way of making sense of a dataset by the production of networks of categories and concepts within the dataset (Krippendorff 2004), and through this process qualitative data can be quantified. The process by which coding was undertaken in this research is further addressed in the sections describing the different methods below (4.7.1).

In order to address the main issues presented by the research questions it was considered necessary to use both qualitative and quantitative information. There was a need to investigate the complex relationships that people have with landscapes, and discover the roots of these relations. Qualitative data collection and interpretation techniques are most appropriate to explore these relationships, as they require questioning which is open ended and allows people to express unprompted viewpoints which may not be discovered by the more closed types of questioning found in quantitative surveys. Another aspect of this research was the need to compare various strands of influence on an individual's landscape perceptions, and this cannot be easily undertaken using a purely qualitative approach. It was therefore appropriate to mix techniques, and convert some of the qualitative information to quantitative information through formal content analysis which allows this comparison. Other information, about personal backgrounds, residential status etc. can easily be collected using quantitative techniques, and as such a mixed methods approach appears to be ideal for this research. These different types of information can be combined and compared using triangulation. There are two different types of triangulation (Brannen 2004, Flick 2002), in one the single case is focussed upon and in the other the dataset as a whole is examined. In the individual case a person's responses to different exercises they have carried out (for example interview and questionnaire data) are compared, and their answers are related to each other. At the level of a group frequencies of observations can be examined, and again these different types of response can be interrelated. Statistical tests can be carried out on the dataset in order to determine the relatedness of these concepts (Zuur et al 2007).

It is therefore no longer entirely appropriate to think of quantitative and qualitative methods entirely separately. Instead it is necessary to think about the appropriateness of the method regardless of the different epistemological roots of the two schools of thought. There has to be a logical combination of the two types of data, they have to have true interrelatedness, but there is no reason why both qualitative and quantitative techniques cannot be combined to great effect in the research process.

4.5. Methodology Requirements

In order to address the two research questions outlined above (section 4.2), in a manner which took into account the issues highlighted in the previous sections, the methodology developed for this research had to fulfil a variety of requirements. This section will outline these criteria, and describe in more detail the reasons behind their necessity.

The methods used had to be workable with a large cross section of the population, something which most of the previous studies into this topic fail to address. Studies into landscape preferences tend to select a sample population from the electoral roll, or work with a single subgroup of the population (e.g. Brown et al 2002, Clark & Stein 2003, Fjortoft & Sageie 2000). This means that many population subgroups, including children are automatically excluded from the decision making process. Also, using the public version of the electoral roll to recruit participants means that only residents of the study area who have chosen to have their details made public are selected. For landscapes such as the Scottish Highlands, this local resident focus is an important oversight, as the Highlands are an iconic landscape valued globally, by more people than just those who inhabit the area, and have large numbers of visitors annually (Patterson 2002).

It is necessary to determine the qualities of a landscape people react to, both in positive and negative ways, rather than just commenting on the landscape as a whole. People value a whole landscape, but their reasons for valuing this landscape may be contingent on a few features within it, or certain characteristics of it. It is also necessary to discover in what ways people care about the landscape (why do they like, or dislike, or feel a special connection to a feature?). The elements of landscape that people value are interesting in their own right, and are a useful source of information for making planning and preservation decisions. It is, however, imperative to investigate the influences on these attitudes, in order to examine how much these attitudes will be affected by changes to the physical landscape, and to understand whether these attitudes are something which have been long held by the individual, or whether they are just transient opinions, caused by events on the day of questioning (see section 2.5 of literature review for further discussion of this).

This research works with the idea that how people think about and value landscapes is governed by aspects of an individual's identity and their place in the world. This is an idea which has been forwarded by several social researchers (e.g. Cosgrove 1984, 2006, Bender 1993, Johnston 1998). Therefore, to fully understand where landscape perceptions are rooted it is necessary to explore aspects of a person's background.

Previous research into people's landscape values has examined causal relationships between aspects of people's identity and their attitudes to landscapes (e.g. Haartsen et al. 2003 Perez 2002). Studies such as these helped identify a number of particular facets of identity that may be important in determining people's landscape values which should therefore be addressed as part of this research. One of the main factors which has been suggested as influential in determining landscape values is use relationship. Use relationship can be defined as what a person does within the landscape, and would wish to do within a landscape, their wants and needs. It includes several particular aspects, including a person's employment, their place of residence, their hobbies and interests. One use relationship related study is Perez's (2002) research, in which he compared participants' responses to paired landscape photographs. Despite issues with using photographs as a proxy for landscape (see section 5.4 of results chapter for further details), this study has interesting results which demonstrate the different attitudes to landscape of those who regularly go out walking and those who do not, this is a conclusions shared by Prentice and Guerin (1998) who examined people's relationships with Ben Lomond. This is just one facet of the use relationship and other studies such as Tesitel et al (2003), Dupont (2004) & Herzog et al (2000) examined other elements of people's relationships with the environment and landscape, and how these affected perceptions. It was therefore decided that it was necessary that methods used in this research were able to examine how individual's use relationships with the landscape affect their landscape perceptions and preferences.

Another aspect of a person's identity that has been suggested to affect a person's landscape perceptions is age. Haartsen et al's (2003) study demonstrated that people of different ages conceived 'rural' differently, with different aspects of the countryside being prominent in forming peoples' opinions of rurality. Their research showed that people of different age groups had different perceptions of the countryside, with young people commonly citing it as being '"silent" and "nothing to do" and intermediate and senior people mention the "nice quietness" of the countryside' (Haartsen et al 2003: 250), so certain aspects which are valued by some age groups are seen as negative by others. They also discovered that people at different stages of their lives valued different aspects of the rural landscape, depending on their particular needs at these stages of their lives. The authors stressed the importance of looking at a number of different ages when examining people's attitudes to rural areas, because these values can differ greatly across people's lifetimes. This is something that was seen to be very important to this study, and as such it was decided to work with participants of a number of different age groups.

Another aspect of people's relationships with landscape is what in this study I have chosen to call 'landscape biography'. This is the sum of all the places that people have visited and have experience of, it also includes other indirect experiences of landscape such as those seen through visual media, which can be said to have been 'experienced' indirectly. Landscape biography is closely linked to use relationship. Several studies (e.g. Matthews et al. 2000, Robertson et al. 2003, Stedman 2002, Ward-Thompson et al. 2005) have investigated this idea, and it will also be investigated in this work.

All of these previous aspects (age, use relationship and landscape biography) are part of a person's knowledge. Landscape knowledge in this sense can be defined as the sum of all that you know that may affect how you think about landscapes. It includes knowledge of history, geological processes, biology, botany, past landuse and the present day situation in the landscape. This knowledge is not necessarily 'academic' or 'book' knowledge, instead a broader definition of knowledge is required, one which includes the variety of types of knowledge that a person can have of the world, one which cannot be tested by a series of questions about a person and the landscape. Therefore it is necessary to develop a methodology that allows for the assessment of as broad as possible a spread of these different attributes which combine to create a person's knowledge.

4.5.1. Working with Different Population Sub-groups

The previous section discussed some of the different aspects of a person's identity which can affect attitudes to landscape. As these landscape values can all be different, it is necessary to look at the perceptions of a cross section of the population, rather than one population sub-group. This research is unlike many earlier research programmes in that it investigates people's responses to a particular area of landscape rather than a particular group of people (e.g. Robertson & Fox 2002, Rye 2006). It was therefore necessary to determine who exactly comprised the 'population' of the study area, something that is not straightforward as both of the study areas are popular tourist destinations.

How do you define the population of the Scottish Highlands?

Scotland's Highland landscape is globally renowned (Paterson 2002). It is a place visited by far more people than actually live there. Still more people just have an 'imagined' Highlands within their personal landscape (the landscape which exists within a person's mind which consists of all the experiences they have of places, including places which they have not visited but still have experience of (Ermischer 2004)), and as such it is not immediately clear who are the 'population' of this study. This is further complicated by the fact that the study area is in part within the Loch Lomond and the Trossachs National Park (LLTNP) and as such it is an area of land designated for the nation.

By definition National Parks are areas of land which have been designated by the government for their outstanding natural beauty and for the enjoyment of the nation (Nationalparks.gov.uk 2006). Therefore, theoretically the entire nation should be consulted on the best way to manage these areas: in practice, the National Parks are administered by National Park Authorities (NPAs), who include members of the local community in their make up (for a more detailed review of the remit of LLTNP see section 2.7.3.of the literature review). NPAs have the remit to:

- Conserve and enhance the natural beauty, wildlife and cultural heritage; and

- Promote opportunities for the understanding and enjoyment of the special qualities of National Parks by the public.

If there is a conflict between these two purposes, conservation takes priority. In carrying out these aims, National Park Authorities are also required to seek to foster the economic and social well-being of local communities within the National Park. (Nationalparks.gov.uk 2006). These actions are undertaken on behalf of the nation, rather than just the local community, therefore the constituency for decisions to be made about the National Park can be seen as being the entire nation.

Within the scope of this research it was decided that it would be best to work only with certain subgroups of the population, in order to be able to look in detail at their landscape perceptions. Also, the structure of the research project meant that it was possible to work with children, they have been overlooked in landscape research, and as such they were a novel group focus upon. The reasons for this exclusion are further discussed later in this chapter (4.5.2 & 4.5.3).

4.5.2. Excluded Groups & Landscape

A vast number of population groups can be seen to be 'excluded' both from academic research and the Scottish Landscape. It is not possible for a piece of academic research within the scope of a PhD project to account for all excluded populations[4], so projects such as this tend to focus on one particular population subgroup (e.g. Mc Cormack, Prentice & Guerin 1998), and it was decided, for reasons outlined below that this research would work with children as well as adults, to integrate children's attitudes into a wider framework of values for the areas' landscape.

As outlined previously, the studentship which funded this research was associated with a Heritage Lottery Funded project. One of the requirements of the funding was that the project had a significant amount of community involvement. In order to fulfil this criterion, the NTS developed an education programme where the local primary schools were introduced to the area's history and the work of an archaeologist. These schools were approached by myself and a NTS representative, and agreed that their primary 6/7 (10-12 year olds) could participate in the study. Contact was made with a teacher in a second study area school, and pupils of a similar age participated in the same study in a different location (Luss, Lochlomondside) the following year.

Until recently the way that children interact with and understand landscape was not well understood. Children[5] are often seen as being miniature adults, or as being completely at the mercy of adult actors (Matthews 2003). In the past they have been seen as thinking in the same way and having same life world as their elders (Jones 2001). In a 1992 paper Philo demonstrated that there were very few studies that dealt with the views of children in rural areas. In the intervening decade and a half there have been a number of studies which have examined children's relationships with rural areas (for example Halfacree 2004). This has been part of a wider trend for studying 'children's geographies', which included the founding of a Journal of that name in 2001. Many of these studies which work with children tend to focus solely on the experience of the child, rather than studying the perceptions of children in parallel to those of adults.

In the policy arena, children are often seen to have limited economic/decision making powers, and it has been suggested that attempts to involve children's opinions in policy formation have been ill thought out at best, with no real thought being put into methodologies which will best engage young people, and at worst tokenistic afterthoughts (Beale 2006, Smith 2004). It has also been suggested that children cannot form lobby groups without adult help, and as such their cares, wants and interests are not evident until they are researched (ibid). However, if marketing literature is examined (e.g. Hastings et al. 2004, John 1999) it is apparent that children are key players in family decision making processes. Many decisions about days out, and holidays etc. are made specifically with children in mind and in a dialogue with them. As such decisions about landscape are influenced by children's views. It can be argued that as key decision makers in the landscape consumption process, landscape policy decisions should always involve children.

Children think of the landscape in different ways to adults, these ways are linked to their identity as a child, in terms of their interests, interactions, knowledge and use relations with the landscape (Fjortoft & Sageie 2000). It appears that often children have different landscape values and therefore different landscape needs/wants to adults. The way that children interact and discover the landscape is also very different to that of adults. Because of these differences it is

---

[4] Other excluded groups, in terms of the Scottish Landscape include ethnic minorities, and other social groups which for many reasons may feel that the rural landscape is not somewhere that they can visit and experience. The Black Environmental Network (www.ben-network.org.uk) is one of several organisations dedicated to increasing the types of access people can have to the countryside.

[5] It is realised that the identity 'child' is a complex cultural construct. You cannot talk about children as being a single entity any more that you can about adults. However, all children have been excluded in matters of landuse policy and as such this generalising term is justified in this case.

desirable to carry out a study of both adults and children's perceptions for the same landscape, to attempt to discover more of what differences and similarities there are in thinking. Otherwise, landuse change decisions which are made solely using the opinions of adults may be to the detriment of children's relationships with land.

It can be argued that it is important to study children's perceptions to discover how their perceptions formed as a child can be taken on into adult life, as many of people's attitudes to landscapes are formed in their childhood (Yamashita 2002). However, without doing a longitudinal study (which would not be practical within the timeframe of a PhD) it is not possible to determine which of a child's attitudes will be taken into adulthood. Also, to only see a child's attitudes as interesting and important in relation to opinions of adults is to ignore a child's rights to an opinion now rather than in some uncertain point in a future. It also sets up a false dichotomy, which suggests that a person will think in one way throughout their childhood and another through their adulthood and that these opinions will not change within this time.

The idea of age based and cultural differences in landscape perceptions was researched by Herzog et al (2000) in a study which focussed upon the landscape perceptions of a variety of Australian population sub-groups (from primary school age to adulthood) and American college students. This study examined participants' attitudes to a number of photographs of the Australian landscape, and found that different groups found different elements of the images appealing or unappealing. This was one of the first studies that attempted to examine the landscape perceptions of a wide range of constituent groups, rather than just the inhabitants (or frequently just one section of the inhabitants) of an area, and is one of the few (along with Yamashita 2002, Kenny 2002) which specifically includes both adults and children in a study. The majority of studies that have examined children's attitude to and use of landscape have only focussed on children (e.g. Fjortoft et.al 2000 & Robertson et al. 2003). This is often a consequence of the original research remit. For example Robertson et al's study on the landscape perceptions of East Anglian school children grew from a nationwide initiative concerned with children mapping their local area. There can be seen to be a worry that studies that involve solely children's geographies will become a sub discipline which is not integrated into wider ideas of people's interactions with landscape (Catling 2005). By far the most common type of landscape study, however, are studies which completely avoid the issue of children's perceptions of landscape. In most cases children are invisible.

4.5.3. Working with children: challenges and opportunities

It is clear that the inclusion of children in a research design raises many ethical and methodological issues, and the following section will outline some of these issues. When designing a methodology for this study, it was essential to find techniques that could be used with both adults and children to assess their landscape perceptions. There were a number of techniques which would not have worked with the children. After conversations with the NTS education specialist (Jackson pers comm.) and local school teachers, it became clear that children work best in studies that involve their active participation, and all written material has to be worded carefully, so that the language is simple and the tasks that the children have to carry out are very clear. A literature search was undertaken to examine methods that had previously been used successfully to engage young people and discover the values they hold for their environment. It was established that many of the most successful studies have involved the production of images by children, either by drawing (e.g. McCormack 2002) or photography (e.g. Yamashita 2002, Young & Barrett 2001). Young and Barrett (2002:151) suggest that *'Visual methods have been demonstrated to be a good way of including children of all ages and both genders into the research process without discriminating between those of different abilities, confidence levels and educational attainments.'* It was therefore decided that this study should involve an element of image creation. It was realised that photography would appeal equally to both adults and children in a way that drawing would not (some individuals think that they 'cannot draw', few worry about being unable to take a photograph). Also the fact that asking participants to produce a number of drawings would take much more time than taking a number of photographs meant that photography was the more practical option.

When producing a photograph of a landscape, the individual is producing a record of a landscape feature, or a particular view which is of meaning to them. This is not an objective record of the landscape, instead it is produced within the context of the individual's subjectivity (Mirzoeff 2000). For a researcher to analyse a person's image of a landscape, they have to make a secondary interpretation of that participant's interpretation of that landscape. The feature or idea that the participant wished to capture may be invisible to the researcher, who is viewing the image through their own subjectivity. This is something that became evident in Young and Barrett's (2001) study of street children's perceptions of landscape. In this study the researchers gave children cameras, and asked them to capture scenes typical to their everyday life. They then discussed the photos taken with the children who produced the images. One of the scenes depicted appeared to be a view of a typical bustling street. However, when the photographer was questioned he said that he had been told to photograph his everyday life, and what he had been doing was taking a photograph of his friend pick pocketing. Without this extra information the photograph would have been wrongly interpreted. It was therefore decided that any exercises in this research should involve captioning as well as the creation of images, and the text used to demonstrate the meaning of the photograph to the photographer (Dennet & Spence 1975). This photographic methodology is discussed in more detail as the 'landscape workbook' below.

There are practical, legal and ethical considerations which have to be taken into account when working with children. When the idea of working with children was first mooted, the researcher was made aware of the legal requirements for working with children. As such, enhanced disclosure was applied for before fieldwork commenced. All visits to the field were accompanied by a trained first-aider, and were led by the class teacher, and the NTS education officer for the Lochtayside schools, or National Park ranger for Lochlomondside. The schools agreed to provide the number of adult helpers that were necessary for trip safety standards set by the local authorities. At no point was the researcher responsible for the safety of any of the children, nor did the researcher ever have one to one contact with the children. The schools sent a letter home to parents explaining the nature of the project that allowed the parents to choose whether or not their child was involved in the work. All parents agreed to their child's participation.

The exercises that children could undertake were constrained by the timetabling of the school day. It was first thought it may be possible to work with children from Breadalbane High School, but the rigid timetabling of the secondary school curriculum meant that this was impossible to organise. Children could only be expected to be outside for a short period of time, as even though the work took place in late spring, good weather could not be guaranteed in the Scottish Highlands. These constraints shaped the methodology that was eventually used for the study.

All materials used in the fieldwork process had to be carefully worded so as to be accessible to children, whilst not being viewed as overly simplistic by other groups. This ended up being very useful for the research project as a whole as it ensured that all materials were clearly worded and easily understood by all participants, and there was no confusion evident in the written responses generated from the materials, although certain elements of the study did require additional explanation to participants by the researcher. Materials developed for data collection were used with both adults and children although in the end it was found to be necessary to use two different questionnaires, as there were certain questions that could be asked to adults that would be irrelevant to children (for further discussion refer to section 4.7.3).

4.6. Developing a Methodology

It is necessary to undertake research on landscape within the actual landscape you are talking about. This may seem obvious, but as technology improves there is an increase in methods which gauge people's perceptions through 'visualisation' techniques, where they are guided though a flyover or walkthrough of a landscape and then asked to comment upon this. Such methods mean that the full sensory experience of landscape, including smells and sounds and tactile feelings of the texture and temperature of the surroundings is lost, and people will be commenting on a small sub-section of their true landscape experience.

Recent research with blind people, who go walking in National Park areas for the landscape experience (Macpherson 2005) serves to demonstrate the importance of senses other than sight. There has also been a reaction against 'ocular centric' views of landscape in anthropology where the preoccupation with visual qualities of landscape is seen as being particular to western modernity (Bender 1999). For these reasons it was important to include an experiential exercise in the methodology used.

4.6.1. Appropriate Techniques

When examining culture purely quantitative techniques are of limited use for examining a group of people's thoughts and feelings (Yarwood 2005). Instead qualitative, creative, imaginative sources are necessary, but it is then hard to assemble a methodology which can be seen to be both 'explicit and transparent'. Instead a mixed methods approach was taken working with quantitative and qualitative methods. Three different exercises were developed to generate information about the values that people had for landscapes, their relationships with these landscapes and their personal biographies. These three techniques (a landscape workbook, image workbook and a questionnaire) will be further discussed in section 4.7.

4.6.2. Participants

The following section describes the participants in this field research, in terms of who they were (where they came from, whether they local or visitors to the area) and the processes that were undertaken to recruit these volunteers. A more detailed profile of the study volunteers is given in section 5.2.1 of the results chapter.

The timetable for this research was constrained by it being a part of the BLHLP (as outlined above in section 3.1). The first season of fieldwork for this project (2005) coincided with the last season of volunteer involvement in the BLHLP. It was therefore decided that in this season, only conservation volunteers and local schoolchildren would be worked with, meaning that local adults, and a second study area would be worked with in the second year of the project. In retrospect, this decision led to some of the issues with recruitment of local adults being more problematic than they needed to be, if this process had started sooner. The issues with recruitment of participants and the resolution of these is discussed further below.

General ethical issues

All work with volunteers involves a consideration of ethics, some of the particular ethical concerns of working with children have been discussed above, but more general ethical issues applied to this work. For all social science research (indeed all research involving human subjects) consent is required, participants have to be aware that they are participating in this research, and what potential uses/outputs this research may have (Ryen 2004). Participants also have the right for their identity to remain confidential, and as such a system has to be devised to allow the participants to keep their anonymity whilst the researcher can determine 'who has said what'. Researchers enter into a trust relationship with their research subjects, and must make sure not to abuse this trust in any way, including avoiding misrepresenting participants' responses, presenting all responses in a balanced way and not using their data for outputs other than those discussed (Boss 2001). There is also a requirement to ensure the safety of all participants during field research, in this case the main dangers were physical dangers caused by the Scottish climate. All participants were warned that the field site had no shelter, and were recommended to bring waterproofs with them when visiting the site. On certain occasions the exercise was finished early when the weather got too bad to keep participants outside any longer.

Children

As discussed above, this project involved children who had worked as part of the BLHLP outreach programme. I met with the teachers of Killin and Kenmore schools to discuss my ideas, show them samples of the survey material and discuss with them which age group it would be most appropriate to work with. They suggested that the exercises drafted would be most appropriate for older primary school children (primary 6-7, 10-12 years old).

A second study area of Lochlomondside was selected and a comparative school was found with an enthusiastic teacher who was keen to find out more about the project. This was a slightly smaller school than the ones in Lochtayside. It only had two classes and as such there were also pupils present from the P4/5 (8-10 year old) age group in the class selected to participate in the research. It was decided to allow them to participate in the exercises, and simply to discard the data if the younger children were unable to complete the exercise. In the event pupils at that school were all very able, there were no issues with non-completion and all the data was retained. In total 49 children took part in the study.

Adults

It was initially envisaged that this research would work with both residents of and visitors to the Scottish Highlands. In the first field season research was carried out with visitors: participants on Thistle Camps[6] run by the National Trust for Scotland, which were again part of the BLHLP. These volunteers included camp participants who were interested in archaeology and those working on habitat conservation. It would be wrong to assume that their sole reason for being in the area was related to the activity they were carrying out at the camp, and as such it was necessary to determine their other reasons for being in the area. They cannot, however be seen as being typical of all visitors to the Highlands, as they have all came to

the area for some of the same specific reasons, and were all spending the same length of time in the area, none were there for short day visits or for longer stays. Some of the participants were first time visitors whereas others had long standing relationships with the area and were knowledgeable about its past. Because of the fact that the adult visitors were all in the area on educational camps, they could not be seen to be typical of all visits to the area. Participants in these camps, however, cannot be seen to be only interested in ecology, or history or archaeology, and as such a questionnaire (see section 4.7.3 & appendix 3) was designed to assess their interests and motivations for being in the area. The second (2006) field season, focussed primarily on local adults in the area.

It was not possible to outline an exact research question to use when recruiting participants (in terms of 'this exercise is seeking to find opinions on the proposed wind farm development in Lochtayside'). Instead participants were asked whether they would be willing to give up an afternoon of their time to participate in a study about people and landscape. It was not feasible to be much clearer than this as it was thought best for people to come to the study with no preconceived ideas about the exercise they would be completing. Therefore several people excluded themselves from the study on the grounds that, 'I [the researcher] would not want to speak to them'. This is always going to be a problem that occurs with non issue based landscape research when there is not a hook for people to think, 'this applies to me', and as such it can be difficult to recruit participants for such studies.

Various attempts were made to recruit participants in the study areas' resident populations. Letters were sent out via the schools to the parents of children who had previously participated in the research. Posters were printed and displayed in the villages, and articles were placed in local newspapers, and in the case of Killin, on the community web page. In the end word of mouth (snowball sampling) was found to be the most successful way of recruiting adult participants (Gobo 2004). Contact was made with certain members of the community, who in turn were able to direct me to others who might be interested. This was possible in Killin, where there is a strong community ethos and many local environmental and social organisations and clubs whose members were keen to participate. The same was not true of the second study area of Luss. Luss is a smaller village than Killin, with an ageing population (many of whom are housebound), many of the younger members of the community commute to Glasgow, and are not involved in village activities. All efforts at recruiting adult participants in Luss proved unsuccessful.

In Killin, the indoor parts of the exercise were carried out at the NTS building at Lynedoch. The NTS have a good relationship with the Killin community: the property manager has lived and raised a family in the village for the past twenty years. Several local community groups use the facilities, and other members of the community do occasional contract work for the Trust. In Luss the exercise

---

[6] These are residential conservation volunteer camps run by the NTS where participants learn a new skill (such as archaeological fieldwork, dry stone walling, or footpath repair) on one of the NTS properties, in return for a small fee (generally less than £100 per camp which lasts 1-2 weeks)).

was carried out at the National Park centre there. As outlined in section 1.3 of the introduction the NTS received some of the funding to support the CASE studentship from the Loch Lomond and Trossachs National Park Authority, and as such, the rangers based in Luss offered to help with time and resources for the fieldwork. It was therefore decided to use the Park Centre classroom for carrying out the indoor exercises. Contact was made with the local church and Pilgrimage centre as the two organisations in the village which had community involvement, but both were unwilling to help. I later discovered, from conversations with the park rangers and the local school teachers, that the Park and the community had a somewhat difficult relationship, rooted in the decision to make to make Luss a 'gateway centre' for the National Park, and to build a car park which is almost the same size as the village. The influx of tourists that this has brought to the village, has been perceived as detrimental by many of the community, and as such they have been very reticent about any involvement with the Park. The head ranger for the area told me of the difficulties they had engaging with the local community, and the fact that they had been unable to form a community futures groups locally. A previous attempt had been made (by the LLTNP board) to work with the community, but the group formed decided to exclude the Park from their discussions. Despite my best efforts to engage with the community, through letters to parents of the school children, posters in local buildings, and contact with local organisations it proved impossible to attract adult volunteers for the Luss case study site. In hindsight these issues could have been recognised earlier in the study, if the second case study site had been selected in year one of the research and attempts made then to recruit participants, and a different study area selected.

All of the local adults worked with in this research came from the Killin area because of the difficulties outlined above. The comparative element of the study of adults' perceptions of landscape is in essence a comparative study between visitors to and residents of Loch Tay, and it is also possible to compare the responses of adults and children, and children from Loch Lomond with children from Loch Tay. The research population samples are therefore Loch Tay adult residents, Loch Tay adult visitors, Loch Tay children and Loch Lomond children.

4.7. Information collection - Methods Used

Three different exercises were developed to explore participants' landscape perceptions. The first method, the landscape workbook, was designed to investigate what aspects of the landscape people valued or disliked. Two further exercises, an image workbook and a questionnaire were designed to discover what aspects of an individual's identity influenced these values. The following section will outline these exercises, and how the data from these were triangulated in the analysis process.

4.7.1. Exercise 1 -Landscape Workbook

The landscape workbook method was designed to create

data based on an individual's experience of the landscape and about their attitudes to the landscape. All participants already had some experience of the landscapes– this research did not take anyone to the study for the first time (and even if it had then they would still have had an 'imagined' idea of the landscape in their heads), and these previous experiences would colour how participants responded to the landscape of the study site (as describe in the previous chapter section 3.4).

In this exercise, people had a set time to explore a tract of landscape. This specific field location was known to some but not all participants. Many of the people had been to the surrounding area but not to the particular site, and others just to the neighbouring villages. Participants were given time to explore the study sites in order to gain an impression of what could be seen from the site, and to investigate features of the field site itself. Participants were then asked a set of standardised questions about the landscape, they were asked to give reasons for their answers and also to explain why they felt the way they did. The specific questions they were asked were:

These questions were compiled to discover what aspects of the landscape are valued in terms of physical elements and more intangible characteristics (such as spiritual reasons, or feelings such as peace, tranquillity or contentment). Participants were also asked what it was about these aspects they valued, and whether there were any features that detracted from their landscape experience. Question 4 was asked to determine more of what individuals use relationships with the countryside were, and what they would wish to do in the surroundings. Participants were asked the final question to determine where their interests in the landscape lay, outside the knowledge that they already had of the area. This provides information about the type of information that people would desire from any interpretation of the landscape, and as such is of interest to organisations such as the NTS, who have education as one of their main aims. It is often unclear what information individuals seek from interpretative materials, and as a result much on site interpretation focuses on giving the individual an 'origins' or 'scientific' history of the 'importance' of a site or landscape. For example, information given on signage often focuses upon how old a site is, or how a landscape is formed, and what rare species can be found there. This may not, however, be what people necessarily wish to discover about an area. This final question is also of interest when examining the second research question (What are the main influences on people's landscape perceptions and values?), as comparison of responses given for this with information from the questionnaire section of the exercise (see section 4.7.3), will examine whether people's existing knowledge of the landscape affects what else they wish to discover of the area.

When they had completed the questions, participants were given a camera and asked to photograph things that represented the two responses that they felt most strongly about for each question. For example, if the activity they most wanted to do was hill walking they would photograph the hill slopes that they most wanted to walk on, or if the thing they liked the most was the sheep then they would photograph them. This provided an idea of the varying strength of values that people held for the various landscape features.

One major drawback with the photographic element of the study was that it introduced an ocular-centric bias to the results. Sometimes people felt strongly about a non-visual element of the landscape such as the 'peace', smells, or feeling of the weather, which could not be photographed. When I was questioned about this in the field, I asked the participants to photograph something which they felt represented this for them. However, in the first season of fieldwork non-visual aspects of the landscape were found to be underrepresented when people refined their preferences, this is further discussed in section 6.3.1 of the discussion chapter. Use of the camera was a good way of engaging children in the study, eliciting more responses and more detailed information from them. Many of the children tired of the amount of writing that the exercise involved, and the chance to have a break when taking the photographs renewed their interests. All participants were issued with the camera, after completion of the first part of the exercise, and this acted as a 'reward' for the children for the successful completion of this. The production of photographs made all participants think twice about the same issues, perhaps more deeply, and express their thoughts more fully. Also, some participants, particularly children, were more comfortable about expressing their attitudes through the creation of an image rather than the written word, and expressed their feelings more fully in the captioning of this image than they did through their response to the first part of the workbook.

Landscape Workbook Field Method

Participants were taken to an area of the centre of the field (study sites described in previous chapter section 3.4) from where they had a clear view of the surroundings, and were invited to take about ten to fifteen minutes to explore the area.

All participants undertook this exercise in small groups; adult group sizes varied between two and six individuals. This was done in order to minimise the interaction between participants during the exercise. The school children had to undertake the activity as a whole class due to time and personnel restrictions although they were divided up into smaller groups of about six or seven children, escorted by one adult leader whilst they explored their surroundings. Children were asked not to speak to each other whilst looking around the landscape and not to follow their friends, but inevitably there was some interaction between participants. In order to produce some record of this, children were asked to note which sub-group they were part of, and a record was made of any children whose answers were similar, but this did not appear to be a significant issue.

Whilst participants were filling in the first part of the landscape workbook, records were made about how many participants were in the field, what the weather conditions were on the day (including wind direction if strong wind) and vegetation cover in the field. Also, brief notes about the path that participants took around the field were made. In some cases participants approached the study field from the northern rather than the southern exit, this was noted when it occurred. All of these factors affect what is visible to individuals as they undertake the study and therefore what features individuals could draw their preferences from. This was particularly important during certain days when there were gale force winds, which forced people to look away from certain views of their surroundings or on foggy days, when large sections of the area were hidden by clouds. The field in Kiltyrie, Lochtayside had widespread bracken cover in the late summer months (July, August, September) but this was not present in the spring time. This bracken obscured some of the archaeological and geological features which are evident in the field at other times of the year. These seasonal effects were unavoidable, as it was necessary to carry out fieldwork at times which fitted in with the availability of volunteers (when the schools were available, and when the thistle camps took place).

Landscape Workbook Analysis Methods

1. Thematic Coding

A content analysis of individual's responses was undertaken (Bauer 2000). Content analysis was developed as a tool for undertaking qualitative analysis of extensive tracts of texts (Spencer et al 2003) by determining key themes which recur through the text. In essence, a numerical dataset of quasi-variables is created from the rich qualitative data (Richards & Richards 1994) which can be linked to variables external to the text; in the case of this study, responses from the questionnaire and image workbook.

When the landscape workbook information was coded, categories were determined for both the subjects that individuals referred to when answering the questions posed and the reasons that they gave for their preferences. An inductive approach was taken, in that the data were given a preliminary examination, and the coding framework was derived from this, with new codes assigned as and when required (Cloke et al 2004). Analytical categories were allowed to grow organically from the data. After the initial coding of the raw data took place, all the responses were checked again, and recoded with the full framework in place.

People's responses were divided into two sections: the subject they were referring to, and the reason given for the reference:

e.g. Dislike the large pylons in front of me [subject] ruin the scenery [reason] (T39)[7]

---

[7] Throughout the work quotations appear with a letter with a number following it (e.g. (T39) as shown above). These are codes given to the participant by the researcher, in order to maintain the participant's

Each respondent's subjects and reasons were given a code and entered into a SPSS database. Each individual subject and reason was given an individual code, however these fitted into broad themes. The codes given were hierarchical, entered first at a detailed level which could then be clustered at a thematic level (e.g. streams and rivers were given the code 221, within water (code 220) which was within topography (code 200)). All of the different water features could be reassigned the code 220, and treated as a whole and all different topographic features could be recoded and treated as a whole, depending on the level of detail required). This facilitates a multi-tiered analysis of data: an examination of both the specific and the general. Some of the titles of these themes are self explanatory but with others it was impossible to find a single phrase which encapsulated the whole category and when this is the case, they have been discussed more fully below.

The themes and sub themes used for 'likes', 'dislikes', 'special', and 'more about' were (for full coding structure see appendix 1):

Reasons given for responses were also coded thematically (again a hierarchical coding scheme was designed, please refer to appendix 1) for full list.

The things that people said they would like to find out more about were also divided into two categories; a subject and what they wanted to find out more about. (*e.g. sheep* [subject] *breeds and farming practices* [what they wanted to find out]) The subject categories were the same as those used for the other questions (what like, dislike, special), but a different set of themes was developed for what people wanted to find out about these.

2. Analysis of Photographs

Photographs taken by participants were not analysed separately to the captions given to the images. The captions gave information about what area of land or aspect of the landscape was photographed and these were felt to be important. Had images been analysed separately to the caption, in all likelihood different features in the photographs would have been seen than those that the participants meant to capture. The photographs did, however, prove a useful tool when determining what features were being referred to if the description given by the caption was vague. (e.g. *the rocks running across the field* – the photograph could be checked to examine whether the caption was referring to a geological or built feature).

3. Statistical Analysis of data

Once coded the data from the landscape workbooks were imputed into the SPSS statistical package, and frequencies (counts and percentages) were run on the data, at both a thematic and individual code by code basis. Cross-tabulations were also run, as follows:

---

1. Is there anything you like about your surroundings? Please write down up to four things that you like about your surroundings and write down why you like them

2. Is there anything you don't like about your surroundings? Please write down up to four things that you dislike about your surroundings and why you dislike them.

3. Is there anything in your surroundings that makes the area special to you? It could be something that makes you think about other things or places, or something which you think is only found in the local area or the Highlands of Scotland, it may even be something which is connected to your family. Write down up to four things that you find 'special' and what it is that makes them special to you

4. Think of your favourite outdoor activities. Write down what activities you would like to do in this area, and where they could take place.

5. Is there anything of your surroundings that you would like to find out more about. Write down up to four things that you would like to find out more about, and what you would like to know about them.

Figure 4-1 Questions asked in the Landscape Workbook exercise

• Subjects and reasons (this was undertaken with the full dataset, for all other cross-tabulations subjects and reasons were analysed at a thematic level.)

• Subjects/reasons and gender

• Subjects/reasons and age group (from questionnaire)

• Subject/reasons and house type (whether they came from urban or rural areas)

• Subject/reasons and residence (whether they lived in or were a visitor to the area).

• Subject/reasons and employment status

• Subject/reasons and why in Ben Lawers area (either archaeology volunteer, conservation volunteer, school, or worker)

The distributions produced by cross-tabulations was tested using the Chi-square statistical test. This test allows you determine whether there is an association between different variables (so for example, whether what an individual likes about their surroundings is influenced by their gender?) (Zuur et al 2007). If once the test is carried out there is a p-value of less than or equal to 0.05 then the test can be said to be statistically significant for the purpose of this research. This test allows the determination of whether the differences observed in the data are statistically significant by comparing them to the frequencies which would be expected if there was no variance between groups. This tool therefore tells you whether differences observed in data can be ascribed to the variables

anonymity but allowing the researcher to have an individual code for each participant.

tested. However, it may be that there are multiple variables that influence people's landscape perceptions (e.g. age AND gender AND employment status), and the Chi-square test cannot tell you which of these influences is strongest. Had a larger dataset been collected, it may have been possible to undertake more sophisticated statistical analysis in order to determine the relative strengths of these different influences. However, this research focussed on discovering what has an influence on individuals' landscape perceptions, rather than the relative strength of particular influences, and as such the Chi-square test was sufficient to give an indication of these relationships.

4.7.2. Exercise 2 - Image Workbook

The landscape workbook was used to assess people's perceptions and preferences for landscape. Reasons behind the reactions to specific landscape features were also given (for example *I like the mountains because they make me feel peaceful*). It was possible to examine what aspects of the landscape are most commonly liked or disliked, and to examine the most common reasons for these. However, this does not allow a determination of where these perceptions are rooted (what makes one person value a landscape for its peace, whilst another values it for memories, or the potential of using it for recreation). Why are elements which some people like disliked or unnoticed by others?

This exercise was designed to examine which elements of the landscape individuals actually derived their preferences from. There is a large body of literature which deals with the concept that not everyone views the world in the same way, and indeed some features which are evident to certain individuals are invisible to others (e.g. Berger 1980, Mizoreff 1999). Vision is not an objective sense (Ingold 2000). What a person sees of a place depends on where they choose to look, which is in turn affected by a multitude of factors connected to a person's identity (Dennet & Spence 1975). It is therefore possible to study the interrelationship between landscape values and identity (and therefore what influences an individual's landscape values) through examining what people see and how and why they see it. This exercise also allowed the researcher to determine what type of knowledge individuals had of certain landscape features, in terms of the language they used to describe them (e.g. what may be a ruined farmhouse to one individual, may be a pile of stones to another, or 'the ruins of my grandfather's house' to another, to others still this feature may be unimportant and not require naming). Individuals were also asked questions about what they would do in the landscape, to gauge how they would use the wider landscape, rather than just the surroundings visible from the study sites for the landscape workbook exercise. The images shown were a mixture of ground level and oblique aerial photographs (provided by LLTNP and RCAHMS). Previous research (Plester et al. 2003) demonstrates that children of the age worked with in this study can understand aerial photographs and extrapolate features present in the photograph as being particular features on the ground.

Image Workbook Analysis Method

The image workbook exercise provided five different types of information about people's relationships with the landscape. These were:

• The features people identify in the landscape.

• The knowledge that they have of landscape features.

• The familiarity that people have with the landscapes shown.

• People's use relationships with the landscape.

• People's emotional reactions to spending time within these landscapes.

As with the landscape workbook section of the study, an inductive approach was taken during the analysis of this data, using content analysis. The features 'seen' were coded using a framework similar to that developed for the landscape workbook. The key themes to emerge from this analysis were of natural history (flora and fauna in a 'natural' or 'semi' natural state rather than geological features), topography (including all geological and water features), landuse (including farm animals, and all 'modern' features including modern buildings, crops and infrastructure), history (including ruined buildings, field boundaries, and prehistoric landscape features) and weather. By examining the wording used in these responses, it was possible to examine something of the knowledge that people had of the area. Activities suggested by respondents were coded using a similar framework to that used for activities in the image workbook, although additional categories had to be created for activities that could take place outside the field site (for example going to the pub, a tea shop or a local visitor attraction). It was noted when participants recognised certain places, geological features and historical sites. These were integrated with answers given in the questionnaire to examine the types of knowledge participants had of the area. Three different types of knowledge were identified: place knowledge (when people had noted specific place names), livelihood knowledge (where people had spoken about farming processes, the lives of inhabitants etc.) and academic knowledge (including knowledge of history, geological processes, names of plants etc.). These were loose groupings, but gave an idea of the amount of and types of knowledge people had of the area.

It was possible to examine the words selected to describe photographs from the given lists by different groups, and therefore compare different groups' understandings of these features (for example whether they were more likely to see an area as wild and natural, or managed and lived, or whether they saw the area as being beautiful or ugly). The analysis of people's very different responses to two images that portray a similar area led the researcher to realise the full implications of commentary on a photograph rather than directly to an actual landscape. This led to the rejection of much of the dataset as a useful tool for

---

Thematic coding framework for features and activities
- o **Natural history (later renamed Flora and Fauna)**
  - Vegetation
  - Wildlife
- o **Topography**
  - Hills and mountains
  - Water
  - Geology
  - Topography of field
- o **Landuse**
  - Farm animals
  - Modern features
  - Activities
  - Air quality
- o **History**
- o **Weather**
- o **Entire area** (generally assigned when no specific subject was given (e.g. *the atmosphere* [no specific subject] *tranquillity and peaceful* [reason] (T40))

Types of activity were also split into themes. These were:
- o **Sport**
  - **Hill sports**
  - **Water sports**
  - **Other sports**
- o **Work**
- o **Investigation** (this category took in all interests which involved a further exploration of the landscape – for example archaeological fieldwork, wildlife watching etc.)
- o **Hobbies**
- o **Recreation** (something of a 'catch all' category for all activities which did not fit in any other, including: play, camping, picnicking etc.)

Figure 4-2 Thematic coding framework used for features and activities cited by participants in landscape and image workbooks

assessing perceptions and preferences, as the answers given were found to be a reflection of a person's views about a photograph, rather than a landscape (this will be discussed further in sections 5.4 & 6.3.1). The exercise did, however, serve to demonstrate the shortcomings of using a purely image based methodology for the assessment of landscape preferences. Several of the images shown depicted the same area, but were taken from different vantage points, including one photograph of a snow capped hillside taken from the village of Killin and another taken on that same hillside during the previous day's blizzard. For these images, participants were asked to '*Describe what you see in this scene. How would you feel about spending a day in this picture? Write about what you would do if you were in this picture for a day and how being there would make you feel*'. As these images are viewed in isolation, and out of their landscape context an holistic idea of the landscape could not be gauged. Instead participants were forced to make decisions on a small area of the whole, selected by a researcher who cannot be completely objective about their selection. As such, participants gave very different emotional responses to two pictures which were of the same landscape features, and these responses were clearly linked to the individual's ideas of that contextless picture, rather than their ideas of the landscape itself. The use of visual proxies in landscape research will be more fully

discussed in the next (results) chapter, and the following two discussion chapters.

The image workbook section of the methodology was developed to expand upon the data generated by the landscape workbook by providing more information about emotional attachments, use relationships and visual recognition of the landscape. In order to understand these preferences and values for landscape it was necessary to find out more about the backgrounds of participants. This is why the third, questionnaire based element of the study was developed.

4.7.4. Exercise 3 - Questionnaire

The questionnaire was developed to discover more about study participants' backgrounds, knowledge and use relationships with the landscape. This information was collected in order to determine what aspects of an individual's identity affected their landscape values.

The questionnaire was the one element of the exercise which was different for adults and children. This was because it was realised that children would not be able to fill out a complex questionnaire, including likert scale type preference questions etc. but to not get this information from adults would have been to miss an opportunity to

Themes for reasons behind likes, dislikes and what people held to be special were:
- o **Aesthetics:** the sensual aspects of/experience of landscape, such as beauty, ugliness, smell and sound.
- o **Mnemonics:** Personal memories provoked by the surroundings, whether they be of people, places, or events in a persons life.
- o **Use relationships:** linked to the physical relationship that people have with the landscape. This includes the potential of the surroundings for specific uses, and the physical experience which comes from this use (in terms of hazards, comfort etc).
- o **Emotional:** the variety of emotions provoked by the surroundings, both positive and negative.
- o **Interest:** the elements of landscape which hold or provoke a persons' interest; including history, botany, geomorphology etc.

Figure 4-3 Themes used in coding of reasons cited by participants in landscape workbook exercise

What participants wished to find out about the area
- o **Nothing specific**
- o **Present landuse:** including the ownership and administration of the land, and the lives of present day inhabitants.
- o **Formation of landscape:** a large category, broken into sub-themes, which contains all aspects of the landscape's past.
  - • **Geomorphological processes**
  - • **Vegetation**
  - • **History of area**
- o **Geographical Facts:** empirical facts of an area including directions, place names, and sizes of mountains etc.
- o **Natural History**

Figure 4-4 Themes used in coding what participants wished to find out more about in landscape workbook exercise

gain a greater insight into their relationships with the landscape.

Description

The children's questionnaire (appendix 2) contained a number of both tick box and open ended questions. These questions sought to elicit information about where the children lived, how long they had lived there, what their hobbies were, and what sort of experiences they had with their parents, including specifically visits to historical sites in order to determine their exposure to the historic environment. A knowledge of history was particularly focussed upon in order to examine the affect that the outreach work undertaken as part of the BLHLP schools project (which Killin and Kenmore had participated in) had on informing the children's ideas of landscape. It was necessary to examine whether children from Luss school also had any exposure to history, so that a comparison could be carried out. With the modification of the second research question to a more general examination of the factors which influence individuals' landscape values other aspects of knowledge and identity were examined, but it was decided not to overcomplicate the children's questionnaires with further questions about other activities they may participate in, or attitudes to the countryside. The questionnaire had some open ended questions about sports and hobbies, in which children wrote several of their different activities and clubs, which allowed the determination of other aspects which may affect their landscape perceptions.

The adult questionnaire (appendix 3) was subdivided into two sections, according to different themes of identity that were to be investigated. These were:

Personal Information:

Participants were asked basic demographic questions about themselves (including age, gender, employment etc), their reasons for being in the area (or their reasons for settling in the area). They were asked about what places they were familiar with (including places they had lived before). Participants were also asked about their family situations, including where their families grew up. This information was collected so that it would be possible to undertake triangulation of these responses with those responses from the landscape workbook to determine whether these factors affected people's landscape perceptions and values.

Experiences of the countryside, knowledge and interests.

The final section of the adult questionnaire addressed knowledge and interests. A series of questions were asked about people's experiences of the countryside, where they would go and what organisations they were a member of. This was undertaken to determine more about an individual's knowledge, use relationships and landscape biography (discussed in section 4.5). I also asked what aspects of landscape people found out more about through popular media, as this also influences people's landscape knowledge.

Image Workbook Questions

Individuals were shown eight different images, all of local areas, on PowerPoint and asked to comment on them in different ways. The questions asked to participants were:

1. Write down everything that you see in this picture.
2. Describe what you see in this scene. How would you feel about spending a day in this picture[children's workbooks said would you be happy or sad, excited or scared]? Write about what you would do if you were in this picture for a day and how being there would make you feel.
3. Which of the words below would you use to describe this picture?
4. Look at what this picture shows. Describe a day that you could spend in the landscape. Mark on the picture where you would stop, and write what you would do in these places.

These questions were each applied to two different images which were shown to the group using a data projector. Participants were also given a black and white copy of the images for them to examine and in certain cases annotate. They were not asked directly whether they knew where the scenes pictured depicted were. However, a note was made when it was apparent that a participant was familiar with, and could identify the location of the photograph.

Figure 4-5 Questions asked to participants during the image workbook exercise

Analysis Method

Data from the questionnaire were inputted into the SPSS statistical package along with coded data from landscape and image workbooks. Frequencies were calculated to create a demographic profile of the population which could be compared to national averages to determine the representativeness of the information collected. The information was collected to answer the specific research questions and as such only types of analysis that would aid in the answering of these questions were attempted. The questionnaire was designed to provide information on participant's backgrounds, which could then be cross-tabulated with their landscape workbook responses to determine what influences their landscape values. In order to examine this certain aspects of the data set were cross-tabulated against information from the landscape workbook, to determine their influence on people's landscape perceptions as outlined above. Also, on a case by case basis, information that participants had given about their interests and purposes for visiting the countryside could be compared to their landscape workbook responses to determine individual links between knowledge and landscape experience. Sometimes an individual would have referred to a specific place or interest in their responses to the landscape workbook, and it was possible to correlate this with biographical information from their questionnaire responses.

The information from all three of these exercises was triangulated to determine what aspects of a person's identity govern their landscape values, and this is discussed in the next two chapters.

4.8. Methodology chapter summary

This chapter has presented an overview of the research questions guiding this work and the methods used to address them. A rationale for the methodology has been presented including a description of the process of recruiting research participants. The inductive approach taken to this research has also been discussed, along with how this lead to certain elements of the method used (much of the information from the image workbook) being rejected as unhelpful in addressing the research questions.

These methods have been situated within contemporary debates about assessing landscape value, and within the constraints and opportunities presented by this particular research project. A mixed methods approach was taken in insofar as participants have not been observed in their everyday situations: instead exercises have been developed to gauge people's opinions of the landscapes of two separate areas. These exercises generated both qualitative and quantitative data. Through a process of thematic coding the qualitative data were transformed into quantitative data which could be triangulated with the information on individual's backgrounds and interests to determine how these may affect landscape perceptions.

The results of this research will be discussed in the next two chapters. Chapter 5 will present the dataset to give an impression of the information that was collected. Chapter 6 presents a more detailed account of the findings. In this the information is discussed, theorised and imbedded within current discourses on landscape preferences.

5

Results

5.1. Introduction

This chapter will present an outline of the primary information collected for this PhD research. The information from the three exercises: the questionnaire, landscape workbook, and image workbook will be outlined in turn.

The questionnaire dataset is introduced first, and a demographic profile of the participants is outlined. As discussed in the previous chapter (section 4.6.2) there were issues with the recruiting of participants which meant that they came from very particular sections of the population, rather than spanning a representative cross section. This will be further examined here, as well as participants' interests and experiences of the countryside. Information from the landscape workbook will then be discussed. This exercise (outlined in chapter 4 section 4.7.1) generated qualitative data that was coded. The coding process will be outlined, before the coded information is presented, which will be discussed in more detail in the following chapter. The final exercise presented is the image workbook. When the image workbook information was examined, there were found to be some issues with the answers that individuals gave, insofar as they did not reflect people's perspectives of the landscape, but instead their perspectives on the images they were shown, and only these images. These problems will be introduced in this chapter, and then discussed further in chapter 6. The information from all three exercises is used in the following chapter to examine the main influences on individual's landscape perceptions.

5.2. Questionnaire

Both adult and child participants were asked to complete questionnaires to investigate more about their backgrounds, interests and experiences of the countryside. This information was used to create a demographic profile of participants and to provide information about their perceptions of landscape. This data can be compared with information gathered from the other two exercises to suggest what elements of an individual's identity affected their landscape perceptions and preferences. Adults and children were given different questionnaires as there was some information that it would be possible to get from

adults that children would not be able to give. Certain questions had to be worded differently for adults and children, in order to gain the desired information. The two questionnaires can be seen in Appendixes 2&3.

5.2.1. Study Sample Profile, from Questionnaire

In this section, basic characteristics of the research participants are presented, followed by information from adults and children's questionnaires. The results are presented with the actual number of participants followed by the percentage that this figure represents. The percentage figure is given in brackets and represents solely either the percentage of adults or children depending on which section of the population the question is referring to. The following table (5.1) provides a summary of participants, including age, gender, and where they participated in the study

5.2.2. Review of findings from Adult questionnaire

Adult participants were asked about their employment status and levels of education, these are summarised in tables 2 & 3 below.

The adult sample was not representative of the population as a whole. Most participants were in the area as volunteers on archaeology and conservation camps and had an interest in conservation or archaeology. There were a large number of students and young adults on the camps including a number of archaeology students (participants were asked what subjects they had studied at university, as well as their current employment). The majority of participants lived in one or two person families and had no dependents.

Adult Landscape Biographies

A section of the questionnaire was designed to find out more about individuals' experiences of landscape. Studies such as that carried out by Robertson et al (2003) suggest that the places and landscapes you are familiar with influence how you think of other landscapes. It was therefore important to determine participants' 'landscape biographies'.

Participants were asked where they were resident and what

	Age Groups	No. of individuals	No. Male	No. Female	Loch Tay	Loch Lomond
Children	8-12	49 (37 %)	25 (44)	24 (33)	36 (32)	13 (72)
Adults	16-17	6 (4.6)	32 (56)	49 (67)	76 (68)	5 (28)
	18-24	29 (22.3)				
	25-40	23 (17.7)				
	40-54	9 (7)				
	55-64	12 (9)				
	65 +	2 (1.5)				
Total		130	57 (44)	73 (56)	112 (86)	18 (14)

Table 5-1 Demographics of sample population, and location of study participants (in this table percentages are for both adult and child participants).

Employed full-time	18 (22)
Employed part-time	4 (5)
Self Employed full-time	6 (7.5)
Self Employed part-time	5 (6.3)
Retired	10 (12.5)
Unemployed	5 (6.3)
Student	29 (36)
School	3 (4)

Table 5-2 Employment status of adult participants

Completed secondary schooling	2 (2.5)
O level/GCSE/ Standard grade (or equivalent)	5 (6.25)
Highers/'A' levels	33 (41.25)
Completed a HNC/HND	2 (2.5)
Completed a University or College degree	23 (28.75)
Hold a postgraduate Qualification	15 (18.75)

Table 5-3 Level of education of adult participants.

Rural (on a farm)	6 (8)
Rural (not farming)	8 (11)
In a village/small town (up to 10,000 pop)	26 (34)
In a large town (10,000 – 80,000)	12 (16)
In a city	24 (31)

Table 5-4 Locations of adult homes, as mentioned in the questionnaire

Once (this is the only time)	26 (34)
2-3 times	21 (27)
4-5 times	5 (7)
More than 5 times	13 (17)
Not Applicable	12 (15)

Table 5-5 Number of times adult participants had worked as conservation volunteers or on archaeological research projects.

areas of the UK and abroad they had lived in previously. Almost three quarters of respondents were from Scotland, half of whom lived in the central belt or southern Scotland. A number of people had spent time living elsewhere: only 25% had lived in the same area for their entire life. Almost 25% of participants had lived abroad at some time in their life, and about 70% of participants had moved about within the United Kingdom (participants were able to name a number of locations that they had lived in previously and as such the sum of percentages is greater than 100%).

Adult participants were asked what sort of community their present home was located within. Through examining this and the locations of individuals' home it was possible to determine whether participants lived in urban or rural areas (using the Scottish Executive 6 fold division see http://www.scotland.gov.uk/Publications/2004/06/19498/38787 for details). The adult participants' residence were split nearly equally between urban and rural areas, with 41 (50.6%) living in urban areas and 40 (49.4%) living in rural areas. Living on a farm was included as a separate

category, as several of the children came from farming backgrounds, because it was thought that this could lead to a different relationship with the landscape than that had by most.

How you think in adulthood is affected by your experiences as a child, particularly interactions with your family (Giddings & Yarwood 2005, Jackson & Scott 2005). Adult participants were therefore asked where (if known) their parents grew up. The majority of the parents grew up in the UK and almost 50% of parents had a Scottish background.

Experiences of the Countryside

Following on from the previous section on landscape biographies participants were asked several questions to determine their experiences of the countryside, including their experiences of the study area.

	Very high	←	Neither high or low	→	Very low	Not applicable
A cheap holiday	5 (7)	7 (10)	11(15)	10 (14)	17 (23)	23 (31)
A chance to learn a new skill	35 (46)	17 (22)	6 (8)	3 (4)	1(1)	15 (20)
Helping the environment	18 (24)	16 (21)	8 (11)	10 (13)	4 (5)	19 (25)
A chance to new people	19 (25)	11 (14)	23 (30)	5 (7)	4 (5)	15 (20)
A chance to spend time in the countryside	29 (38)	17 (22)	7 (9)	3 (4)	6 (8)	15 (20)
A chance to 'give something back' to the countryside	16 (21)	11 (15)	21 (28)	3 (4)	6 (8)	18 (24)
A chance to spend time in the Loch Tay/ Lomond area	7 (9)	18 (23)	17 (22)	12 (16)	8 (10)	15 (20)
It may lead to a career in conservation or archaeology	26 (34)	3 (4)	9 (12)	6 (8)	12 (16)	19 (25)
Work experience for University or College course	26 (35)	3 (4)	3 (4)	1 (1)	13 (18)	28 (38)
Something to add to your CV	20 (26)	11 (15)	4 (5)	14 (18)	9 (12)	18 (24)
A fun activity	25 (33)	20 (26)	13 (17)	2 (3)	2 (3)	14 (18)
Other reasons (Please state below)	12 (35)	4 (12)			2 (6)	16 47)

Table 5-6 Factors influencing people's choice to work as a conservation volunteer.

	Very high	←	Neither low nor high	→	Very low	Not applicable
A chance to spend time in the Loch Tay/Lomond area specifically	7 (10)	3 (4)	15 (20)	12 (16)	21 (28)	16 (22)
A chance to spend time in the Scottish Highlands	13 (18)	23 (32)	8 (11)	4 (6)	5 (12)	16 (22)
A chance to spend time in Scotland	19 (26)	7 (10)	8 (11)	1 (1)	15 (21)	22 (31)
The activity on offer at the camp	32 (43)	11 (15)	7 (10)	3 (4)	5 (7)	16 (22)
A chance to meet old friends	5 (7)	6 (8)	6 (8)	1 (1)	26 (35)	30 (41)
Other reason (please state below)	18 (44)	1 (1)	1(1)		4 (5)	17 (21)

Table 5-7 Factors which influenced the choice of a specific Thistle Camp.

Participants who were visitors to the area were asked about the number of times they had worked as conservation volunteers, and the main reasons that they chose to work as a volunteer (as all of the visiting participants were taking part in either Conservation or Archaeology Thistle Camps). This was done to examine their familiarity with the study area, and the work that they were undertaking as a conservation volunteer.

Table 5-6 above shows the relative importance of different reasons for working as a volunteer. The reasons most commonly rated 'very high' and 'high' were career related including, for example, learning a new skill, and the possibility of getting a career in conservation or archaeology. The activity being fun was also rated highly, as was the chance to spend time in the countryside. The chance to spend time in the Loch Tay or Lomond area was seldom rated highly. This was also highlighted in the next question where participants were asked to rate various reasons as to why they had chosen the specific Thistle Camp. Participants were most likely to choose a camp by the activity on offer, or the time of the camp, rather than its specific location, suggesting that most participants were in the area to learn a particular activity, and enjoying the landscape was secondary to that.

Participants were then asked a series of questions to determine more about their experiences of the countryside.

They were asked which outdoor activities they regularly participated in. Activities commonly carried out included walking (82% of participants regularly participated), sightseeing, photography, and a variety of outdoor sports. They were also asked to rank the importance of various reasons which determined their decision to visit the countryside generally and to visit specific locations. Reasons which ranked highly were 'getting away from civilisation' (71% of respondents ranking this 'high' or 'very high'), fresh air, and reasons linked to specific sites and sights that they wished to experience.

Participants were also asked which 'heritage' activities they had carried out in the past year. Responses to this are shown in the table below.

The table above demonstrated that the majority of the adults visited historical sites within their spare time, although fewer had visited nature reserves. This may reflect the interest in history that was prevalent within participants on the Archaeology Thistle Camps. The final part of the questionnaire was designed to determine more about people's experience of the countryside and history in the popular media. The majority of participants watched and listened to programmes on history and natural history, fairly regularly, with *Country File* and *Time Team* commonly cited. The majority of participants also sometimes read books about history and the British countryside, and two

In the last year have you…….	10+ times	4-10 times	1-4 times	Never	Don't know
Visited a Museum	20 (27)	22 (29)	30 (40)	2 (3)	1 (1)
Visited a National Park	5 (8)	14 (23)	32 (52)	6 (10)	5 (8)
Visited a historical site with an attached interpretation centre (e.g. Stirling Castle)	13 (17)	15 (20)	37 (19)	7 (9)	3 (4)
Visited a historical site where there is an information board but no interpretation centre (e.g. a stone circle with a board telling you about its history)	11 (15)	22 (30)	38 (51)	1 (1)	2 (3)
Visited a SSSI/Nature reserve	11 (16)	10 (15)	22 (32)	17 (24)	9 (13)
Been to a 'living history' centre (e.g. Scottish Crannog Centre)	3 (5)	1 (1)	41 (61)	20 (30)	2 (3)

Table 5-8 Number of times that respondents have visited specific heritage sites.

thirds of participants regularly read history magazines such as BBC History, History Scotland etc, this also reflects the interest in history that many Thistle Camp participants had.

Adult Questionnaire Overview.

The information presented above has given a profile of background and interests of the adult study participants. The majority of participants were from Scotland, were relatively young and had at least completed their secondary education. Most participants spent time in the countryside, generally for recreational purposes and had some interest in the countryside and history, and many have continued this interest or had it stimulated by studying archaeology and history in further education. The majority of adult participants were in the area as volunteers on conservation and archaeology work camps, which partially explains the interest in history shown by participants (although many of the local participants also had an interest in history and ecology). For this reason the adult participants in this sample cannot be seen to be representative of the population as a whole. This is not seen as problematic within the context of this research however, as it focuses upon the examination of influences on landscape values, rather than trying to get a representative cross-section of the population's landscape values.

5.2.3. Review of findings from Children's Questionnaire

The children who participated in this study were aged between 8 and 12, and the following section outlines the information recorded in the children's questionnaire. The questionnaire can be viewed in appendix 2.

		P 4	P5	P6	P7	Total
Loch Tay	Killin			13	8	21
	Kenmore			6	8	14
	Glen Lyon			1		1
Loch Lomond	Luss	4	2	4	3	13
Total		4	2	24	19	49

Table 5-9 Ages and locations of child participants.

In total there were 49 child participants. All of the children from Lochtayside were aged between 10 and 12 (in Primary 6 or 7). Luss primary was a smaller school with only 2 composite classes and all pupils from P4-7 were

taught together. All these pupils participated in the study, as it was thought that if they were unable to complete the exercise then their work could be discarded. In the end, all children were capable of completing the exercise and all data was analysed.

There was a near equal gender split between participants, with 23 female and 26 male participants and all of the children lived in rural areas, with 27 living in villages, and 22 living in the countryside (13 of whom lived on farms). The majority of children had lived in the area for an extended period of time and even if they had lived in more than one place most had spent most of their lives in the central Scottish Highlands (four children had spent time in England, one in Africa, and two elsewhere in Scotland).

Children were also asked what jobs their parents did. This was asked in order to find out whether there was anything of the children's backgrounds which would mean they were more likely to know about the landscape (e.g. have a parent who is a countryside ranger or a farmer). It was discovered that a number of children lived on farms or had parents who worked in the agricultural industry, and in hospitality and service industries. The employment profile, as recorded by the child participants, of the two areas was similar, and is broadly similar to figures for all of rural Scotland (Scottish Executive 2000).

Children were then asked a series of questions to determine their exposure to history outside of school classes. They were asked how many times they had visited specific types of historical attraction, whether they ever read books about history, or watched history programmes on television. Ideally the children would have been asked more questions about other aspects of their interaction with the countryside, but the length of questionnaire had to be kept as short as possible, both because of children's concentration spans and time constraints. Children were given the option of answering whether they had done these activities lots of times, once or twice a year, or never or 'don't know'. Information from these showed that the majority of children had visited historical sites and watched television programmes about history at least once or twice in the past year.

Children were also asked to list the hobbies that they regularly participated in and the clubs that they were

How often in the past year have you…..	Never	Once or twice a year	Lots of times	Don't know
Visited a museum	3 (6%)	26 (53%)	12 (25%)	8 (16%)
Been to a historical site with no information board or interpretation centre?	3 (6%)	15 (31%)	22 (35%)	9 (18%)
Been to a historical site with an information board but no interpretation centre?	5 (10%)	20 (41%)	12 (14.5%)	12 (14.5%)
Been to a historical site with an interpretation centre?	3 (6%)	29 (59%)	9 (18%)	8 (16%)
Been to a living history centre?	8 (16%)	21 (43%)	12 (25%)	7 (14%)
Read history books outside of school?	7 (14 %)	25 (51%)	17 (35%)	0
Watched history programmes on television?	18 (37%)	21 (45%)	8 (16%)	1 (2%)

Table 5-10 Children's out of school history based activities

members of. Almost 90% of all children regularly participated in sporting activities and almost half of the children participated in outdoor activities, including hill walking, horse riding, mountain biking and helping on their parent's farms. It can therefore be suggested that they had a use relationship with the landscape which included various forms of recreation, and in some cases, work.

5.2.4. Questionnaire Summary

The questionnaires given to adults and children have provided information about people's backgrounds, in the form of their home and family life and their employment and education. The questionnaires also gave information about individual's relationships with the countryside, in terms of their landscape biographies, activities in the countryside, and experiences of other landscapes. 'Knowledge' or interest in history and other aspects of the landscape was also examined.

Information from the questionnaire and certain exercises in the image workbook was used to determine what knowledge participants had of the area. As outlined in the previous chapter (4.7.2) three types of knowledge were outlined. These were:

• **Livelihood knowledge** (whether people had knowledge of farming processes etc in the area) **(9.9% yes, 90.1 % no)**

• **Place knowledge** (whether people had knowledge of specific place and topographic names, or other knowledge of the area) **(67% yes, 33% no)**

• **Academic knowledge** (whether people had knowledge of history, geological processes, names of plants etc) **(yes 29 %, no 71%)**

This information has been used to suggest factors which influence people's responses to the landscape workbook element of the exercise.

5.3. Landscape Workbook

The landscape workbook (outlined in section 4.7.1. of chapter 4) was designed as a way of finding out participant's landscape perceptions and preferences. In this exercise people were taken out to a field site and asked to answer questions about various aspects of the landscape that they liked, disliked, were interested in etc. Participants answered these questions by writing in a workbook, which was collected from them when they were finished. The responses for the landscape workbook were coded using a content analysis technique (as discussed in section 4.7.1.2 of methods chapter). The themes created for individual items that people commented on were: natural features (flora and fauna), topography, landuse, history, weather and 'entire area' (used when no particular item was cited). Themes were also created for why people liked, disliked or found certain elements of their surroundings 'special'. The themes created were: aesthetics/sensory, mnemonics (the feature invokes memories for the individual), use relationships, emotions, and interest. The complete list of all of the codes used can be viewed in appendix 1. The following text box shows a worked example of the coding for one participant's likes.

In this section the themes and individual items that have been featured most often in each of the questions will be discussed. Information from the landscape workbook has been cross tabulated against information from the other two sections of the exercise (image workbook and questionnaire) to determine what influences people's perceptions of landscape, this is discussed in chapter 6.

The above chart (5.2) shows the main themes that people cite as liking within the landscape of the study area. Within these themes, the items most commonly liked were hills and mountains (within the topography theme), ruined buildings (the history theme), trees (flora and fauna theme) and farm animals (landuse theme). The main reasons that people gave for liking a feature included aesthetics (26.7%) and emotions (33.2%). Within the theme of aesthetics, the most commonly invoked reasons were aesthetics (general) (10% of all 'like' responses) (usually phrased as *'because it is nice to look at'* (participant S49) or similar), beauty (10%) and colour (5.8%). The most commonly cited emotions were peace (7.7%) and pleasure (generally) (5.6%). Other common individual reasons for 'likes' were interest (general) (5.4%) and interest (history) (5%).

Example Coding – Participant T33

What do you like about your surroundings?

1. The colour! I love how the landscape **[subject – entire area (colour) 5.1]** is such a lively green colour **[reason – aesthetics (colour) 1.1]**. It looks alive. Different shades of green, yellow and brown everywhere

2. I like the valley and the hills **[subject- topography (hills and mountains) 2.1]** because I know how they were formed **[reason – knowledge (geomorphology)5.3]** and I can pick out features left by glaciation.

3. I like the isolation- can't see a house for miles because I don't particularly like busy built up areas **[subject – entire area (open landscape) 5.0]**. I like the open free feeling. The feeling of being the only person in the world**[reason – emotional (isolation/remoteness) 4.22]**.

4. The water – loch **[subject – topography (water (loch)) 2.2.3]** – very pretty **[reason – aesthetic (beauty) 1.2]**.

Each of these codes functions on 2 levels. The first number is the broad theme, so for example with the 2nd response the subject fits within the primary theme of Topography (2.00) and with in the sub-theme of Hills and Mountains (2.1), which allowed crosstabulations and frequencies to be carried out at both of these levels. The sample size was not large enough to allow crosstabulations to be carried out at a sub thematic level and produce results that could be seen to be statistically significant, as in certain cases only one or two responses were given within a particular sub-theme The reasons are also coded on 2 levels, again with the 2nd response the reason fits with in the primary theme of Knowledge (5.00) and Knowledge of Geomorphology (5.3).

As well as facilitating the crosstabulation of variables such as gender and preferences for landscape features these codes also allow for the crosstabulation of subjects and reasons, allowing questions such as 'why do people like mountains?' to be addressed.

Figure 5-1 Example coding, participant T33's likes for landscape

Participants were asked to photograph the features that they liked the most about their surroundings, and the most commonly cited strong 'like' was topography which featured in 42% of all responses, and the entire area (15%). Commonly cited individual items include hills and mountains (19.5% of all responses), the entire area (14.7%), ruined buildings (10.4%) and farm animals (8.7%).

The 'entire' area did not feature nearly as commonly in photographs as it did in the first answers. There are a variety of potential reasons for this, one being that some people cited the entire area as a 'like' more than once. Otherwise people may feel more strongly about certain features within the area than the whole area itself, an alternative explanation is that people photographed features that were easiest to record, and individual features such as buildings, animals or vegetation were easier to record. When questioned by participants about this (questions such as 'how do I photograph peace?'), I asked them to photograph something which represented the whole area, or the non-visual element they were referring to.

The main dislikes for the case study areas' landscapes cited by participants in the landscape workbook exercise were (thematically), landuse (65.8%) and natural features (15.8%). Within the landuse category the main dislikes were pylons (19.2% of all responses despite pylons only being present at the Loch Tay site), rubbish (7.9%), roads and tracks (7.6%) and conifer plantations (5.7%). Two different types of roads and tracks were disliked; farm

vehicle tracks, and large public roads, such as the A82, which runs along the West side of Loch Lomond. Another feature commonly disliked was bracken (7% of responses). In total 'modern features' (including pylons, roads, barbed wire etc.) account for over half (51.1%) of what was disliked about the environment. The main reasons for people's dislikes fell within the categories of aesthetics (39%), use relationships (35.5 %) and emotional responses (24.5%). Within these categories, the main reasons for disliking features were ugliness (23.7%), discomfort (10.7%), pain (8.9%), and feeling that a feature was unnatural (11.0%).

The most commonly cited strong dislike for the landscape (from the photographs taken by participants) was landuse, with 144 (71%) responses. Within this, the individual features mentioned most often were pylons (26% of responses), rubbish (11%), animal dung (9%) and conifer plantations (6%).

Participants were asked: '*Is there anything that you can see that makes the area special to you?*

It could be something which makes you think about other things or places, or something that you think is only found in the local area or the Highlands of Scotland, it may even be something that is connected to your family'.

Topography was the theme most commonly cited as being 'special' to individuals (36.3%). Within the general themes the features most commonly cited were hills and mountains (17.7%) and lochs (5.1%) (both of which were within the topography theme) the entire area (16.6%), ruined buildings (7.4%), (within the history theme), farm animals (5.7%) (within landuse theme). The two most common reasons for finding items 'special' are mnemonics (37.3%) and emotions (26.4%). Mnemonics involve the 'associative values' that people have for places, because of the memories they associate with them; of their own past, personal relationships or other geographical locations. Beauty (9.0%) was the other reason commonly cited for finding features 'special'. No single emotion rated highly within people's perceptions of landscape, however between them emotional reasons accounted for over a quarter of all reasons for the landscape being 'special'. Emotions experienced included pleasure, belonging, pride, peace, excitement and a feeling of the place being 'unique'.

Topography was also the most commonly cited theme as being the most 'special', in terms of what participants photographed. Within this hills and mountains (45%) and the loch (6.2%) were the features most commonly named. Other features often noted as being the most 'special' were the entire area (15.2%) and ruined buildings (11%).

Participants were asked 'In the box below write down up to four outdoor activities that you could do around here. Describe the activities and where they could take place'. In response they described a number of activities that could be carried out in the landscape. These ranged from 'work' based activities such as farming, to sports and relaxation. Sports were by far the most common activity cited by participants. These were divided into three categories, hill sports, water sports and other sports. Together these comprised 70% of the total responses to this question, with hill sports (30%) and water sports (26%) in the majority. The other category of activities commonly cited was recreation (16% of responses), a group which contained activities such as picnicking, relaxation and children's play. Other activities cited came in the categories of hobbies (3%), investigation (10%), and work (1%). Frequencies for individual activities were also examined. The most popular activities were hill walking (19% of responses), sailing/canoeing (7%), play (7%), walking (7%), cycling (5%) and wildlife watching (4%).

Participants were also asked what activities they would be keenest to participate in (the photographic element of the exercise, where participants were asked to photograph potential locations for carrying out activities). Responses to this question were similar to the first question about activities, in terms of proportion of responses. Hill sports were again the most common response (38%), followed by other sports (22%), recreation (19%), water sports (11%) and investigation (7%). The figure of investigation may not be typical of the population as a whole and may instead be because the visitors to the area were mainly there to carry out archaeological investigation and conservation work. In the next Chapter the relationship between use of landscapes and people's attitudes to them will be discussed further.

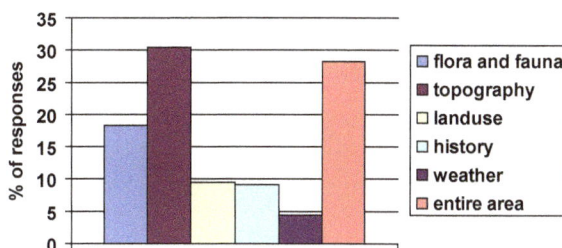

Figure 5-2 percentage of 'like' responses for each landscape theme

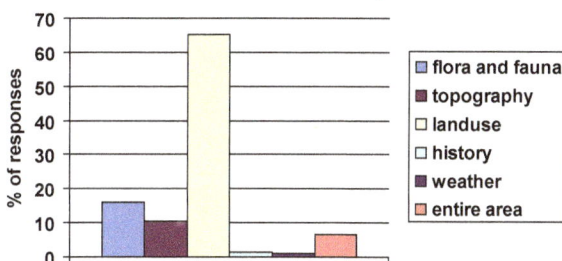

Figure 5-3 percentage of 'dislike' responses for each landscape theme.

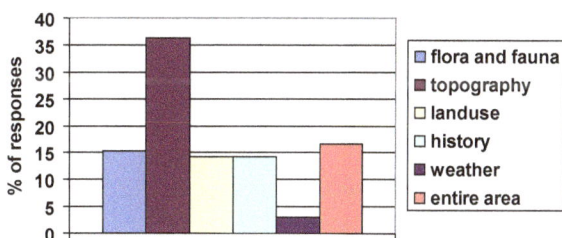

Figure 5-4 percentage of 'special' responses for each landscape theme

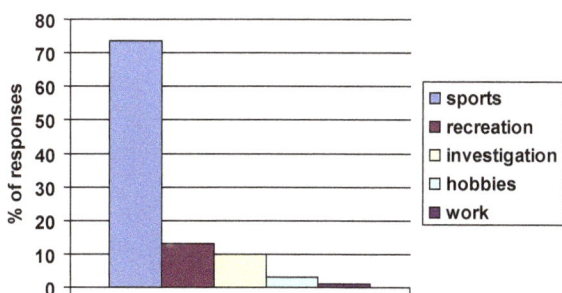

Figure 5-5 Types of outdoor activity by percentage of responses

More about

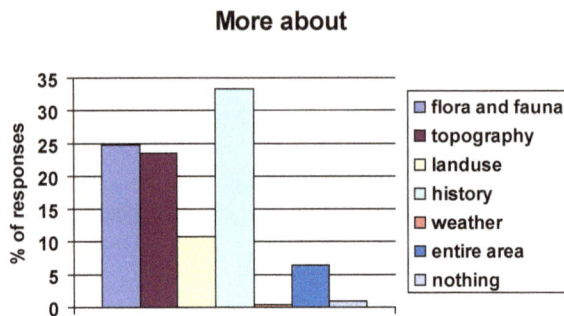

Figure 5-6 Themes people would most like to find out about by percentage of responses.

Participants were also asked whereabouts they would carry out their chosen activities. This was asked in order to determine their use relationship with particular areas of the landscape (and therefore what areas (if any) of the landscape were most important for them in terms of direct use). 25% of all responses did not suggest a specific place for activities, 59% suggested specific topographic features, 9% mentioned specific man made features, 4% mentioned specific weather conditions and 3% mentioned vegetation. The specific locations most commonly mentioned were hills and mountains (28%), lochs (10%), in the field where they currently were (9%) and roads and tracks in the surrounding area (6%).

The finally question asked to participants in this section was: *Is there anything in the area around you that you find interesting and you would like to find more about?* The theme that most respondents wished to find out about was history (33.3%). Within this theme ruined buildings were the most common item (14.2%) followed by all historic features (7.4%) and the past of the area (7.1%). Natural features (24.7%) and topography (23.4%) were also commonly cited as features that people wished to find out more about. Within these themes geology (7.4%) wildlife (6.8%), hills and mountains (6.5%) and vegetation were mentioned. Individuals wanted to find out different things about the formation of the landscape (41.9%), natural history (12.0%) & present landuse (10.7%) and the most common questions asked within these themes were about geomorphologic processes(8.8%), people in the past (7.8%), wildlife species (4.2%)and plant species (5.2%). When asked what they would most like to find out about, the most common theme (38%) was history, followed by topography (28.3%) and natural features (20.2%). Individual features that people most wanted to discover more about included ruined buildings (21.2%), historical features generally (9.1%), hills and mountains (8%) and boulders (7%). These were the large erratic boulders found in both the fields at Loch Tay and Loch Lomond.

5.3.5. Landscape Workbook Summary.

The landscape workbook was used to discover which aspects of the landscape people liked the most, disliked the most, and were most attached to. This exercise produced

quantitative data, which was coded using the processes described above to produce themes and sub themes of subjects and reasons that participants gave in their responses. Cross-tabulations were computed to examine what elements of people's identities appeared to most affect landscape perceptions. The results from this are discussed in section 6.2 of the next chapter, where they are situated within wider theories of people/landscape interactions.

5.4. Image Workbook

Four different types of question were used in this exercise, with participants asked to answer each question twice, based upon two contrasting images. All of the images shown were of the Loch Tay or Loch Lomond areas, depending on the field site that participants were taken to.

The image workbook was designed to provide five different types of information about how people saw the landscape (as presented in methods chapter section 4.7.2). These information types were:

• the features people identify in the landscape,

• people's knowledge of landscape features,

• the familiarity that people have with the landscapes shown,

• people's use relationships with the landscape,

• people's emotional reactions to spending time in the landscapes.

It was realised, however, that the responses that participants gave were directed at the fragmentary moment of landscape as depicted in the photographs rather than the entire landscape, which are two completely different things. It was possible to look at the responses individuals gave to examine what knowledge they were drawing upon when answering the questions (in terms of the features identified in images, see section 5.2.4 above), but any attitudes expressed about the photographs were just that, attitudes about the photographs, rather than the landscape.

The photograph is an artefact of a moment in time, created by the researcher, and is not a landscape, whereas the landscape contains all of the thoughts, memories and associations that a person has with their world. In this section the responses which demonstrate that individuals were responding to the limited scope of the photograph rather than the whole landscape will be presented.

5.4.1. Case Study

Question Type 3 *Which of the words below would you use to describe this picture?* Participants were given a list of adjectives and asked to circle as many as they thought applied to the images they were shown.

Lochtayside

The image used for this question was a photograph taken

Figure 5-7 Image 3 shown to Lochtayside participants, looking west along Loch Tay from Kiltyrie (author)

at Kiltyrie, on the north shore of Loch Tay, on a clear cold day with farmland in the foreground looking west along the loch to the snow-capped Breadalbane hills in the background.

Loch Lomond

The image used for this question was a vertical colour aerial photograph of Glen Luss; it depicts Edentaggart farm, and its deciduous trees. There are deciduous trees in the valley bottom, and open hillsides and rock outcrops.

The words used most commonly to describe these images were; countryside (67% or responses), open (64%), natural (54%), beautiful (52%), light (51%), relaxing (46%), colourful (44%), rural (42%), fresh (39%), familiar (37%), agricultural (37%), interesting (35%), happy (34%) and unspoiled (33%).

Image 6

Both images in this section were selected to contrast the pictures shown as image three. They both show more evidence of features in the landscape that are clearly 'man made'.

Loch Tay

Image 6 is an aerial photograph of the north shore of Loch Tay showing the area of Edramucky and Milton Morenish.

The photograph was taken in winter or early spring and as such the vegetation is low, and the sun is at an oblique angle meaning that several earthwork features such as disused quarries and peat tracks are visible on the hillside. Holiday cottages and caravans are evident on the slopes south of the road, and there is a small harbour filled with pleasure craft.

Loch Lomond

The photograph shown to Loch Lomond participants was an aerial photograph of Luss and Loch Lomond, it shows the mouth of Glen Luss and the island nearest to Luss, and the A82, the main road up the lochside. The area photographed borders the area shown to Loch Lomond participants as 'image 3'.

The words most commonly chosen by participants to describe these scenes were: countryside (46% of participants using this word); open (42%); light (38%); managed (32%); manmade (30%); interesting (29%); living (29%) and working (28%).

Scrutiny of the responses to the two photographs showed that the adjectives that people circled can only be seen as a reflection of their attitudes to the landscape as depicted by the photograph, rather than the landscape itself. Several words were used far more often for Image Three than for Image Six, and many of these were aesthetic and emotional

Figure 5-8 Image 6 shown to Lochtayside participants Image 6 oblique aerial photograph of Milton Morenish, N. Lochtayside (RCAHMS)

adjectives. Image Three was more often described as open; colourful; wild; rural; fresh; light; interesting; countryside; relaxing; gentle; dramatic; natural; unspoiled; untouched; agricultural; stunning; tranquil; historic; beautiful and happy. Therefore, positive adjectives were more generally used for this image, along with adjectives which stressed the 'unspoiled' (anti-modern?) nature of this image. This is despite the fact that both images show the same area, just from different vantage points.

Examining the differences between things that are seen as 'unspoiled' and those which are seen as 'untouched' is interesting. In both images unspoiled was used more often than untouched (33 vs. 20% for image 3) and (10% vs. 4% for image 6). This suggests that people are willing to accept that a landscape can be 'touched' by human hand without being 'spoiled', but clearly too much human intervention can 'spoil' a landscape. The biggest differences are in the words 'natural' (54% vs. 23%), beautiful (52% vs. 23%) and unspoiled (33% vs. 9.6%). Image 6 was far more often described as 'man made' (30% vs. 10%), managed (32 vs. 17%), working (28 vs. 16%), dull (18% vs. 13%) and boring (15% vs. 9%). One other word used more often for image 6 than 3 is 'homely'. No positive aesthetic adjectives are used more often for image 6 than 3. This dislike of manmade features will be further discussed in chapter 6, where it will be discussed in the context of cultural themes stemming from the Picturesque and Romantic Movements and Nationalism of the eighteenth century.

Analysis of the information gathered has led me to examine more fully the importance of the context of landscape. As demonstrated above, perceptions and preference of landscapes are governed by the embodied cultural and identity based relationships with place, rather than by a reaction to the visual aesthetic of a space (these relationships will be further discussed in chapter 6). Therefore there are issues with using visual sources as a proxy for the entire landscape, and this section will discuss how these issues were encountered within my own research.

Two of the questions in the image workbook asked individuals to comment on what they would do, if they were to spend a day in the areas depicted in the photographs and whether they would like to spend time in the area. Participants worked with two images of the same physical presence (the west end of the Tarmachan Ridge), but were commented on in very different ways.

The first photograph participants were shown was taken from the Bredalbane Park in Killin and shows Meall nan Tarmachan with a covering of snow on a sunny winter's day. It also shows some of the buildings of Killin, including the Dall Lodge Hotel and the sports pavilion. Around three quarters of participants said they would be happy to spend time in the area, that they liked it and would use the area for recreation. The second photograph was taken on a cold stormy day near to the summit of the Tarmachan ridge, and showed the Neolithic axe working area of Creag Nan Callich, with the fields of Glen Dochart

Figure 5-9 Image 2, Tarmachan Ridge, taken from Bredalbane Park, Killin (author)

5-10 Axe quarry on Creag na Caillich, part of the Tarmachan ridge (author)

in the background. Only half of participants questioned were keen to spend time in this area, and almost two fifths expressed negative emotions about spending time here and very few participants were indifferent to spending time in this area.

These two images which depicted small areas of the landscape which looked very different. The images were artefacts created by the researcher (myself), and were contextless for the participants. Therefore, people's reactions to the images were just that, reactions to the images rather than to the wider landscape. The 'moments' depicted within these images were the only information that participants had of the landscape (which was itself lacking in all the other non-visual aspects of that landscape's moment), and as such made their decisions on the whole landscape solely from this image. Therefore, even though their reactions to the images may have been affected by their prior encounters with similar situations, the comments made were comments about this one very specific scenario.

This is reinforced by the reaction to another image shown to Loch Tay participants, which depicted part of the north side of the loch including the area where many of the participants had undertaken archaeological or conservation fieldwork. Participants were asked to say what activities they would like to undertake in the area. In the written section of the exercise, one participant said that they did not wish to spend any time in this area, and expressed regret at this comment when they were informed of the location shown by the photograph. Several other participants said that they would have answered the questions differently if they had known where the landscape depicted actually was. Out of context, this view of the landscape had been an unappealing picture, rather than the lived landscape which people enjoyed.

The same problems arise with all methods which involve the use of a proxy for 'landscape' rather than the landscape itself when seeking to examine individual's perceptions of landscape. This will be discussed further in section 6.5.1 of the discussion chapter.

The idea of all images being artefacts rather than 'mirrors of reality' has been discussed by a number of researchers. John Berger (reprinted 1980) was one of the first researchers to discuss the idea that the a photograph is only a record of the environment as the photographer has chosen to portray it. The photographer has chosen the time and the place, and the size of the scene to be photographed, and therefore is not an objective record. Ingold (2000) elaborates on the idea that vision is not an objective sense. What a person sees in a place depends on where they choose to look, which is affected by factors of time, culture and identity. In addition qualities of light and weather mean that only certain elements of landscape are visible to be viewed at any given time, and there are certain times where not all of the physical landscape is available to be seen. Therefore photographs, and any other visual proxies of landscape

produced by the researcher can only be seen as reflections of the identity of the researcher and the time which they produced the image. People's perceptions of these images can only be understood as their perceptions of the researcher's landscape (or how the researcher portrayed their landscape) rather than perceptions of the participant.

This issue of the context of proxies for landscape (such as photographs or visualisations), and whether they are valid in landscape research will be discussed further in section 7.2.1 of chapter 7.

5.5. Summary – Results

This chapter has briefly presented the information collected through fieldwork. Questionnaire information was the first to be outlined, and within this it was noted that the adult sample was weighted towards visitors to the area, almost all of whom had an interest in the area's history and/or ecology as participants were attendees on National Trust for Scotland Thistle Camps. The children's questionnaire represents all of the children of that age group (10-12) who were resident in that area, with no visiting children. The children from Lochlomondside had all learnt something of the history of the area's landscape through participation in the BLHLP schools' outreach programme.

The second set of information outlined was that from the landscape workbook. The process by which the information from this had been coded was outlined, and results presented. This particular exercise gave information on participants' landscape preferences and what it was that they liked or disliked (etc.) of these landscape features. The original intention was to compare this information with that gained from the other two exercises, but analysis of the image workbook information lead to the realisation that much of the data from it was essentially unsuitable for this purpose.

Some information from the image workbook was presented above and it was explained why the information from this section of the exercise has had to be discounted with regard to how people think about the landscape as a whole. It has, however, served to demonstrate how people offer attitudes based on available evidence, and if the photographs are contextless images, then people can express opinions of them which are not linked to how they think of the landscape as a whole. This raises wider questions about the use of contextless visual proxies for landscape which will be discussed further in chapter 6. Information from the image workbook has still allowed for the determination of the type of knowledge that individuals use to describe landscape features, which gives an idea of their knowledge of and familiarity with the landscape. It is possible to compare the values for landscape expressed by people in the landscape workbook with information from the questionnaire exercise, and the 'knowledge' expressed in the image workbook to examine what influences individual's perceptions of landscape. This will be carried out in the following chapter.

6

Discussion

6.1. Introduction

The previous chapter outlined the information gathered in the fieldwork element of this study. In this chapter, this information will be discussed within a theoretical framework which examines how values are created. It has long been realised (e.g. Derby 2000, Proshansky et al 1983) that differences in peoples' perceptions of landscape are associated with differences in identity, which creates subjectivities. Equally it is understood that similarities in identity are associated with similarities in landscape values. However, individuals with very different identities can express similar values for similar features. This has led to the suggestion that it is the landscape itself which makes the 'same' through materiality (Stedman 2003, Tilley 1994; 2002). This produces a circular argument whereby the physical landscape affects how people think about the physical landscape. This research, and an examination of the history of the Highlands, suggests this is not the case. Instead there are broad cultural influences which create similarities in landscape values as well as similarities in individual's identities (e.g. children, tourists, adults) which also can be shown cluster responses. Culture, landscape and identity are temporally situated and this time takes different forms. These factors can be described as the 'context' of the individuals' landscape values, and this context must be understood to understand the influences on people's landscape values.

This chapter will develop this argument, using examples drawn from my research and evidence from historical attitudes to Lochtayside (outlined in chapters 2 & 3). At times and by different people Loch Tay has been seen in different ways (as wild, home, tame, hostile etc) whilst having the same 'bones' materially. Therefore individuals attitudes to landscape, rest not within the landscape, but within the individual. The individual 'sees' and 'looks' at what they want of the landscape depending on the context of their relationship with these and will react to landscapes which are seemingly physically similar in very different ways because of this. This renders problematic studies which are based on visualisation scenarios which involve the creation of an image which is a proxy for a real landscape, or a photograph which is a decontextualised fragment of a view of a landscape.

The different influences on values will be discussed with reference to trends and responses evidenced in my own research. It will also be suggested that there are broad sociocultural hegemonies which have affected landscape perceptions. All perceptions of landscape happen within a temporal context, and the relationship between time and landscape values will be unpackaged. Examining landscape perceptions in a way which is not rooted in one which assumes that the material land is what influences people's perceptions involves a reconsideration of methodologies for assessing landscape values. This chapter will address methodological issues involved in assessing landscape values, without relying on materiality as a causal explanation including issues within my own research.

6.2. Contexts of landscape perceptions

This section will examine the roots of people's landscape perceptions, including the contexts of encounter which help to determine these perceptions. As outlined in the methods chapter (section 4.7.1.2) participants responses to the landscape workbook were crosstabulated with aspects of identity worked shown in the questionnaire. All of the relationships discussed below are ones that were statistically significant at a 95% confidence level when a Chi-square statistical test was carried out. Other potential influences (such as gender) were examined, but were found to have little effect on people's landscape values and as such are not discussed here. The following table shows the Chi-square tests that were carried out to determine the significance of the distributions shown in the crosstabulations. Only tests (and therefore crosstabulations) which were found to be significant are listed.

6.2.1. Identity

This section will examine the context of people's landscape values, in terms of examining the relationships between culture, identity and time and landscape perceptions. In some senses the separation of culture and identity involves the creation of a false dichotomy, but in this work identity is taken to be factors pertaining to the individual, whereas culture can be taken to be wider social phenomena.

The first strand of influence on an individual's landscape perceptions is 'identity'. Identity is a term which is much

Adults and Children

Age group: what do you like about the landscape? Chi-square = 25.729, p=.041

Age group: why do you like this? Chi-square = 50.509, p=.000

Age group: what do you dislike about the landscape? Chi-square= 36.398, p=.002

Age group: why do you dislike this? Chi-square = 27.508, p=.007

Age group: what is special about the landscape? Chi-square = 27.747, p=.023

Age group: why do you find this special? Chi-square = 38.999, p=.000

Age group: what activities would you like to do in the landscape? Chi-square =40.501, p=.000

Age group: what activities would most like to do? Chi-square =.59.206, p=.000

Age group: what information do you most want about these landscape features? Chi-square = 55.703, p=.000

Adult vs Child: what do you like about the landscape? Chi-square=16.510, p=.006

Adult vs Child: Why do you like this? Chi-square= 29.587, p=.000

Adult vs Child: what do you dislike about the landscape? Chi-square=14.321, p=.014

Adult vs Child: what do you dislike the most about the landscape? Chi-square = 11.948, p=.036

Adult vs Child: why do you dislike this? Chi-square = 27.508, p=.007

Adult vs Child: what is special about the landscape? Chi-square = 17.815, p=.003

Adult vs Child: why do you find this special? Chi-square = 38.999, p=.000

Adult vs Child: what activities would you like to do in the landscape? Chi-square =29.735, p=.000

Adult vs Child: what activities would you most like to do? Chi-square=31.758, p=.000

Adult vs Child: what information do you most want about these landscape features? Chi-square = 48.570, p=.000

Solely Adults

Interest in history?: what do you like about the landscape? Chi-square = 39.890, p=.000

Interest in history?: what do you like the most about the landscape? Chi-square = 20.958, p=.001

Interest in history?: what do you dislike about the landscape? Chi-square = 21.906, p=.001

Interest in history?: what do you dislike the most about the landscape? Chi-square =13.740, p=.017

Interest in history?: what do you find the most special about the landscape? Chi-square = 13.740, p=.080

Interest in history?: what do you want to find out about the landscape? Chi-square =22.188, p=.001

Interest in history?: what information do you most want about these landscape features? Chi-square = 11.691, p=.039

Urban vs Rural: what do you dislike about the landscape? Chi-square = 12.996, p=.023

Urban vs Rural: what information do you most want about these landscape features? Chi-square = 15.615, p=.008

Solely Children

Lochlomondside vs Lochtayside: what do you like about the landscape? Chi-Square =16.01, p=.007

Lochlomondside vs Lochtayside: what do you dislike about the landscape? Chi-square = 15.816, p=.003

Lochlomondside vs Lochtayside: what do you want to find out about the landscape? Chi-square = 24.329[a], p=.000

6-1 Significant crosstabulations (and Chi-square values) for different aspects of identity and landscape preferences.

debated in the social sciences, it can be seen either as something which exists within the self, or as ascribed to you by another individual (Mauss 2000). It can also be a certain aspect of an individual's self, such as their identity 'as a woman', 'as a child', 'as a sportsman'. In this instance I am using the term 'identity' to describe the individual and who they are in the world. By this I mean the multiple facets of their biography which make them a person, including their relationships, experiences, and thoughts of themselves. In this sense identity can be seen as being related to subjectivity insofar as it involves particular qualities of an individual which make them think differently to other people. It is differences in identity (in terms of who they are and what experiences they have of the world) which can create differences in people's perceptions of landscape. Also, similarities in people's identities can create similarities in perceptions of landscape, as demonstrated by group identities, such as that of 'a child', 'a tourist', or 'an archaeologist'.

This section will discuss some of the trends evident in individual's perceptions and preferences of the Highland landscape as evidenced in this research. Perceptions which are unique to the individual, borne out of their individual experiences will be addressed first, followed by trends in a perception which have been recognised, and are associated with 'collective identity'.

Individual aspects of identity

This section will examine some of the individual aspects of identity that provide a context for the differences in people's landscape values.

1. Memories

Memory is a key influence on individual's landscape perceptions (Schama 1996, Butler & Hall 1999). When participants cited elements of the landscape that they liked, disliked or saw as being special, they often invoked memories as a reason behind these preferences. Memories are unique to the individual (Murphy 1985), even if a number of people have had similar landscape experiences, and these memories create individual perceptions of the landscape. Individuals' relationships with landscape are formed by 'doing' rather than just seeing the landscape, (Ingold 1993, Soliva 2007, Møller Madsen & Adriansen 2004). Responses given in the landscape workbook suggested a strong link between people's use relationships with the land, and what of the land they value. Memories of activities carried out in the landscape of the case study area, and other places within their past lead certain areas to be valued, or disvalued because of the individual's particular relationship. The quotations presented in the following paragraph provide examples of these.

[Something which is special to me is the] *Sheep pen near our dig site where our path lies every day.* (T46). The individual here has started to value an area of landscape which they have grown familiar with through its presence in their everyday experience of this landscape. Equally, the landscape can hold memories of past places of activity, such as this following response: [something which is special to me is the] *Remains of building – excavation of longhouse .... in 2003 reminds me of wonderful fun two weeks where I met many brilliant people.* These examples demonstrate how the individuals see these places as nodes (areas of specific value) in their particular taskscape (Grasseni 2004, Ingold 1993). These places hold value for these specific respondents, not because of their physical properties (or materiality) but largely because of the memories they have of the places through passing pleasant time in the area.

It appears that memories of other places with physical similarities can cause people to think of the landscape in certain ways as indicated in the following statements. *The view of Ben Lawers is pretty special. It reminds me of all the other Munroe's [sic] in Scotland I have climbed with my outdoor club* (T33). *Northern Scottish countryside always reminds me of walking the West Highland way with 2 friends and what an enjoyable experience it was* (T41).

In the above cases the individuals are interpreting the Lochtayside landscape through the lens of previous experiences, in similar landscape settings. The physical presence of Ben Lawers causes the individual to remember events which have happened in her past, and these previous experiences led the individual (T41) to value a landscape that they have never before experienced. In the following example the respondent is interpreting landscape features by referring to personal relationships; this time of something which reminds them of a parent. *Sheep! They are special because I've had sheep all my life. My mum has kept sheep about 18 years. So they have special connotations and remind me of my mum.* (T35). However others with no experience of this particular landscape, even though they had visited similar ones, found nothing of their surroundings to be special. *I don't believe the area is particularly special to me and nothing in the landscape changes this view. Sorry?!* (T5) was one of a number of responses that showed that landscape features having similar physical forms does not always make them similarly valued, showing that material similarity is not always enough to make people value certain landscapes.

This idea of certain landscapes or landscape features acting as mnemonics was most prevalent in terms of what elements of the landscape people said they felt were special to them. The category of 'special' was designed to determine what features, places, or elements of the landscape people felt an attachment to, rather than just 'liked'. This can be described as 'place attachment' (Prohansky et al 1983), which is when a person has an embedded relationship with a landscape, one which is borne of experience rather than just immediate reactions to a place (Johnston 1998, Brown 2006).

Elements of the landscape can also be valued for reasons pertaining to their use. In the following example the participant had photographed trees before, and valued a similar tree as they may return at a later time to photograph it. *The tree in the bottom left corner – has an interesting shape. I like to photograph interesting trees* (T42). Another individual described a particular activity (that of hill walking) as something which makes the landscape special to him. *Going up a hill with my dad - the special feeling you are on your own and the only 2 people that exist* (S16). To this child the hills are 'special' because of past experiences he has had there. Another child found fields special because of helping his father in the fields. [The field is special to me because] *I help my dad in the field, just the ones that I see.* (S39). With both of these comments, the suggestion is that the features are only special because of these activities, and if they had not taken place, the features would not be of value. Therefore it is the actions which have taken place within elements of the landscape which mean that they are valued, rather than any inherent value of the landscape itself.

Landscape Biography.

Part of an individual's subjectivity is derived from where they come from, what their everyday world is like. This includes the places they currently inhabit, which in turn affects how they think about other landscapes. One child had recently moved to the area and commented that *I like that it has hills or mountains because where I used to live there was no mountains.* (S25). Other people who were visitors to the area compared the area favourably to where they lived and worked: *Very beautiful to look at and be in – completely different to the industrial estate that I work in* (T64). *Quiet and peaceful (relatively) different from busy city (Edinburgh) where I live* (T21). Conversely others appreciated the area because it was home, or had similarities to where they lived e.g. *The ruins make me think of home because there is one right next to me* (S9). Others saw the area as being part of a national biography, and appreciated it as such *It makes me feel good to be in the highlands because all my family lives in Scotland* (S32).

The landscape can also be disliked because it is different to a personal ideal landscape such as this example from one North American visitor [I dislike] *The lack of trees. I'm from a part of the world (North America) where trees are a vital part of the landscape. And while I can appreciate this place for what it is, I have to admit that I love trees and miss them* (T22).

2. Knowledge

What people know also affects how people value the landscape. Knowledge is inseparable from identity, in terms of the fact that what you know and what you want to know is very personal, and is related to experiences in the past and interests in the present. Participants suggested that certain elements of the landscape were liked because of the knowledge that they had of them and also the potential they had for more knowledge to be generated. A number of children commented on the fact that *Archaeologists can study the landscape and they can excavate and that is good because they can give us information.*(S12). Other individuals value certain elements of the landscape because of what they already know. This includes people who have learned things through formal education e.g. *The geology – some places have rocks that are unique to the area, and knowing that can make a place special to me.* (T3), or through knowledge gained through doing such as the following response from a child from a farming family, [I like] *Sheep poo- because they make they make the grass grow better, the sheep eat more and can have twins and makes more meat on sheep* (S15).

It is rare that elements of the landscape are valued purely because of one facet of an individual's identity. In the following example the individual suggests that the history of the area is important to them both because of their identity as a Scot and because of their academic interests. *Strong sense of Historic feel to the landscape – probably natural as I'm Scottish, studying archaeology and Scottish Ethnology. Ruins of old longhouses etc. nearby* (T39).

Grouping in Perceptions

The examples discussed above have demonstrated how aspects of an individual's identity affect landscape values. Investigation of the landscape workbook responses revealed a clustering of responses which can partially be explained by the fact that a number of individuals share aspects of their identity. In this case, demographic sub-groups, as identified from the questionnaire data, allow the investigation of aspects of identity which affect people's landscape perceptions.

1. Shared Identity

Age

Age is part of identity. How old you are affects your place in the world, what you do and what you know (McCormack 2002). In the first part of this sub-section age will be dealt with as a simple dualism between 'child' and 'adult'. It is recognised that several individuals in the study sample who were teenagers occupy a place as 'adolescents' in between these two groups. They are treated as adults here because they carried out the adult version of the research exercise. After the child/adult comparison is reported I will then discuss some of the differences in perceptions evident from the responses of the different age groups.

Children's and adults' landscape preferences as recorded in the landscape workbook revealed some striking differences. Whilst children and adults exhibit similar likes and dislikes for landscape, different reasoning was exhibited as to what these likes were, in that children were more likely to draw upon aesthetic reasoning and adults on emotional ones (38% vs. 23%). For example a typical adult response may be:

[I like] *mountains – they give me a sense of freedom* (T8)

And a typical child's:

I like the hills because there is a nice view (S32)

In terms of why things are disliked, children's responses almost exclusively focussed upon use relationships with and aesthetics of the landscape (47%& 43% respectively) whereas adult reasoning was split almost equally between aesthetics (35%), use relationships (32%) and emotions (31%). This suggests that children may have a more direct relationship with landscape than adults, they spend more time seeing and doing landscape than adults who appear to see, do and think landscape in equal proportions. Adults may also be more comfortable with the use of emotional reasoning for landscape, as they have been more exposed to a culture where land is valued for emotional rather than functional reasons (landscapes and culture are discussed further below in 6.2.2) . This relationship continues into what adults and children view as being special about the landscape. Adults more often spoke of memories and emotional relations with land while children more often mentioned a direct relationship with the land including aesthetics and use relationships again, which is linked to the idea of children learning about the world through active relationships (Fjortoft & Sagie 2000, Harker 2005).

Adults were more specific than children when questioned about what they wished to find out about that landscape. Over half of all children's responses were similar to *I would like to find out about the old buildings a bit more* (S1) where the individual has given a subject (the old buildings) but not what they want to find out about it. In contrast, the adults questioned were more likely to comment on which facets of the landscape they would particularly like to know (e.g. [I would like to know] *how to look after sheep* [subject] *to care for the needs of a new flock* [particular facts] (T14)). In particular adults wished to discover how the landscape was formed (in terms of geomorphological and anthropogenic processes) (47% of adult responses). There are a number of potential reasons for this. It may be that adults have developed more specific interests than children, or that adults already feel that they know all they want to know about certain features, and just wish to know about others. Otherwise, children may have a more generalised curiosity about the world than adults. It may instead be simply that children had got bored of writing when they came to this question, which was the last one in the workbook.

Participants in the adult version of the study ranged

in age from 16 to 78, and it was thought that there may be differences of opinion within this age group. It was therefore deemed necessary to examine more closely the preferences for landscapes as expressed by different age groups, rather than simply between adults and children, as is suggested in previous studies on age and landscape perceptions (e.g. Haartesn et al 2003). The age groups used were 9-12 (The children's section of the study), 16-24, 25-54 and over 55.

Children and the over 55's were most likely to talk about their use relationships with the land as a reason for disliking landscape. Many of these comments were made about the difficulty of getting around in the landscape, and may be linked to reduced mobility of some of the over 55s, and the children talked about the problem of standing in animal droppings or getting spiked by thistles whilst playing in the landscape.

There were differences as to why different groups deemed different features of the landscape to be special. Children more often cited aesthetic and use relationship related reasons than all the adults. Over 55's were most likely to talk about 'interest' than other groups. This may be related to what discourses of landscape individuals are exposed to and are willing to participate in, in terms of their social groups, and what they view to be appropriate responses. All of the adult groups were more likely to mention mnemonic reasons for finding landscape features to be special (about 43% of all adult responses used this type of reasoning). This cannot be ascribed to the fact that adults simply have more experiences of this type of landscape, as most of the children had spent a large amount of their lives in the Highlands. It therefore suggests that adults and children use a different type of reasoning when discussing landscape.

Perhaps unsurprisingly there are differences in the sorts of activities that different age groups wished to carry out in the landscape. The two older groups (55+ and 25-54) were more likely to mention hobbies (such as drawing or photography) as activities they would like to participate in. These two groups were also more likely to mention 'investigation' (such as archaeological fieldwork or wildlife watching) than younger groups. In contrast the two younger groups more commonly cited sports and recreation than the two older groups. Recreation included 'play' which was often mentioned by children. These same trends in use relationship were also evident in the image workbook where participants were asked what activities they would like to do in different scenes. This information hints that a variance in use relationships with the landscape is linked to people's ages, and how individuals value the landscape. The idea of age affecting landscape values is linked to a wider consideration of time and landscapes, which will be examined more fully in section 6.2.4 below.

Landscape Biography

What one knows of landscapes is part of one's identity. A landscape biography can be defined as the landscapes that an individual has experienced, either physically, through living or visiting, or mentally, through imagining the area. This has already been discussed in terms of the individual, and how individual experiences of place can shape people's landscape values (see section 6.2). Similarities in landscape biography can also mean that people can develop similar landscape values, and this section will examine this relationship, through the use of two different facets of landscape biography: whether people were visitors to or residents of the study areas and whether they lived in urban or rural areas.

Both visitors to and residents of the two areas were involved in the research, and cross-tabulations were computed to determine whether residential status affected people's landscape perceptions. The groupings that were investigated that are relevant to this were visitor/resident, urban/rural and Loch Tay/Loch Lomond (for the children only). These dichotomies are linked to 'place knowledge' which is discussed further below.

All of the children were resident in the areas that were studied, and many of the differences between visitors' and residents' perceptions follow the same pattern as adults and children, as discussed previously. The differences observed were similar to previous studies contrasting children's and adults relationships with landscape (e.g. Matthews et al 2000, McCormack 2002), and therefore were ascribed to this rather than differences in residence. Investigation of the perceptions of more local adults or visiting children would be necessary to gain an indication on how much of an affect residential status has on perceptions of landscape.

Area of Residence/Urban or Rural

The background questionnaire recorded whether adults lived in urban or rural areas (for definition of rural used in this study please refer to section 5.2.2.1 of the results chapter). It was anticipated that people who lived in urban areas would value the landscape for different reasons to participants from rural areas (as evidenced in studies such as Alexander and Riddington 2007 and Halfacree 1994). This was found to be the case, and appears to be linked to different use relationships with the land, and was particularly evident in the dislikes for the landscape which were offered. Participants who currently lived in rural areas were more likely to dislike elements of the areas' flora and fauna (in particular bracken as discussed below in section 6.2.1.3), and participants from urban areas were more likely to dislike weather conditions. Individuals from urban areas were also more likely to express a dislike of animal dung and items of 'rubbish' (fertiliser sacks etc) in the landscape. These differences in dislikes appear to be linked to differing opinions as to what the landscape is there for. For individuals from rural areas the countryside is a lived place, a taskscape where daily life is played out (Ingold 2000). For adults from urban areas, the landscape of the Scottish Highlands may have mainly been known through idealised images presented in tourist literature, and nostalgic media (e.g. television series such as 'Monarch of the Glen' or 'Hamish Macbeth') (Butler & Hall 1999). Therefore items such as sheep droppings, feed sacks and pylons are not present in 'their Highlands' and are disliked as detracting from this idealised picture. The landscapes of the Highlands are seen in opposition to the everyday urban existence, rather than as a 'working countryside', something reported in the questionnaire responses where 71% of adult respondents said that 'escaping civilisation' was an important factor in determining where they visit in the countryside. When items of 'rubbish' are seen or other traces of modernity experienced, they are a reminder of the modernity that participants have sought to escape, as exemplified by the following quotation form a Loch Lomond participant. [I dislike] *the noise of the traffic on the other side of the loch and the chainsaw near by. Landscapes are for peace and quiet!* (T70). The relationship between this 'anti-modernity' perspective and perceptions of landscape is further discussed within the framework of Romanticism in section 6.2.2. In contrast, participants from rural areas were more likely to dislike features because of their use relationships, such as the following participant from a farming background: *the bracken is gradually taking over the good grazing. This provides a habitat for ticks which can cause ill health in animals and humans (T72).* This may be because for a farmer the landscape is, at least partially, a 'tool of the trade' and therefore has to function correctly to be valued. However, it should not be suggested that the farming community has a strictly functionalist relationship with the land (Lee 2007). The same individual who dislikes bracken for functional reasons stated *I just love being in the Hills!* Rural participants from non-farming backgrounds still have a use relationship with the countryside which is based on their everyday existence, rather than any reasons rooted in escaping modernity (notwithstanding any original reasons for moving to a rural area in the first place).

The following statement acts as a caveat against using a simple urban-rural dichotomy when looking at why people value certain landscapes. This child (S35) lived in the village of Killin, but did not see the study area (which was 'only' 5 miles away from Killin) as being part of his landscape. *I liked it because we saw loads of stuff that people who live in the village like me don't see very often unless they go up Stoneaccacin* (S35). However, these divisions allow the researcher to identify clustering in influences across a diffuse range of perceptions that people have for landscape.

The final place-based division to be discussed is the differences in perceptions between participants from Loch Tay and Loch Lomond. In section 4.6.2 the difficulties in recruiting adult participants in Lochlomondside was discussed, and as such a comparison was carried out purely between children from Lochtayside and children from Loch Lomond. It appears that many of the differences apparent in the values that children from the two areas hold for landscape are caused by the knowledge these children have (such as the increased knowledge of landscape history that the Loch Tay children had compared to the Luss children because of their involvement in the BLHLP outreach work)

rather than the physical spaces they occupy. Therefore this relationship is discussed below in terms of knowledge and landscape perceptions.

Knowledge and Landscape Perceptions

Integral to identity is what you know about the world, and indeed knowledge and how you know the world was implicit in all the previous influences in perception which have been outlined. In this section three different types of formal knowledge will be discussed, along with their relationship with people's landscape perceptions. When information from the landscape workbook was coded, trends in perceptions were compared to types of knowledge demonstrated in the questionnaire and image workbook sections of the exercise. The three types of knowledge investigated were 'livelihood', 'place' and 'academic' knowledges.

Livelihood knowledge involves people having an understanding of how the landscape works, including a knowledge of farming, conservation and everyday practices in the area. This appears to alter how people think of the landscape. Individuals who demonstrated this kind of knowledge were more likely to dislike something of the area's flora and fauna (29% vs. 16% of respondents) than those who did not have this kind of knowledge. Many of these dislikes are linked to bracken, which is spreading in the study areas due to a reduction of grazing, for reasons pertaining to the fact that it is an invasive species and damaging the ecosystem, and the viability of the farmland (Marrs & Pakeham 1995). An example is: *The bracken is gradually taking over good Grazing. This provides a habitat for ticks which can cause ill health in animals and humans'* (T70). Having livelihood knowledge also appears to mean that people are more likely to dislike features because of their use relationships with the surroundings (52% vs. 38% of responses) as demonstrated by the response (T70) quoted above. People with knowledge of livelihood were also less likely to dislike features of the area's landuse. This may be because features such as farming equipment, which was seen as 'ugly' and 'unnatural' by a number of respondents, were seen as a necessity to the landuse of the area. This is similar to the division in perceptions evident between participants from urban and rural areas. [I dislike] *The farmer's crap is lying around the field and it appears to have no value or use whatsoever. It is rubbish.* (T3). One child who was unaware of the effects of bracken on the ecosystem suggested *When I see the bracken and trees it makes it quite colourful.... It makes you feel relaxed* (S4).

One aspect of livelihood knowledge is knowledge of working practices in the area. This can change how a feature or landscape is valued, and whether or not it is seen positively or negatively. Forestry plantations were valued differently by participants who knew of their manmade origins and those who thought they were natural. The field at Kiltyrie was bordered by two stands of woodland. To the south there was an area of semi-natural woodland, containing native species, and to the west there was a

Knowledge of Livelihood: what do you dislike about the landscape? Chi-square=13.996, p=.016
Knowledge of Livelihood: why is this special? Chi-square = 12.286, p=.031
Knowledge of Livelihood: what would you like to find out about the landscape? Chi-square =13.415, p=.037
Knowledge of place: what do you like about the landscape? Chi-square=12.356, p=.030
Knowledge of place: why do you like this? Chi-square=11.444, p=.022
Knowledge of place: what do you dislike about the landscape?? Chi-square=16.361, p=.003
Knowledge of place: why do you dislike this? Chi-square =11.107, p=.025
Knowledge of place: why is this special? Chi-square=9.985, p=.041
Knowledge of place: what information do you most want about these landscape features? Chi-square = 18.626, p=.002
Academic knowledge: why do you like this? Chi-square =21.653, p=.000
Academic knowledge: what do you dislike about the landscape? Chi-square = 11.058, p=.050
Academic knowledge: why do you dislike this? Chi-square =12.093· p=.017
Academic knowledge what activities would you like to do in the landscape? Chi-square =22.180, p=.001
Academic knowledge: what information do you most want about these landscape features? Chi-square = 18.898 , p=.002

6-2 Significant knowledge based crosstabulations and chi-square values

large densely planted forestry plantation. Only one of the children made a distinction between these two types of trees, whereas adult responses revealed a dichotomy in values, where the native species were good and the forestry plantation was bad and an *'unnatural' 'manmade'* monoculture. Conifer plantations were also selected for criticism by some adults in the image workbook section of the exercise, where they were described as 'eyesores', which detract from the landscape's natural beauty. It appears that these dislikes are based on what is known of the origins of these plantations, for many of the children who liked the conifer plantations, they were seen as 'natural' rather than manmade features (hence they were no different to the semi-natural woodland in the area). In contrast, the individuals (including some children) who knew about the manmade origins of this feature, as well as the damage caused to the landscape when the trees were removed, disliked them as being unnatural.

Knowledge of livelihood also appeared to affect what things people wished to find out more about. People who knew about working (such as farming) and conservation practices were keener to find out more about the flora and fauna of the area (56% vs. 24%) than those who did not. This may be because the ecosystem is more noticeable to them as they know more about it and as such they are more aware of any gaps in their knowledge, or are just more interested.

Another type of knowledge evident was knowledge of the place itself. This was identified by examining which individuals were able to identify scenes from the image workbook as being from the study area. These participants were judged to be more familiar with the area than those who were unable to identify it from pictures. People with 'place' knowledge had different landscape 'likes' to those who did not, insofar as they were more likely to identify specific, sometimes named features rather than the entire area as being a like. This may be because, as you have more knowledge of a place, you know more individual features of the landscape, rather than just seeing it as a whole 'place'. It is instead a lived landscape, with specific nodes that the individual is more familiar with, spends more time in, and has stronger views (wither positive or negative) about

(Ingold pers comm.). This same knowledge also appears to affect why people like certain features. People who did not know the area were more likely to use emotional reasons for their likes (43% compared to 28%), whereas those who did know that area more often used reasons linked to their use relationship with the landscape (13% vs. 6%) and interest in the area (18% vs. 10%). This may also be linked to the fact that a number of the individuals who had exhibited knowledge of place were children, who tended to speak more often about their values for landscape using either aesthetic or use relationship based reasons than adults.

Knowledge of place also appears to affect what people dislike of an area. Those who know the area were less likely to mention landuse (61% vs. 72%) (linked to knowledge of livelihood as discussed above) and weather (10% vs. 3%) and were more likely to mention flora and fauna (22% vs. 8%). People who live in the area may be more 'tolerant' of the weather of the area and landuse features there, it may be that these features are less important to someone with a deeper understanding of that particular landscape. Also, a number of individuals who commented on disliking the weather of the area were first time visitors to the landscape, and had only experienced the inclement weather (in particular, participants in Loch Tay in April 2005 had to contend with blizzards and hailstones). Therefore, for them the landscape was only 'known' as one of bad weather, whereas participants with more knowledge of place had experienced it through changing climatic conditions, good and bad, and the weather to them was only incidental to the landscape they 'knew'. Another issue with the number of visitors to the area citing weather as a dislike is that most of the visitors were spending the time they had in the area outside, meaning that they were more exposed to weather conditions than many of the local participants who spent most of their time indoors.

The final type of 'knowledge' that was examined through the results from the image workbooks, and responses to the questionnaires was 'academic' knowledge. This was determined through an examination of what subjects participants had studied at school and university, and whether individuals had demonstrated 'specialist knowledge' in describing landscape features (e.g. using technical terminology for geological features etc.). People who demonstrated this kind of knowledge were more likely to cite 'interest' as a reason for liking certain landscape features (26% vs. 11%), suggesting perhaps that the more you know of a landscape, the more you realise there is left to discover and the more you want to know. Academic knowledge also appeared to affect what kinds of activities people wished to carry out in the landscape, insofar as 'investigation' including archaeological fieldwork, wildlife watching and conservation work. For example, *Would be interested in historic aspects such as ownership. Have studied prehistoric aspects at uni* (T39). This may be because people have gained knowledge through these particular activities, and are already part of their landscape experience.

The role of knowledge as an influence on landscape perceptions was investigated further when the perceptions of children in Lochtayside, who had participated in three years of archaeological outreach work, were compared to those of children of a similar age at Luss School in Lochlomondside. The children were from similar small rural schools, and the areas of landscape they were taken to were broadly similar. Comparison of these children's responses to the landscape workbook questions produced some interesting results.

Children from Loch Tay consistently referred to the area's history in their responses, whereas the children from Loch Lomond were more likely to cite flora and fauna. This division may be ascribed to participation in activities at school. The children at Luss had been involved in an 'ecoschool' project and were working towards their John Muir award[8] at the time of my visit and as such had been investigating the wildlife in the area, whereas children in Loch Tay were less aware of this feature. These trends were also evident in the questions about what participants felt most strongly about (e.g. liked the most, disliked the most, found the most special, and most wanted to find out more about). Over 40% of responses from Luss children referred to the flora and fauna as being what they liked the most about the landscape, compared to only 10% of Loch Tay responses. Children from Luss were also more likely to mention flora and fauna as a strong dislike (48% vs. 11%) which may be because the field at Loch Lomond was full of sprouting bracken. The children there were well aware of the dangers of ticks and Lymes disease associated with this plant with several responses being similar *I don't like the bracken because it has ticks in it and they hurt!* (S40). As well as likes and dislikes, there were differences between what features the children from different areas wished to find out more about. Again, children from Luss were keen to find out more about flora and fauna (60% of Luss pupils 10% of Loch Tay pupils), whereas children from Loch Tay looked at a wider variety of features, including (14% vs. 0%) but not exclusively history.

The examples above serve to demonstrate the importance

---

[8] An award for working on environmental and conservation projects.

of 'formalised' knowledge as a facet of the individuals' identity which helps to form perceptions of landscape. For the children of Lochtayside learning about history has brought historical features to the fore in their personal landscape, and they are now part of the suite of features that individuals could express preferences for. For the children of Lochlomondside, these features were largely invisible. Contrarily the children from Luss had focussed on learning about flora, fauna and the 'natural' landscape. Their landscape preferences were therefore heavily by these.

Knowledge of History and Landscape Values

As one of the original research questions, knowledge of history will be dealt with explicitly here.

It has already been demonstrated that children who had learned about the history of the area referenced it more often in all aspects of their values for landscape. This included what they would like to find out more about, where aspects of the landscape's history were cited by over half of the Lochtayside children. Quite simply it appeared that for them the historic environment was part of their landscape experience in a way that it was not for children who did not have this knowledge. The same is true for adults who participated in archaeological research in both Lochtayside and Lochlomondside. These individuals also more often talked of the ruins in the landscape, in terms of them being a 'good' thing in the landscape and something that they wished to find out more about. It appears that the more participants knew of landscape history, the more they valued the historic environment, as exemplified by the following quotations:

[I would like to find out more about] *the ruin –I would love to know the history of the ruin and what life was like there* (S22)

[I would like to find out more about] *The ruins- how many people lived there in the olden days* (S21)

The ruins are special because it is proof that someone used to live there (S32)

Landscape history cannot be treated as a single entity. The BLHLP dealt mainly with the historic period in the area (c.1200 AD to present day), and as such, participants' knowledge of the landscape history was mainly of this period. Aspects of the prehistory of the area, or wider histories of the Highlands such as 'the age of clans' were less commonly commented on, as they were peripheral to people's landscape experience, despite the field in Kiltyrie having a number of prominent features which have been catalogued as potential barrows by RCAHMS.

This sub-section only covers a very strict 'academic knowledge' of history. Every individual has their personal history, comprised of their own experiences and memories: a number of participants talked of past experiences in the landscape, or used reasoning based on personal memories as to why they valued certain aspects of the landscape. These personal histories are outwith 'academic' knowledge, are harder to quantify, and are covered within other aspects of identity described above. For example:

[Something which is special to me is] *Houses – remains I like to experience how other people live, seeing remains makes me wonder how people lived and thought* (T15)

[I dislike] *knowing the history of the area in that many people in places like this were forced off their land in order to make room for raising sheep. I think this was very sad.* (T24)

The ruins are special because someone used to live there (S32)

For some, the landscape was made more special by the fact that it was a lived place (e.g. [something which I find special is that] *I can see that people dwelt on the hillside by the remains of longhouses. I can see that people cultivated this area by field boundaries and the remains of a grain drying kiln* (T76). There were, however, a number of participants who knew of the depth of history in the landscape who still spoke of it in terms of being a 'wildscape', and talked of recent human interventions as having damaged the landscape. For example, the individual quoted above as finding old remains 'special' (T76) stated that *I don't care for the intrusion of Electricity Pylons – they are ugly and spoil the rural aspect.* This participant is making a value judgement about which of the anthropogenic aspects of the landscape are positive and which are negative. In their case, modern landuse is seen as a 'bad' thing, a view held by many participants. This can be ascribed to particular cultural influences, borne out of the Romantic Movement, as discussed in the following section.

Examination of preferences within demographic subgroups has suggested certain influences on landscape preferences. There are, however, some preferences for landscape which are prevalent across groupings, including a liking for mountains, wildlife, and a general appreciation of the aesthetics of the area. These similarities in preference have been noted in a number of studies (e.g. Kaltenborn & Berg 2002, Stedman 2002) and may instead be ascribed to cultural influences, which will be discussed in the following section.

6.2.2. Culture

From the responses given by individuals in the landscape workbook it was evident that some particular preferences and dislikes for landscape were common across all groups. In this section it will be suggested that these similarities can be ascribed to the cultural context in which people are living. Particular cultural influences can be seen that have stemmed from the Picturesque and Romantic Movement (as discussed in the literature review section 2.2.2) which can be seen to be the precursor to anti-modernity and ideas of the rural idyll.

A number of adult respondents mentioned similar themes, in terms of what qualities of the landscape they valued, and why they valued these. Many of these focussed on ideas of 'wilderness' and the free open spaces of the wild landscape. The following two quotations emphasise the size of the landscape, and the feeling of insignificance that the respondents felt in that landscape.

The size – the smallness of me in nature (T33)

Space. Makes me feel smaller than nature, lost in grandeur/ scale. (T61)

These opinions can be said to be rooted in the ideas of the sublime and the vastness of nature. Central to the sublime is the idea that people experience a horror in dramatic landscapes (such as mountains, deserts, or snowscapes), and that this touches upon something elemental within the person's soul (Oerlemans 2002). This experience is pleasurable as it serves as a reminder to humans of the insignificance of their place in nature, and inspires awe within them. In their responses to the landscape workbook individuals mentioned the feeling of 'wildness' of the landscape, and a mixture between pleasure and fear that they felt in the surroundings, which can be seen to be linked to ideas of sublime horror. Both of the responses below (T37 & T40) use wording which shows how elements of the landscape that raise apprehension can add to the landscape's appeal. *Remoteness by the 'menacing' mountains, clouds, sky, sounds. Intriguing and a bit scary* (T37), *Today the mist is haunting* (T40).

Wilderness is also a central tenet of the sublime and the following quotations are three of several which valued the 'wilderness' of the area. [I like the] *Open wild countryside* (T66), [something which is special to me is] *Such a feeling of wildness and a sense of freedom* (T9), [I like the landscape because] *It feels magical, like a wilderness* (S16).

Through the nineteenth and twentieth centuries, Romanticism broadened into a wider trend of antimodernity. Individuals such as Ruskin and latterly Tolkein continued this Romantic ideal, but stressed more the importance of the wild and the natural in response to urbanisation and industrialisation (as introduced in section 2.2.3 of the literature review). This can be seen to be linked to current ideas of the rural idyll where the rural is valued, for beauty, peace, and 'authenticity' which are not found in urban areas.

Many study participants spoke of the 'naturalness' and isolation of the landscape, and how much they valued this of the area. This naturalness is spoken of as something existing in opposition to a built-up landscape:

[The landscape is special because] *It feels isolated from everything else – roads, people, traffic. It makes you forget to worry or be in a rush* (T38)

I like the isolation – can't see a house for miles [and

73

therefore I like it] *because I don't particularly like busy built up areas. I like the open free feeling. The feeling of being the only person in the world* (T33)

[I like the] *natural surroundings – landscape seems unpolluted etc. also scenery is idyllic, impressive.* (T39)

The following quotations talk about the timelessness of the landscape, and the idea that is has not been spoiled by humans; the individual appears to equate all human action to 'spoiling' of the natural landscape. [what is special is the] *Unspoiled landscape- I like feeling I may be looking at a similar scene to people hundreds – even thousands of years ago.* (T39). [Something which is special] *Glacial erratics and other rocky outcrop features – the part of nature that man cannot tame or remove because they are so huge (and ancient)* (T43). The next quotation shows something of the confusion of the anti-modern idea. [something which is special to me is] *The field* [because it] *is natural* (T50). This quotation demonstrates how certain manmade features can accrue 'natural' status if they are seen to have the right anti-modern criteria. Here the idea of natural can be seen to be applicable to anything which is not urban, and fits into an idea of rurality. This is an idea shared by other responses such as [I like] *The wildlife, sheep dotting the hills and mountains* (T46) and *I didn't dislike anything because its natural* (S33).

The land is also valued by many for its 'peace', with many participants disliking anything which disturbed this peace. *Countryside – its peace and quiet and its great just to get away now and again* (T54). Again this peace is often valued in opposition to people's normal existence within towns and cities, and when this peace is disturbed it is spoken of as being a mnemonic of modernity. For example, *The quiet peace. Almost felt like intruder on the land as a human. The only sounds were of nature. Very unlike the city* (T45) *I don't like the faint background noise of passing by cars. It makes it feel like there's civilisation nearby and you're not quite in the wild* (T35), [I don't like that you] *can hear cars on nearby road – again is reminder of urban or modern world* (T39), *The electric pylons spoil the land, cut lines through and seem alien* (T45)

Alongside this dislike of anything that disturbs the peace of the countryside, features that are indicative of modern human activity were commonly disliked by participants, with the reasoning that they make the landscape 'less wild' or 'less natural'. For example: *I don't really like the appearance of human activity. The phone lines, the car tracks. The stone walls are ok because they fit in. I don't think they are an eyesore.* (T33). Again, this involves a value judgement as to which elements of modernity are valued in the landscape, the field walls in Lochtayside are from the improvement period, a time when the landscape of the area was radically transformed. Without this context (or perhaps in spite of this), the participant saw them as part of the rural idyll.

The landscape was also valued because of the 'drama' and 'authentic' setting of the 'picturesque' landscape,

and features are disliked because they detracted from this ideal.

[I like]*The ridges of the mountains. They cut dramatically into the sky and are striking.*(T49),

[Something which is special to me is that] *The land seems more rustic, more realistic* (T52),

Surrounding mountains [are special]. *Very Picturesque landscape* (T12),

[I like the land as it has a] *Restorative effect of body and mind* (T59) (it was thought that the spiritual experience of contact with nature could purify the mind within the ideas of the sublime. (Oerlemans 2002),

I don't like the pylons because they make the view not look right because they just look like piles of metal (S9);

[I dislike] *The pylons as they ruin the overall picturesque landscape and are tall and very prominent* (T3).

A line of overhead power cables running across the landscape. Disliked because I find them aesthetically unpleasant and detracting from, what one might call the 'country ideal' as a haven from modern disturbance. (T7).

These similarities in perception cannot be explained by simple similarities in identity. These views were prevalent across adult groups and were present within some children's responses too, suggesting that they are linked to wider cultural phenomena rather than the individual strands of identity discussed earlier.

Another cultural trend which can be seen to be visible in the responses given to the landscape workbook was Scottish Nationalism. By this I do not mean Nationalism in the narrow political sense, but pride in the Scottish Nation/ Scottish identity as discussed in 2.6.1 of the literature review. Several of the responses cited the Highlands as a symbol of what is good about Scotland, which can be seen to be linked to nineteenth century ideas of rebuilding a Scottish Nation after the Act of Union and the quashing of Jacobite rebellions in the eighteenth century (Hobsbaum & Ranger 1983). In this nationalist movement, and the associated tartanry and Romantic traditions, the Highlands which had previously been seen as wild and ungovernable provinces, were valued as part of the Nation where traditions lived on. Certain responses cited national pride and heritage as a reason for liking the landscapes or for finding them special, such as those below:

Love to think that this area is part of Scotland and helps to define its culture. It's a treasure that everyone can enjoy. (T45) To this individual the landscape of here defines their National Pride, and a sense of belonging.

[something which is special is] *The ruins of old buildings. Its part of Scottish heritage ergo it should be special to all Scots* (T49).

Cultural influences were evident in people's responses to what qualities they liked about the landscape of Lochtayside and Lochlomondside. Within the 'likes' that people expressed for landscape, over a quarter of responses referred to the aesthetic qualities of the landscape, and this is a particular aesthetic developed with Romantic ideas of the Scottish Nation in mind.

Over half of all responses about what was disliked in the landscape involved 'modern features' (e.g. [I dislike] *The traffic sounds. Would prefer none at all* (T23), [I dislike] *Post and wire fences. Not so traditional as the stone walls making it look more modern* (T55). These responses can be seen as existing within the rhetoric of 'anti-modernity', which is a continuum of the Romantic mode of thought, where the new is disliked, in favour of an authentic, traditional way of life. Nowhere is this demonstrated as clearly as through people's responses to the pylon line which ran across the study field in Lochtayside.

6.2.3. The electricity pylons are an obvious dislike (T14)
A case study of pylons and Anti-modernity

The preceding section provided a discussion about how the cultural trends of Romanticism and anti-modernity were evident in many respondents' attitudes to the landscapes of the study areas. Many of the dislikes that people mentioned were of 'modern' features, such as roads and farming machinery, but the most commonly vilified feature was the pylon line which ran through the study field in Lochtayside. The following two quotations illustrate responses about pylons.

Dislike the large pylons immediately in front of me – ruin the scenery – reminder of urban world etc. (T39)

[I dislike] *Power lines. They take away from the peaceful, natural look. Old man made structures are not offensive* (T46).

Pylons were overwhelmingly disliked by participants. Only one individual professed a liking of them: this was a child who said that he liked them because mapmakers could use pylons to tell them where they were in the landscape. In total, over 20% of all dislike responses (which equated to over half of all participants in Lochtayside - there were no large pylons in the Loch Lomond study area) professed a dislike for pylons, although several people commented on their 'necessity' in the landscape. Most of the children who disliked the pylons gave an aesthetic reason for this; statements such as 'they are ugly' or 'not nice to look at' were common. The reasons that adults gave for their dislike of pylons contrasted with this. Although a number of the adults questioned wrote about the pylons being ugly, a greater percentage professed to dislike them because they were 'unnatural'. A number of responses from adults talked about pylons and other man-made features as 'destroying the landscape' (for example tyre tracks from vehicles 'scarring' the fields). A significant number of adults also spoke of the wildness or 'naturalness' of the landscape being a positive feature, and it appears that the pylons

impinge on this naturalness, and therefore are disliked. One of the key reasons for dislikes of modern features is that they can be seen as invoking memories of 'real life' which has been escaped by coming to the 'timeless' highlands, something which is evidenced by the larger percentage of people commenting on the 'unnaturalness' of the landscape coming from urban areas (as discussed in section 6.1.2 above).

Both types of dislike of pylons can be seen to be linked into the aesthetics and sensibilities developed through the Romantic Movement. The Romantics valorised the 'old', the 'sublime', the 'wild' and the 'authentic' in terms of aesthetics and experiences. The pylons in the landscape detract from this 'wilderness' aesthetic, and are therefore disliked for impinging on the beautiful view. The pylons also detract from the 'Romantic' experience of landscape, especially the idea of escape from 'modern' landscape, and are thus disliked because of this. The same reasoning also helps to explain the comments about other modern features, such as forestry plantations and roads.

Pylons are a hot topic in landscape planning in the Scottish Highlands, as there, at the time of writing, controversy about the erection of a 'super pylon' line from Beauly in Invernessshire, to Denny in Falkirk region. It could therefore be suggested that the responses elicited in my research were artificially high because of this debate. However, all of the visiting adults participated in my research in the early summer of 2005, which was before this issue arose (the planning application was submitted in July 2005 (Beaulydenny.co.uk 2008)).

6.2.4. Temporal influences on landscape perceptions

In the two previous sections the idea of the material landscape being the main factor which affects perceptions of landscape has been deconstructed, and instead an idea of landscape values being context specific and linked to an individual's identity and cultural background has been outlined. Throughout the discussion, a third influence has been implicit, that landscapes, identity and culture happen within time. The temporal context of an encounter with, or experience of, landscape can greatly affect an individual's landscape perceptions. This following section will examine how the different types of time (as outlined in literature review section2.5) affect landscape experiences and values.

Linear Time and Landscape Perceptions

As discussed in section 2.5.1 of the literature review linear time is the time in which history happens, and in which cultural movements are situated. Events in a single person's life also occur within liner time and the particular life stages that an individual goes through affect their landscape values. As has already been discussed above, there appear to be differences in landscape perceptions which are linked to age, and the amount and type of knowledge that a person has of a landscape. People's moods on the day, and what they have been thinking

Figure 6-3 features commonly disliked (as photographed by study participants). These are mainly man-made elements of the landscape.

about can affect their responses. It is likely that the people who were on the archaeology Thistle Camps' responses to the landscape would have more information about the archaeology of the area than they would have if asked at any other time. For example, one individual stated *Having participated in the Ben Lawers Project I have learned to see the landscape with better understanding, and now I notice features that at one time I would not have noticed. This makes me wonder about the details of the lives of people who lived here in the past* (T3). 'Current events are also temporally situated, and people's reactions to news items and other happenings will affect their landscape perceptions. These create a 'now' bias which makes it hard to determine which responses people give to surveys are rooted in embedded beliefs and which are more transient in nature, and liable to change. For example, in the past forestry plantations have been seen as 'a good thing' as they provided employment in areas where there were very few job opportunities. Nowadays, in a political and social climate where nature conservation and biodiversity are valorised, forestry plantations are disliked by many as being unnatural monocultures which do little for the environment, e.g. [I dislike] *The coniferous plantation. Dark, gloomy and probably only there for the money. Its too straight edged and feels like it dropped inform above*

(T19). Equally, current aspects of an individual's personal situation can influence their landscape perceptions, such as the views of this one thistle camp participant who liked *The sounds. Birds I don't hear at home. Little traffic noise. No conversation – living in camp it is nice sometimes just to sit on your own and think.* (T23), where the sounds were liked mainly because of the particular situation that the participant was in at that time.

Cyclical time and Landscape perceptions.

Again, as outlined in the literature review (section 2.5.2) there are various cycles of time. There are a number of lengths of temporal cycles, and the effects of some of these are evident in the responses given in the landscape workbook exercise. One particular type of cyclical time is seasonality. In Highland areas the effect of the seasons is particularly strong (Palang et al 2005), with great changes in the physical properties of the landscape, including vegetation and snow cover. The majority of fieldwork with participants was carried out between April and September, but some work with Loch Tay residents was carried out in October and December. Weather is linked to seasonality, although in the Highlands there is no guarantee of fair weather at any time of the year. Some individuals spoke of aspects of the weather both as likes and dislikes. In the quotations below the weather was seen as a negative aspect of individuals' landscape experiences.

No shelter from weather – it is an immediate physical dislike (T39)

Rain has almost nothing to recommend itself on a walk when trying to write (T46)

Grey Clouds – a sunny day with white fluffy clouds would be preferable! (T58)

Certain elements of the weather were also liked by some participants, especially sunshine and warm weather, and related effects of the light on the hillsides.

[I like] *The clouds! Because they are so beautiful and you have miles of visibility and on one side they are fluffy and the other side they are dark and stormy, both gorgeous* (T24)

[I like the fact that] *Today the weather is warm and cloud shadows were travelling across the hillside. I could have sat down a while and enjoyed that.* (T29)

Weather also altered the conditions of the field that participants visited. Water logging of the field was disliked by many e.g. [I dislike] *Waterlogged land, bogs and ditches, make the ground messy, Muddy* (T15), [I dislike the fact that] *Water gathers in certain areas which makes the ground very muddy and wet.* (T18). This water logging was liked by others, such as these children who saw the fun in puddles and mud [I like] *Deep puddles because I can wade through* (S15), *I like the mud because its fun to play in* (S26), and an adult participant who liked the wildlife attracted to the waterlogged areas [I like] *The standing water where I could see the birds preening and bathing* (T29). This example demonstrates how certain features only occur at certain times of year. These features (in this case the water logging of the field) do not act as mediators of meaning for the landscape, instead people interpret the seasonal elements of the landscape through their own particular subjectivities.

Lifetimes are cycles, there is the human lifecycle, and how age affects landscape perceptions has been discussed above. Vegetation has lifecycles and rhythms. Those of grasses, deciduous trees, heather and bracken etc are clearly visible within the seasonal round. For example the bracken in the field at Loch Tay was not present when the first adult volunteers were at the site (in early April 2005). The Scottish midge is a great menace in both study areas in the summer, and when the exercise was carried out on still, damp days many individuals commented on them as a dislike e.g. [I dislike] *Biting insects. I am prone to being bitten and my system reacts strongly to bites. They disturb my sleep when they itch* (T23). At other times the midges were not present in the area, and as such did not feature as a landscape like or dislike. Tourist seasons also create temporal cycles within the Highlands, as many areas are only visited at certain times of the year. Certain participants

realised this, with one suggesting *There is very little that I don't like* [about the landscape]*, except that I regret the apparent necessity of having things like the Ben Lawers visitor centre and in summer the towns and villages are congested with tourist traffic – but then I am part of that.* (T6). Interestingly no residents complained about tourist visitors to the area, perhaps because they are so integral to the area's economy, or because, like weather, they are just an integral 'fact' of the seasons of the Highlands.

All of these temporal contexts combine to create a 'now' bias in terms of landscape perceptions. Perceptions of landscape are grounded in a present which is an amalgam of calendar time and the place of that present on the multitude of different cycles. (so what place the individual is at in their lifecycle, the time of day where the present is, when the season is etc.).

This section of the book has sought to answer the second research question: What are the main influences on people's landscape preferences and values? The different contexts that can be seen to be of influence on how people think about the landscape have been discussed with reference to people's preferences for landscape that they stated in the landscape workbook exercise. The wide spectrum of values expressed by people who have undertaken the same exercise in two similar areas of landscape serves to demonstrate how little bearing on meaning and value the landscape itself holds. This question can therefore be answered by suggesting that the main influences on people's landscape preferences and values exist within the person, and the wider social world with which they engage, in terms of time, identity and culture.

6.3. Methodological Issues

At this point in the work, when all the primary data has been presented and discussed, it is appropriate to return to the methods used to collect this information, and to assess how successful they have been, identify what elements of the method worked well, and suggest what would be changed in future studies. This is important when seeking to address the first research question: What methods can be utilised to understand qualitative preferences for landscapes which work with a large cross section of the population, and can be used in a repeatable and reliable manner? Certain methodological issues have already been discussed, such as the use of photographs as proxies for landscape in the image workbook exercise in chapter 4 and chapter 5. Further on in the next chapter (section 7.2.1) the use of visual proxies as a landuse policy tool will be discussed. The two other methods used, the landscape workbook and questionnaire will be reviewed here.

The problems of recruiting participants for the study have already been discussed in the methods chapter (chapter 4). These led to the sample worked with being quite small and not being what could be termed statistically 'representative'. If this study was to be repeated a greater effort would be made to contact more casual visitors to the area, who were an audience missed completely by this research. It may be possible to offer some form of incentive such as the possibility of winning some form of (monetary) prize by entering all participants into a draw. It would also have been desirable to work with children who were not from the area so that their responses could be compared with those of the local children. However, all projects have limits, and PhD research is limited by time, person power and financial resources. As such, although the profile of participants cannot be seen to be representative, information gathered from participants is interesting and useful in furthering knowledge on the topic under investigation. If the research question had been something like 'what do people value of the landscapes of Lochtayside' then it would have been necessary to have a study population that was larger and more representative of the population as a whole. The research questions addressed by this study are exploratory, aiming to discover methods for assessing perceptions of landscape and understanding what influences these perceptions, and as such the statistical representativeness of any sample is not so crucial, as it is more about understanding processes than measuring perceptions. The population of this study can be seen therefore as an illustrative sample.

6.3.1. Landscape Workbook

This was the section of the study where people were taken out into an area of landscape in the study areas and were invited to respond to various questions (for a full description refer to section 4.7.1 of methods). Of the three sections of the methodology this was the one which was the most successful, in terms of the information generated and the ease of analysing and interpreting the information. One of the major challenges when this exercise was conceived was producing worksheets that could be used by participants of all ages, and the fact that the exercise was completed successfully by individuals aged between 8 and 82 attests to its success. This exercise was designed in order to discover what people liked and disliked about the landscape, what they found to be 'special' in the surroundings, what they wished to find out more about, and what activities they would do there. Information was generated on all of these, and when it was compared to information from the questionnaire it was possible to examine what influenced people's preferences and values for landscape. Participants referred to numerous subjects and provided various reasons to explain their responses to this exercise. Several attempts were made to undertake a content analysis of this information so that it could be imputed into SPSS and examined quantitatively. This was possible as the dataset was relatively small (130 participants in total) and it was possible to check and recheck responses for consistency in the codes used. If the dataset had been any larger then it would have been necessary to use a qualitative analysis software package such as Nvivo to help with this process.

The second section of this exercise involved individuals being given a camera and being asked to photograph the features that represented the responses they felt most strongly about for each section (again please refer to methodology section 4.7.1). The fact that this method appeared to lead to under-representation of non-visual elements of the landscape has already been discussed in both the results and methodology chapters, but the information from the photographs proved invaluable in clarifying what elements of the landscape people (particularly children) were referring to in their responses, as this was often unclear in their written responses. The value of the camera exercise as an incentive/reward for children completing the exercise has also been discussed. It is therefore suggested that if the exercise is carried out with adults then the photographic element is unnecessary (despite the extra richness provided by it) but is a vital component when working with children.

One of the issues with the landscape workbook was that despite an effort being made to ensure that participants had a similar experience of the landscape of the study site, there were differences caused by the times in which people carried out the exercise. All participants experienced a different landscape 'now', when conditions of weather, vegetation and light changed the physical form of the land. In order to understand differences in the landscape as experienced by study participants a note was made of the weather conditions and vegetation cover when participants were undertaking the field exercise. This could be compared to people's responses when they referred to weather conditions or items in the field, especially when it was not abundantly clear from their responses what aspect they were referring to (e.g. some responses were worded in ways similar to *'I like the weather, because it is exhilarating'*, but there was no mention of what type of weather it was). Bias was also introduced through the different social climates within 'nows' in which people experienced landscape. Depending on what current affairs had been at the forefront of people's minds when they carried out the exercises people may have thought about the landscape differently. If a similar study was undertaken again it would be advisable to undertake all of the sampling within as small a window of time as possible in order to overcome variation caused by this 'now' bias. When the first fieldwork was undertaken for this PhD research it was uncertain as to how well the field method would work, and as such the first season of data collected was analysed before the next phase of fieldwork was undertaken. A second study could be undertaken with the knowledge that this is a technique that 'works' and as such the data collection would not need to be staged. In order to more fully address any 'now bias' in results (rather than ensuring that all participants were subjected to as similar conditions and therefore similar biases as possible) it may be desirable to undertake a longitudinal study, where participants undertake the exercise a number of times and their responses are crosschecked for consistency. This may not be practical, however when working with participants in the field (particularly when some are visiting the area), and when resources are limited.

6.3.2. Questionnaire Exercise

As an inductive approach was taken to investigating the research questions, it was not immediately obvious which elements of an individual's identity it would be necessary to investigate in order to understand people's landscape values. Certain sections of the questionnaire (such as those about places of residence and places visited regularly) were very useful, whereas others (such as why people were attending Thistle Camps) were less useful. The comprehensive approach taken to data collection at this stage cannot be regretted, but if the research were repeated it might be possible to carry out a more focussed questionnaire which investigated more fully aspects which had previously been found to be significant, and disregarded others which had found not to be. The questionnaire used for the children used a number of more open ended questions, as with the landscape workbook codes could be developed for the different types of responses given, and with only around 50 child participants this dataset could easily be handled manually. Had the number of participants been any larger, again, a computerised data analysis package could be used to help with this.

6.4. Summary and Conclusions

After presenting the information gathered in the study in chapter five, this chapter has examined in more detail what are the main influences on people's landscape perceptions. This was undertaken in order to fully investigate the second research question of this study: what are the main influences on people's landscape perceptions and values? In this work it has been argued that the main influences on perceptions of landscape exist within the context that the landscape is experienced rather than within the land itself. In this chapter the link between context and landscape perception has been discussed further with reference to answers given in the landscape workbook exercise (where people expressed preferences for certain landscape features) and corresponding information from the questionnaire and image workbooks. It has been demonstrated that aspects of people's identity, cultural context and temporal situation all have bearings on a person's landscape perception. Two people can experience the same landscape, at the same time, but have very different perceptions of this landscape because of their individual subjectivities that exist in these contexts. This serves to demonstrate that people's perceptions of landscape are primarily rooted within the person, rather than any inherent materiality of the land.

Issues with the methods used in this study have also been discussed, and this will be expanded upon in the following chapter where the integration of people's landscape values into current polices for landscape protection and planning will be examined.

7

Landscape Values, Landscape Policy and the
Academic Study of Past Landscapes

7.1. Introduction

The previous chapter discussed the different factors which affect individuals' perceptions of landscapes and the values they hold for them. The context specificity of landscape perceptions was demonstrated. Perceptions of landscape are not governed by the material fact of the land, but instead by various factors pertaining to how the individual encounters the landscape. This has implications for landscape management and planning, which will be discussed within this chapter.

In the literature review chapter current policies and designations for protecting landscapes in Scotland were introduced. This will be discussed further within this chapter, with particular reference to public participation within the landscape planning and designation process. It is suggested that current measures for assessing values for landscape do not take context into account, instead operating on the premise that the landscape has essential physical qualities that give it intrinsic values.

In addition to this, current policies and regulations for safeguarding landscapes and heritage rely on criteria made on typological grounds, and as such are based on expert notions of what is important, of value, or significant (for example, designations such as SSSI or SM rely on the site having certain material properties such as the presence of a rare species or a certain type of structure). This section will make recommendations for alternative ways of assessing landscape value and of legislating for landscapes and heritage. These alternative models and methods proposed for working with value aim self-consciously to draw on my own research rather than established pragmatic understandings of landscape management. As well as having implications for landscape policy decisions, the idea that landscapes have no intrinsic value, or essential meaning also affects the methods that archaeologists can utilise to understand past landscapes and people's attachments to them. Currently the phenomenological approach to understanding landscape is very popular (Johnson 2007, Tilley 1994, 2002) and issues with reliance on this approach will be discussed within this chapter.

7.2. Current landscape designations and Policy Needs

Section 2.7 of the literature review has outlined the various types of designation that are currently in place for protecting Scotland's landscapes. It also outlined certain elements of the planning process, including the development plan process, and the ways in which the public are consulted on these planning decisions. Currently there is a need for councils to produce consultative copies of these documents. The Scottish Executive Planning Advice Note 81 (PAN 81) (*Planning With People* 2007) offers some guidelines as to what form these consultations must take. A set of guiding principles (or 'standards') are introduced in this document for widening participation in the planning process. It is suggested that consultations in the planning process should reach a broader audience than just middle aged and elderly white middle classes, who (it says) are the main respondents to planning consultations. Marginalised groups in the planning process are identified as including young people, travellers/gypsies, women and ethnic minorities and links are given to case studies where these groups have been worked with. Examples of different forms of engagements are included, including the use of visualisations, photographic prompts, workshops and e-consultations. An internet site http://www.communityplanning.net is recommended within the advice to discover more about methods of engaging. This site, as endorsed by Hazel Blears (at the time of writing Secretary of State for Communities and Local Government in England) outlined a number of different case studies of different methods for consultation. These methods were described, with no critique of their suitability or workability. PAN 81 also suggests that participants in landscape planning should always be informed of the outcomes of any consultations, including whether points made by participants have been taken into account in the revision of plans.

Results of consultations, and an outline of the consultative process undertaken have to be submitted to the Scottish Parliament, but there is no statutory requirement to take account of individuals' view-points in the formation of these plans (Planning etc. (Scotland) Act, 2006). Scottish Ministers can also 'call in' any planning decisions that they are unhappy with, and can carry out audits on the performance of local planning authorities. National Scenic Areas can be designated by the Scottish Ministers after consultation with SNH and *'such other persons as are prescribed'* [by SNH] (Planning etc (Scotland) Act 2006:86) but there is no clarification as to who these people should be, and quite what they should be consulted on. It therefore appears that, in reality, many landscape management decisions can be made with minimal consultation with the people that these will affect.

I would suggest that there is a need for policies that allow for people's landscape values to be taken account in all landscapes, not just those which have been designated as 'special'. These views may not be based on the same material that has been currently seen as being important by the landscape experts who work on the designation of areas. This should be coupled with increased consultation on landscape planning decisions, which allows people to express opinions based on immaterial grounds that have traditionally been dismissed as 'Nimbyism'. There also has to be a wider debate about who the 'public' are for landscape consultation purposes, as currently many consultative exercises only work with a small subset of the population, both through the methods used to circulate information on consultations, and the communities of interest identified for consultation.

As this PhD was funded by a CASE studentship, from the outset it was decided that the work undertaken had to have a practical element, that it had to have some relevance to the policy community. I also thought very strongly that it was important to do this research more than just for research's sake. Therefore the final section of this chapter will examine how elements of this research suggest that a change is needed in the ways that landscapes are currently curated, legislated and celebrated as current mechanisms do not adequately reflect people relationships with the landscape.

The following section will discuss some potential alternatives to current processes of landscape planning, designation and consultation, using ideas that have been formed through my research. This will be discussed through an examination of the methods used in consultation, in terms of inclusion, context and practical methodological issues, and then in terms of types of legislation for safeguarding people's landscape values.

There is a need for genuine public consultation (not just a bit of an afterthought, or to fulfil expectations) at all stages of landscape planning. This should include the opinions of a wide cross section of the population, not just a subset of a narrowly defined 'community' (either based around one geographical location, interest, or age group). The opinions of 'the general public' should be in the centre of landscape planning, and the questions asked should be broad in scope, rather than just leading respondents in certain ways. This will be discussed further below.

As has been outlined in chapter 6 (section 6.2.1) age can

have a great bearing on what people want from landscapes, and how people value landscapes. As such a consultation which is carried out just with adults cannot be seen to be representative of the population as a whole and should be complimented with research with children of all ages as well. This should not just be restricted to areas which are particularly to do with children (such as the design of parks or playgrounds etc.) but all landscape management decisions, as being under the age of majority does not preclude people from having opinions about the places they live in, and a right to be consulted on these opinions (Kelly 2006, Woolley 2006). This study is one of several (e.g. Giddings & Yarwood 2006, Robertson 2000, 2003 Rye 2006,) that have demonstrated that children value landscapes in different ways to adults, and to not account for these in the planning process.. Equally, consultations that involve the selection of names from the electoral roll for study only involve that sub-group that is both of voting age and has allowed for its details to be circulated. Without suggesting that others should be coerced into participation in surveys, a greater effort should be made to publicise consultation exercises and encourage wider participation. This could be undertaken though the use of novel methodologies which are more likely to engage participants rather than straightforward questionnaire surveys. Novel modes of publicising consultation exercises could also be used, for example, social networking sites could be used to increase young people's participation in the planning process. Sites such as Facebook are already home to groups interested in planning issues[9] and it may be possible for official bodies to also use these sites to publicise and provide links to e-consultations.

This work has also discussed that more people care about the landscapes of the Scottish Highlands (and landscapes in general) than just those who are resident in these area. These include people who are visitors to the area, as tourists or workers and also people who care about places through 'option' and 'existence' values, insofar as they may want to visit the place in the future, or they never want to visit but value the landscape in its present state and wish to see it managed in certain ways only because of this. There is therefore need for debate as to who should have a say in landscape management decisions, within the different communities of interest. It is currently standard practice to consult members of the local community through various means, including public meetings, public enquiries and web based consultations. It is also standard practice to inform special interest groups as 'interested parties' in planning debates, and enquiries over legislation, and many of these groups (such as the RSPB or the Council for British Archaeology) have dedicated staff who advise on potential impacts to their particular interests, and campaign for changes to be made to plans to

---

[9] At the time of writing, there is much debate surrounding Donald Trump's plans to build a large golf resort on protected coastline in Aberdeenshire. On Facebook, for example, there are two opposing groups one supporting, and one against the development. Both groups, whilst inherently biased, provide members with information about the public enquiry as it progresses, and provide a forum for debate on the merits and issues with the plan.

protect these interests. There is, however, currently little consultation carried out with people who live outside the area and are not a member of any interest groups. This means that people who value an area may discover it has changed in ways in which they object to simply because they were unaware of any plans, and because they do not belong to interest organisations who would be informed of any plans. Internet based consultations do go some way to closing this gap, as they can be accessed globally (and are thus available to all interested parties with internet access), although thought has to be put into the way that information is presented, in a non-biased way, and questions asked that will not lead the participants in a certain way. However, many internet based consultations use illustrations and visualisations of landscape, and these can be problematic, as discussed below. I do not believe that there is any 'magic formula' for determining how much influence the various interest groups should have in planning decisions, instead a cross section of all opinions should be gathered and then conflicts in interest examined and then handled on a case by case basis.

The need for an understanding of the context of people's landscape values also has to be addressed within the landscape planning process. This is important in terms of what methodologies are utilised to determine landscape values, and the ways in which people's values are used to form policy. A seemingly disparate group of individuals may be affected by very similar circumstances, leading them to have similar landscape perceptions, whereas other individuals from similar backgrounds may be affected by different contexts.

As has been outlined above, there is evidence from this study to suggest that people's landscape perceptions are context, rather than material specific. It is therefore necessary to understand the context of people's relationships with landscape in order to understand people's landscape values. This raises several issues about methods for examining landscape perceptions in order to make informed planning and policy decisions and this subsection will examine some of these issues. In order to understand the context of people's landscape perceptions it is important to understand which elements of identity are influential in their formation. It is therefore necessary for studies investigating landscape perceptions to explore people's relationships with landscape as well as the perceptions and preferences themselves. This involves investigating people's biographies, including their landscape biographies, knowledge, and use relationships with the landscape.

In order to tackle the issue of landscape preferences being affected by the context of encounter with landscape, methods for determining landscape preferences have to use the landscape itself. Throughout this work the problems of using a contextless visual proxy for landscape rather than the landscape itself have been discussed. They include the fact that non-visual elements of the landscape (the experiences of senses other than sight) are not represented,

and without a person knowing what places are represented in visualisations they do not have the associations that provide the context for values. However, methods which rely on them are still widespread, and in certain cases the use of a visual proxy is unavoidable. When landscape planning decisions are being made, visualisations are often used to demonstrate how developments would sit in the landscape, or how changes in landuse policy would lead to changes in landscape character. Independent consultants (Macdonald, 2007) have analysed the images created by developers (companies erecting wind farms appear to be a main culprit) and have demonstrated that these images are often made in ways which show the development looking as small or unobtrusive as possible. These angles selected are often ones where it would be physically impossible to view the landscape from (often in mid air), rather than from ground level which is how most people would encounter the landscape. Although any visualisation is far from ideal, there should be legislation to ensure that when required visual proxies used should be as 'representative' as possible, and guidelines for this should be published by planning authorities. SNH (2007) has now produced guidelines for the visualisations used in wind farm developments, but this has not been extended to any other type of development. This document stated that the guidelines have only been provided for use by landscape architects and other 'landscape experts', and as such no guidelines exist (in Scotland) for the use of visualisations with the general public. I believe that guidelines for this are needed and that any visualisations should be created by a third party who is independent to anyone with interests in the results of the planning decision (these should be funded using the 'polluter pays' principle). Regardless of the 'representativeness' of images shown any consultation the fact remains that only the visual aspects of landscape will be represented. Another alternative would be to work with the idea that as landscapes exist within the mind, people recall places through mental images they have of them (even if individuals have never visited an area they will have some form of mental image of a landscape they value), so it may be possible to carry out consultations without any visual prompts, and allow individuals to use their own recollections of landscape to guide them in the decision making process.

7.2.1. Selection of Methods for landscape assessment

This work has demonstrated that it is necessary to use both qualitative and quantitative techniques for the assessment of landscape values within a policy context. Section (6.3) of the previous chapter has discussed the methods used in this research, the good and bad points of these, and how they could be revised for further research. This section will address methods for the assessment of landscape values more generally.

Quantitative techniques are often too focussed on specific aspects of people's relationships with landscape. It is not possible through the use of specific questions to investigate the different aspects which create people's landscape values. Economic methods such as Contingent Valuation and Willingness To Pay can put a financial figure on the strength of people's feelings for a landscape, and when this figure is compared with total household income the strength of participants responses can be compared with each other. This does not, however, provide any indication of what aspects of the landscape are forming these opinions, and what aspects of a person's identity (and the wide context that they occupy) are instrumental in the formation of these opinions.

Qualitative techniques alone are too time consuming to work with a large cross section of the population, if there are the usual constraints on time and finances that are imposed by work done in a time frame that is required for public enquiries/policy consultations. Therefore to research people's relationships with landscape, the roots of these attitudes and how they may react to potential future changes a mixture of qualitative and quantitative data is required

7.2.2. Legislating for landscape values

If it is the case that people's landscape perceptions are affected more by the context of their encounter with the landscape than the material fact of the land then current legislation cannot be seen to protect landscapes in a way that is necessarily meaningful for the public. As outlined in the literature review (section 2.7) current rules for conserving landscapes and heritage features are based on features and landscapes having inherent value, based on their material properties or more 'formal' cultural associations (such as battlefields, or a house being a famous person's birthplace). For example, ancient monuments are scheduled as being of national importance (to people) but on the basis of their physical elements.

In terms of determining what legislation should exist for curating landscapes and heritage it is helpful to look at the different kinds of values that exist for these (As outlined in literature review section 2.3) and examine whether current legislation fulfils these needs, and what alternatives exist.

Current legislation, and planning decisions do not account for the types of preferences, dislikes and attachments to landscape that have been uncovered by this research. Instead criteria are used within a system which relies largely on expert views of what material aspects of the landscape, heritage and natural history are important. This is not how most individuals think about and value landscape. At the moment all of these current designations are made on material grounds. Landscapes can be designated as SSSIs because of the presence of a rare species habitat, or a particular geological formations. Scheduled monument status is also conferred upon sites because of outstanding material. When 'intangible' (e.g. things which are not related to the material fabric of the landscape/heritage feature) properties are taken into account then these tend to be about formal literary, folklore or artistic associations, rather than simply sites which are valued greatly by the public. This does not mean, per se

that sites that are designated in these ways are not valued by people, rather I am suggesting that people do not value these sites necessarily *because* of the material remains, or their designated status.

I would suggest that there has to be legislation which means that people's (context laden) personal opinions of landscape are accounted for. Areas which are highly valued by people but are not of 'importance' on natural or heritage grounds, or of exceptional scenic value (as covered by current NSA legislation) should still be given equal weighting in the planning and legislation process. This could be undertaken by designating areas as Areas of Great Landscape Value (AGLV), a designation which used to be used in Scotland, but was replaced by the NSA designation in 1980 (Macaulay Institute 2007). These designations were made on similar grounds to NSA designations, but the name is of use because it encompasses all the values that people may have for a landscape, and the designations could be made using techniques that identify all these values. This may be problematic, as it would involve a fossilisation of things that were seen to be of value at the time of designation, and these values may no longer hold. It may be possible to avoid this by reviewing designations every few years, at a set interval, but this would be very costly, and involve a large amount of administration. Also, as with all legislation, it is then implied that areas which do not have AGLV designation are therefore valueless. Instead I would suggest that there is a need for public opinions on landscape change to be taken into account even if they are not based on rational grounds. Otherwise people's opposition to developments or other landscape changes will only be taken into account if they are based on material factors such as the habitat of a rare species that they may fundamentally not care about, their attachments being to other aspects of the landscape. This type of opinion should no longer be denigrated as Nimbyism, but instead celebrated, and people should be encouraged to speak about their attitudes to landscape without risk of being stigmatised. Opinions about landscape values should not just be solicited at times when the landscape is facing some sort of change, as then opinions may be artificially strong because of the threat. If there was a background knowledge of people's landscape values then it would be possible to work out how much of people's responses to landscapes under threat are affected by a 'now bias' and potentially not their everyday views.

The worth of current designations based on material grounds should be debated. It has already been suggested that they are of limited worth in reflecting people's actual landscape values, people may greatly value areas and features that have no official designation, and not value others which are protected. It could therefore be argued, that if all values are contextually based, and not rooted in any intrinsic worth then there should be no formal designations for landscapes and heritage, and all planning and landscape future decisions should be made on a case by case basis, rather than relying on formal criteria. On one level this seems like an attractive idea, if all worth is within people's opinions then a democratic assessment of this should allow the determination of what is of great value, and what is not. Quite apart from the fact that it would be a logistical near impossibility to manage land in this way, there is another value based reason for the retention of formal landscape designations, as they currently exist: the temporal context in which decisions are made for landscapes. There is nothing to say that things which are not valued now will never be valued in the future. This in itself may be seen as a reaction to planning decisions in the mid twentieth century, when Victorian and earlier buildings, which would now be valued were torn down to make space for functional modernist architecture. Much of this modernist architecture is now itself valued, after decades of vilification, with the Twentieth Century society being established to celebrate modernist architecture. At a landscape scale, the planet's biodiversity is declining faster than at any time in the past, largely as a result of land management decisions made in, or resulting from actions in, the nineteenth and twentieth centuries. This supports Thompson's (1979) rubbish theory (section 2.3.1) in that, through increased rarity and the passage of time and the changing of cultural contexts things that are at one time seen as rubbish, accrue value and become treasured. In order to try and conserve features which may be of value it is therefore useful to have experts in their field making decisions on which things which may be as yet valueless, are preserved for future generations. This is not, and cannot be a failsafe way of preserving everything which may be of value in the future, but lessons should be learned from previous planning decisions which have been made using the dominant set of values at the time which have since been regretted.

Rather than this being a bequest value (the desire to preserve something of value for future generations) this is what could be termed an option value, within a formalised system of values (as outlined in chapter 2 section 2.3.2.3). This option value is about the realisation that is necessary to give people the option of deciding that something that is not of worth now may be of worth in the future. As Sir Neil Cossons (the then chair of English Heritage) said in a 2006 speech *Most of the public that value what we do today are yet to be born* (Cossons 2006:70).

7.3. Archaeological Approaches to Past Landscapes

As well as having implications for how policy makers and planners make decisions on a landscape scale, the results of this research also have implications for the tools that archaeologists have at their disposal for understanding past relationships with landscape.

Since the 1994 publication of *A Phenomenology of Landscape* (Tilley 1994), the use of a phenomenological approach to examine past landuse and attitudes to landscape has been common in archaeology. The main idea of phenomenology is that there is an essence to all experiences, and that by recreating an experience that essence can be understood (Johnson 1999). Thus phenomenological

approaches attempt to undertake an objective study of a subjective experience. Advocates of this approach attempt to encounter landscapes in ways similar to how they have been experienced in the past, suggesting that thereby past attachments to landscape can be understood (e.g. Johnston 1998, Jones 2006, Thomas 1999). Whilst accepting that the past is ultimately unknowable, the suggestion is made that a personal interpretation of the past produces one of a number of possible 'readings' of the landscape and how it may have been experienced (Johnson 2007).

This way of interpreting the past draws on the transcendental phenomenology of Heidegger which involve the suggestion that there is something essential to all experiences (Gregory 2000). In the case of landscapes, the suggestion is that this essential truth can be accessed through experiencing the landscape in a similar way to people in the past, i.e. authentically. For this to be a meaningful tool of enquiry into the past the writer must possess special poetic powers to transcend the cultural context of experience. In his book Tilley includes examples from walks he has taken through archaeological landscapes (for instance along the Dorset Cursus). From these walks he suggests how the setting of certain monuments reflects how land was used and thought about in the past. To do this, however, not only involves a reliance on the physical landscape being relatively unchanged through millennia but also the idea of the physical landscape having an agency, which remains unchanged through time, and guides people's ideas of it. There is thus an idea that there is an essential meaning to landscape which can be accessed through experience of it. This research demonstrates that this is not the case, and perceptions of landscape are linked to the context the experience of the landscape.

Any interpretations which grow solely from a modern (or perhaps post modern?) researcher encountering the landscape and having a think about their feelings and past feelings are going to be firmly situated in the writer's cultural present. As the archaeology of ritual, meaning and emotion is always going to be a comparative science this may not at first seem to be too problematic, but it is important to remember that the views of a solitary, often middle class, middle aged male researcher are unlikely to be very similar to anyone's in say, the Neolithic. Whilst researchers may, and do, suggest that the past is open to multiple readings, and theirs is only one reading of it, it is difficult to see how at this extreme the phenomenological approach to understanding the past is anything other than a self indulgent dead end. This is particularly true if you also work with the idea that landscapes themselves are subject to so many multiple understandings at any one time. The chances of one researcher thinking a past landscape in the present and that landscape being anything similar to that thought in the past are highly unlikely. As has been argued in the past (Edmonds 2006), the process of a solitary researcher taking a walk through a landscape with no other purpose than trying to form an understanding of past landscape perceptions is rooted in the Romantic tradition of 'wandering lonely as a cloud'. This method of engagement with the landscape was novel to this time, and the experiences would have little in common with any earlier modes of engaging with the land. The undertaking of specific tasks (such as flint knapping, or other craft activities), gives the researcher an idea of the physical processes which would have been undertaken in the past, and how it would have felt physically to undertake a task. There will be a shared context of shared experience. However, taking a walk across a much altered physical landscape, for a purpose different to that for which any prehistoric person would be undertaking that route is too different an experience to be able to say anything about the prehistoric mindset.

I would suggest that the results of this research call into question the phenomenological approach to the past, and any other approaches which rely on materialities and essentialism as an 'epistomological crutch' on which to hinge interpretations of the past. Instead, it should be recognised that there are always going to be multiple understandings of past belief and religion, and no one should be given primacy because of a presumed transcendental link.

7.4. Conclusions

In the previous chapter, methods used for data collection within this research have been discussed and critiqued. Issues with the representativeness of the sample population had already been discussed in the methods and results chapters as had the use of visual proxies for landscape in the image workbook section of the exercise. Therefore, in this chapter three key issues were discussed, the need to avoid a 'now bias' in further research into landscape perceptions, the use of visual proxies more generally in landscape research, and the need for wider participation in the landscape planning and designation process.

Current legislation for the protection of sites, monuments and landscapes uses criteria based on the material properties of the land to determine their significance. This significance is assessed by landscape and heritage professionals who only then carry out consultation with the wider community about their values for these landscapes. This situation is untenable as people's landscape values are based on knowledge and experience of places and associations with the area, rather than their material fact.

Certain elements within landscapes (mainly physical but also more esoteric elements such as smells, lights, and feelings) act as mnemonics for these associations, and create new relationships and values. Currently legislation does not exist which preserve's landscapes because of their 'intangible' qualities even though these may be the strongest values that people have for places. There has to be increased public involvement in all stages of the landscape management process, so that public values are at the forefront of landscape management decisions. To rely solely on public opinions in the now, however, is to ignore the fact that values change through time, and is here that there is a need for the 'expert'. We have a responsibility to leave things that may not necessarily be valued now for people to make decisions about valuing in the future.

There is also a requirement for impartial experts to inform the public of the consequences of particular landscape decisions and policies. More thought has to be given to the best ways of presenting this information, so that it can be understood by the entire population. In addition to this, attention needs to be paid to who the 'public' is for the assessment of landscape values. Certain landscapes are valued by more than their inhabitants, some are even valued by people who have never visited them. Quite aside from issues of ownership there has to be debate as to who deserves a say in the future of this public good.

Throughout this work I have stressed the importance of examining context and meaning of values for particular landscapes, and suggesting that that value is not inherent within material forms. However while meanings and values shift in time, material elements of a landscape remain, albeit often in an altered state. It is for future generations to invest further meaning and value into this material, or to decide that it is not of value to them. Time after time Rubbish Theory has been proven as architectural styles are valued when new, then derided as ugly, impractical or unfashionable before being celebrated once threatened and rare. Similarly wildlife, at times only valued as game, or food or wildflowers seen as weeds are now protected and habitats managed for their conservation.

It is necessary to realise that the same is true now, the values of the present are not absolute, and are constantly changing through the passage of time and the transformation of context.

8

Conclusions

This study has sought to explore and understand the values that people have for the Scottish Highlands, and the influences on these values. This has been undertaken through a case study at two separate sites, Lochtayside and Lochlomondside. The perceptions of both children and adults have been examined, and those of visitors to and residents of the Lochtayside area. This has been explored in the previous chapters, and in this concluding chapter the two research questions that were set out at the start of the book will be returned to. These will be discussed with reference to the strengths and weaknesses of the approach used and issues that arose from this research (as introduced in previous chapters) which could be explored further in future projects.

8.1. Research Question 1

Question 1: What methods can be utilised to understand qualitative preferences for landscapes which work with a large cross section of the population, and can be used in a repeatable and reliable manner?

To address this research question there was a need to develop an understanding of the methods currently used for the assessment of landscape perceptions, their strengths and weaknesses and their suitability for this research. It was realised that no existing methods were suitable to meet the needs set out in this research question:

• The methods must be able to understand qualitative preferences for landscape;

• They are workable with a large cross section of the population (including both children and adults); and

• The methods used are both repeatable and reliable, so could therefore be used with different people in a number of different situations.

It was therefore necessary to develop novel methods for assessing landscape perceptions. This research used three different methods to examine the perceptions of a cross section of the population.

The landscape workbook was developed to find out participants preferences for the landscapes of the study

areas. In this section of the method participants were taken to an area, given time to explore and asked to answer specific questions about what people liked, disliked and found special about the landscape and why they felt like this (as outlined in section 4.7.1). They were also asked about their use relationships with the landscape and what it was about the landscape they were interested in. This provided a way of examining people's landscape perceptions, and the reasons behind these perceptions. This was found to work with a large cross section of the population (with participants ranging in age from 8 – 84 and from different social backgrounds). The method was repeated successfully about 30 times, with a total of 130 participants, in two different locations apart from one occasion when the exercise had to be abandoned due to blizzard conditions it worked every time.

The second method used was an image workbook (see section 4.7.2) where participants had to answer different questions about photographs of the study area. This was undertaken to find out more about people's use relationships with the landscape and their attitudes to different types of landscape. The image workbook was the one element of the methodology that was unsuccessful, as has been outlined above in sections 5.4 because it was discovered that individuals were commenting solely on the landscape as depicted in the photographs rather than on the entire landscape. Discrepancies were discovered between people's attitudes to the photographs, and their attitudes to the landscape. When these were discussed with participants, people said this was because they were unaware that the photographs represented the landscape of the study area, and as such their responses only reflected their attitudes to the photographs, rather than the landscape they depicted. This raised wider questions about the use of photographs and other visual proxies in landscape research. Visual proxies for landscape do not and cannot contain all of the associations, memories (or context) that a landscape does, and therefore people's attitudes to these proxies are not reflective of all the attitudes people can have to landscapes.

The third method used to assess people's landscape preferences was a questionnaire. This was undertaken in order to examine the second research question 'what are the main influences on people's landscape perceptions and values?'. Different questionnaires were used for the adult and child participants as it was realised that this was one exercise where it would be possible to get more information from the adults than the children, and this opportunity should not be wasted. Both questionnaires were designed in order to gain a lot of information about people's backgrounds and attitudes to the countryside (see section 4.7.3 and 5.2) and these were crosstabulated against the preferences revealed in the landscape workbook. In further studies it may be possible to 'target' the questions asked in the questionnaire in order to discover more about the influences on landscape preferences.

All of these methods had to be repeatable, and all of them (regardless of the validity of the image workbook responses) worked with all of the sample population. In this way they can be said to be repeatable. There is, however, an issue intrinsic to all research: that it takes place within a particular temporal context. This research is no exception to this and as the actual landscape is being examined rather than a proxy, every time the research is repeated the different participants have a different landscape experience. Through the passage of time society changes, the world changes, and the physical landscape changes. Therefore, through this passage of time people's attitudes to the landscape change. The first volunteers worked with in this study participated in spring 2005, and the final participants in autumn 2006. Between these times the physical landscape of the study area had gone through some changes (mainly due to the changing of the seasons) and the cultural 'now' in which people encountered the landscape changed. In addition to this through this time the attitudes of the researcher can also change, as field experience and confidence grew, the way that participants were introduced to the study changed. This can be seen to be an issue with the reliability of the method, as people are no longer commenting on the same landscape and the same situation. However, this 'here and now' bias is inherent in all research, and as long as it is acknowledged and efforts are made to counteract it, then it cannot be seen to entirely invalidate the research.

A particular advantage of all of the methods used in this research was how well they worked with children. The landscape workbook enabled children to discuss and express complex ideas about their relationships with landscape, and the questionnaire exercise allowed the determination of what aspects of the children's identity influenced their landscape values. Perhaps the strongest indicator of the success of these methods for engaging children was the fact that all of the children completed all of the exercises. Indeed, the landscape workbook and questionnaires were completed successfully by all participants. Therefore, in terms of developing a method which can be used with a broad cross-section of the population, this work was successful. This statement could be tested by using these methods again in different landscapes and with different population groups.

The information collection techniques used in this study are repeatable in different locations. There may be issues with letting children explore certain places alone (such as more urban landscapes), but with increased adult supervision this should also be possible. The frameworks used for analysis of the dataset are not transferable, however.

As an inductive study, where the analysis framework grew from the dataset rather than being imposed upon it, the coding frameworks developed were specific to this study. The particular blend of Romanticism and Nationalism evident in people's responses is only found in the Highlands. Other responses are about factors completely unique to the study area (such as responses that make reference to a person's individual relationship with the land). Therefore, though the data collection techniques are applicable to other contexts, an inductive approach would have to be taken to the coding of data collected in a different study area. Whilst one may assume that reactions to areas with similar landscapes and historic contexts may contain similarities this may not be the case, due to differences in attitudes of the participants.

8.2. Research Question 2

Question 2 What are the main influences on people's landscape perceptions and values?

The methods used, as discussed above were designed to examine this question, as well as discovering what peoples' landscape values were. When individuals speak about their relationships with the landscape they are clearly commenting upon perceived attributed of the landscape or its overall character which lead them to think in a certain way. It has previously been suggested that properties inherent within these features make people think of and value the landscape in certain ways (Tilley 2006, Stedman 2002, 2003). This research suggests that instead of this, people's landscape values are contextually rather than materially driven. In other words people's landscape values are rooted within the socialised self rather than within the landscape and the influences on people's landscape perceptions are influences on the socialised self rather than influences on the landscape.

Certain particular contexts have been identified as key influences on landscape values. These contexts overlap, and are not discrete entities. Instead time, culture and identity were used as terms for discussing the large number of different influences on a person's landscape perceptions.

The first context that was discussed was identity. Within this research identity was used as a shorthand for the numerous subjectivities that are linked to a specific aspect of the self. Aspects that were found to be influential in terms of landscape perceptions (through analysis of results in this research) include age, personal biography (in terms of interests and occupation), and landscape biography (places that people know, are familiar with and the ways in which they have experienced these places). Aspects of a person's identity are associated with the 'differences' in landscape perceptions, differences in people's identity appear to lead people to think differently about the landscape. Similarities in identity (for example people of similar ages from similar backgrounds) can also lead to similarities in landscape perceptions, as was evidenced within this work. Similarities in landscape perceptions were also evident in the responses of people with very different identities. These can be ascribed to the second type of context that was discussed: the cultural context.

In this research culture was used to describe the dominant social discourses that participants were exposed to. Ways of seeing developed in the Picturesque and Romantic movements of the eighteenth and nineteenth centuries were to found still have a great influence upon how people thought of Highland Landscapes. Ideas of the Highland landscape being beautiful, and valued for wild, timeless qualities were still evident in many people's attitudes to landscape. An examination of earlier attitudes to these landscapes shows that these were valued in different ways in the past. This leads onto the final context which influences landscape perceptions, that of time. Time has been discussed within ideas of linear time (calendar time) within which history 'happens' and cyclical time (in terms of the seasonality, times of day, and lifecycles). The temporal context in which people encounter landscape affects the physical form of the landscape and a person's attitudes, and as such can be seen to be the overarching context which affects all aspects of landscape perceptions.

In order to better understand the effect of time on landscape perceptions it would be desirable to undertake a longitudinal study into landscape perceptions. This is something which is outwith the scope of this (time limited) research. Because of the differences in perceptions witnessed within participants of different age groups landscape perceptions it was assumed that people's landscape values change throughout their lifetimes. A longitudinal study, working with the same participants at different life stages would determine whether or not this assumption was valid as it is not currently known quite how dynamic values are within a person.

8.3. Implications of this study

The methods used in this research have allowed for a discussion of the perception and preferences that people have for Scottish Highland landscapes, and the influences on these perceptions. The previous chapter was devoted to examining how the ways that people relate to landscape tally with the ways that landscape planning decisions are currently made.

The main issue that was revealed in this work is that there is a clear difference between current policies that legislate for landscape and how people value landscapes. Currently legislation to protect landscape is based largely on material properties and/or formal cultural associations, whilst people's landscape values are largely derived from the context of their encounter with the landscape. Therefore legislation currently assumes that people derive landscape values from a certain set of landscape features, regardless of the context in which individuals encounter these features. The types of value that are covered by this legislation are only a narrow set of the full range of values individuals have for landscapes. Landscape and heritage designations tend to be made on account of the rarity of a resource or feature, or the 'national importance' or 'informational value'. These designations do not reflect people's everyday relationships with landscape and heritage features. It appears that people's landscape values are far more varied and dynamic than legislation can account for. In chapter 7 it is suggested that changes are made to the landscape planning and public enquiry processes so that 'the general public's' landscape values have the same level of importance as expert values which are currently covered in landscape designations. Whether people's landscape values should be covered by formal designations, or by statutory requirements to legislate for them in the planning process has been discussed. Both options have their merits and drawbacks, the dynamic nature of people's values through time means that designations could become rapidly out of date as society, and therefore people's values, changes. However, it is impractical to have widespread consultation on every planning decision which needs to be made. Regardless of this, it is still important to take formal measures to integrate public values into the landscape planning process.

The results from this study also have implications for methods currently used within landscape archaeology. As discussed in the previous chapter the phenomenological approach currently in vogue with the theoretical archaeology community, relies on there being an essential sameness to landscape experience. This work has involved rethinking of experiences of, and values for landscape and it is suggested that these are wholly contingent on context of encounter with the landscape. It therefore follows, that there is no essential sameness which allows a researcher in the present to think the same thoughts as a person in the past.

Appendix 1
Coding framework

Codes used for features mentioned by participants in the landscape and image workbooks

1.0. Flora and Fauna[10]
1.1. Vegetation
    1.1.2. Trees
    1.1.3. Flowers
    1.1.4. Nettles/thistles
    1.1.5. Bracken
1.2. Wildlife
    1.2.1. insects
    1.2.2. birds
    1.2.3. Animals
    1.2.4. Bones
    1.2.5. feathers
2.0. Topography
2.1. Hills & Mountains
2.2. Water
    2.2.1. Streams/rivers
    2.2.2. Puddles
    2.2.3. Loch
2.3. Geology
    2.3.1. Stones
    2.3.2. Boulders
    2.3.3. Rock outcrops
2.4. Topography of field
    2.4.1. Mud /dirt
    2.4.2. bogs
3.0. Landuse
3.1. Farm animals
    3.1.2. Animal dung
3.2. Modern features
    3.2.1. Fences
    3.2.2. Pylons
    3.2.3. Man-made portable objects[11]
    3.2.4. Roads and tracks
    3.2.5. Modern buildings
    3.2.6. Dams
    3.2.7. Telegraph poles
    3.2.8. Conifer plantations
3.3. Activities
3.4. Air quality
4.0. History

4.1. Historical features
    4.1.2. Old buildings
    4.1.3. Field boundaries
    4.1.4. Prehistoric features
4.2 Area's past
    4.2.1 Clearances
5.0. Entire area
5.1. Colour
5.2. Sound
5.3. Peace and quiet
5.4. Scotland
6.0. Weather/Climate
6.1. Sun
6.2. Wind
6.3. rain
6.4. snow
6.5. warmth
6.6. cold
6.7. clouds
6.8. sky
6.9. mist

Activities that participants said they would like to carry out, in response to landscape and image workbook questions

1.0. Sports
1.1. Hill sports
    1.1.1. hillwalking
    1.1.2. climbing
    1.1.3. fellrunning
    1.1.4. abseiling
    1.1.5. skiing/snowboarding
    1.1.6. sledging
    1.1.7. mountain biking
1.2. Watersports
    1.2.1. Swimming
    1.2.2. Diving
    1.2.3. Sailing & canoeing
    1.2.4. Powered craft
    1.2.5. Fishing
1.3. Other sports
    1.3.1. Motor/Quad biking
    1.3.2. Walking
    1.3.3. Running
    1.3.4. Kite flying

---

[10] Previously named 'natural features'
[11] Mainly termed 'rubbish' by participants

1.3.5.   Orienteering
1.3.6.   Horse riding
1.3.7.   Golf
1.3.8.   Team games
1.3.9.   Shooting
1.3.10 Cycling
3.   Work
3.1.   Farming
3.2.   Conservation work
4.   Investigation
4.1.   Archaeological fieldwork
4.2.   Plant hunting
4.3.   Wildlife watching
4.4.   Astronomy
5.0   Hobbies
5.1.   Drawing
5.2.   Photography
5.3.   Model plane flying
5.4.   Writing
6.   Relaxation
6.1.   Camping
6.2.   sitting still
6.3.   Play
6.4.   Sex
6.5.   Picnicking

Specific areas of landscape or weather conditions that people referred to as locations for activities in the landscape and image workbooks

1.0.   Topographic Features
1.1.   Hills/mountains
1.2.   Water features
       1.2.1.   Streams/ rivers
       1.2.2.   Loch
       1.2.3.   beach
1.3.   Low altitude
       1.3.1.   In field
       1.3.2.   Anywhere flat
1.4   Rough ground
2.0.   Weather conditions
2.1.   snow
2.2.   sun
2.3.   wind
2.4.   rain
3.0.   Man made features
3.1.   Ruined buildings
3.2.   Local town
3.3.   Park
3.4.   Shop
3.5.   Pub/restaurant
3.6.   Accommodation
3.7.   Roads and tracks
4.0.   Vegetation
4.1.   Forest
5.0.   No specific place

Reasons given for certain landscape features being liked, disliked or special in responses to landscape workbook questions

1.0.   Aesthetics/sensory
1.1.   colour
1.2.   beauty
1.3.   open landscape
1.4.   smell
1.5.   ugliness
1.6.   Untidiness
1.7.   Sound
1.8.   cleanliness
2.0.   Mnemonics
2.1.   mnemonic (personal past)
2.2.   mnemonic (past general)
2.3.   mnemonic (personal relationships)
3.0.   Use relationships/experiential
3.1.   Potential for use
3.2.   Play/fun
3.3.   Hazards
       3.3.1.   Pain
       3.3.2.   Discomfort
       3.3.3.   Dirt
       3.3.4.   Disgust
3.4.   Warmth
3.5.   Comfort
3.6.   Ease of motion/use
4.0.   Emotional
4.1.   Pleasure
4.2.   Anger
4.3.   Attachment/belonging
4.4.   Solitude
4.5.   Boredom
4.6.   Security
4.7.   Freedom
4.8.   Escape
4.9.   Sorrow
4.10   Inspiration
4.11   Pride
4.12   Calmness
4.13   Peace
4.14   Detachment
4.15   Difference to home
4.16   Excitement
4.17   Natural
4.18   Wild
4.19   Rurality
4.20   Unique
4.21   Unnatural
4.22   Isolation/remoteness
4.23   Fear
4.24   Timelessness
4.25   Spiritual
5.0.   Interest
5.1.   history
5.2.   botany
5.3.   geomorphology
5.4.   livelihood
5.5.   natural history

What people want to find more about features cited in
response to landscape workbook questions

1.0.   Nothing specific
2.0.   Present landuse
2.1.   Ownership
2.2.   Administration
2.3.   Future plans
2.4.   Safety
2.5.   Lives of inhabitants
2.6.   Farming processes
2.7.   Research in area
3.0.   Formation of landscape
3.1.   Geomorphological processes
    3.1.1.   Natural or manmade?
3.2.   Vegetation
    3.2.1.   Development of vegetation
3.3.   History of area
    3.3.1.   People in past
        3.3.1.1.   Clearances
        3.3.1.2.   Recent past
        3.3.1.3.   Medieval period
        3.3.1.4.   Prehistory
        3.3.1.5.   Roman
        3.3.1.6.   Historic period
    3.3.2.   Past landuse
    3.3.3.   Chronology of past
    3.3.4.   Design of features
    3.3.5.   Past structures
4.0.   Geographical Facts
4.1.   Size of mountains
4.2.   Distances
4.3.   Directions
4.4.   Depth of lochs
4.5.   Climate of area
4.6.   Place names
5.0.   Natural History
5.1.   Wildlife species
5.2.   Plant species
5.3.   Ecology

Appendix 2
Children's Questionnaire

Name

| |
| |

Are you

Male		Female	

School and Class

| |
| |

Do you live in:

A city (at least the size of Stirling)	
A town (at least the size of Creiff)	
A village (like Killin, Kenmore or Luss)	
In the countryside on a farm	
On a countryside not on a farm	

How long have you lived where you do now?

| |
| |

If you have lived somewhere else please write down where you lived and how long you lived there for.

| |
| |

Do your parents or guardians work? (tick one box per parent)

	Yes	No
Mum		
Dad		

If your parents work, what are their jobs?

| |
| |

On a day out with your family or friends outside of school time have you (only tick one box per question):

Visited a museum:

Never		Once or twice a year		Lots of times		Don't know	

Been to a historical site where there is no guide or information board? (for example a ruined farm, a war memorial or a standing stone)

Never		Once or twice a year		Lots of times		Don't know	

Been to a historical site where there is an information board but no interpretation centre (for example a stone circle or a monument with a board telling you about its history)

Never		Once or twice a year		Lots of times		Don't know	

Been to a historical site with an interpretation centre (like Edinburgh castle or Bannockburn)

Never		Once or twice a year		Lots of times		Don't know	

Been to a living history centre (like the Crannog centre)?

Never		Once or twice a year		Lots of times		Don't know	

Do you read any history books (including things like 'Horrible Histories') outside of school?

Regularly (one or two books a month)		Sometimes		Never	

What hobbies do you do?

What clubs are you a member of?

Do you watch any history programmes on television (like Time Team, Time Commanders etc.)

Often (once or more a week		Sometimes (once or more a month)		Rarely (a few times a year)		Never	

Thank you for your help,

Camilla

Appendix 3
Adult's Questionnaire

Perceptions of the Countryside Questionnaire

1.1.   Name

1.2.   . Where do you live? (if you have two main places of residence please list both)

1.3 Is your house (tick appropriate)

Rural (on a farm)	6 (8)
Rural (not Farming)	8 (11)
In a village/small town (up to 10,000 pop)	26 (34)
In a large town (10,000 – 80,000)	12 (16)
In a city	24 (31)

4.4.   Please state any other areas where you have spent an extended period of time (lived there previously, or had regular holidays. If you require more space continue on reverse of page)

Places where you have lived in the past:

Places you have visited frequently: (e.g. places you have visited on holiday repeatedly, have worked, or have relatives that you visit regularly)

1.5.   If you are not local to Lochtayside how many times (if any) have you visited the area before?

1.6.   Gender (tick as appropriate)

Male	
Female	

1.7.   Age Group (tick as appropriate)

16-17	
18-24	
25-40	
40-54	
55-64	
65 +	

1.8.   Employment Status (tick as appropriate)

Employed full-time	
Employed part-time	
Self Employed full-time	
Self Employed part-time	
Retired	
Unemployed	
Student	
Other (please state)	

1.9.   Job title (if retired please note the title of your occupation before retirement. If student, please state degree registered for):

1.10   Education Status (please tick highest achievement)

Completed secondary schooling	
O level/GCSE/Standard grade (or equivalent)	
Highers/A levels	
Completed a HNC/HND	
Completed a College or University Degree	
Hold a Postgraduate Qualification	

1.11   If you hold a University degree or a HND /HNC please state which subject(s) you studied in the course of these:

About Your Family

2.1 How many people (including yourself) live in your household? (Tick as appropriate)

1 Person	
2 People	
3 People	
4 People	
5 or more people	

2.2 How many members of the household (including yourself) are in the following age groups? (Write in numbers as appropriate)

Pre-school age	
Primary School age	
Secondary School age	
In Higher Education	
Adults of working age	
Adults of retirement age	

2.3 Do you have any grandchildren? (tick as appropriate)

Yes	
No	

2.5 In what environment (if known) did your parents grow up ? (tick as many boxes as relevant)

	Mother	Father
Rural (on a farm)		
Rural (not farming)		
In a village/small town (up to 10,000 pop)		
In a large town (10,000 – 80,000)		
In a City		

2.6 Where (if known) did your parents grow up?

3.0 Your Experiences as a Volunteer

3.1 How many times have you worked as a conservation volunteer?

Once (this is the only time)	
2-3 times	
4-5 times	
More than 5 times	

3.2 What factors influenced your choice to work as a conservation volunteer?

Please rate each of the following attributes on a scale of 1 to 5 where 1 indicates very high importance and 5 indicates very low importance (circle appropriate responses)

	Very High				Very Low	Not Applicable
A cheap holiday	1	2	3	4	5	
A chance to learn a new skill	1	2	3	4	5	
Helping the environment	1	2	3	4	5	
A chance to new people	1	2	3	4	5	
A chance to spend time in the countryside	1	2	3	4	5	
A chance to 'give something back' to the countryside	1	2	3	4	5	
A chance to spend time in the Ben Lawers area	1	2	3	4	5	
It may lead to a career in conservation or archaeology	1	2	3	4	5	
Work experience for University or College course	1	2	3	4	5	
Something to add to your CV	1	2	3	4	5	
A fun activity	1	2	3	4	5	
Other reasons (Please state below)	1	2	3	4	5	

Any other reasons:

3.3 What motivated your choice of Ben Lawers as a location to volunteer at? Please rate each of the following attributes on a scale of 1 to 5 where 1 indicates very high importance and 5 indicates very low importance (circle appropriate responses)

	Very High				Very Low	Not Applicable
A chance to spend time in the Loch Tay area specifically	1	2	3	4	5	
A chance to spend time in the Scottish Highlands	1	2	3	4	5	
A chance to spend time in Scotland	1	2	3	4	5	
The activity on offer at the camp	1	2	3	4	5	
A chance to meet old friends	1	2	3	4	5	
Other reason (please state below)	1	2	3	4	5	

Other reasons:

Which other organisations have you volunteered with? In the space below please write down the names of these organisations and briefly state what kind of work you did with them (e.g. Woodland Trust, 5 days tree planting near Pitlochry). If you have volunteered for NTS previously, please detail the nature of the work that you have carried out with them.

4.0 Your Experiences of the Countryside

4.1 Are you a member of any of the following organisations? (tick all that apply)

The National Trust For Scotland	
Greenpeace	
RSPB	
World Wildlife Fund	
Historic Scotland	
The National Trust	
Youth Hostel Association	
Friends of the Earth	
Other Wildlife Organisation (please name below)	
Other Heritage Organisation (please name below)	
Outdoor activity clubs (please name below)	

Other Organisations/Clubs

4.2 Which outdoor activities have you yourself participated in over the last year? (Tick all that apply)

	10+ Times	4-10 Times	1-4 Times	Never	Don't Know
Walking					
Shooting					
Heritage sightseeing					
Natural sightseeing					
Art (landscape painting etc.)					
Photography					
Fishing					
Bird Watching					
Cycling					

Ski-ing					
Picnicking					
Mountain Biking					
Dog Walking					
Other sport (please state below)					
Other outdoor activity (please state below)					

Other Sports/Activities

4.3 In the past year have you:

	10+ times	4-10 times	1-4 times	Never	Don't Know
Visited a Museum					
Visited a National Park					
Visited a historical site with an attached interpretation centre (e.g. Stirling Castle)					
Visited a historical site where there is an information board but no interpretation centre (e.g. a stone circle with a board telling you about its history)					
Visited a SSSI/Nature reserve					
Been to a 'living history' centre (e.g. Scottish Crannog Centre)					

4.4 When visiting the country side, which of the following determines where you visit?

Please rate each of the following attributes on a scale of 1 to 5 where 1 indicates very high importance and 5 indicates very low importance (circle appropriate responses)

	Very High				Very Low	Not applicable
'Bagging' a Munro	1	2	3	4	5	
A challenging route to walk	1	2	3	4	5	
Scenic views	1	2	3	4	5	
Fresh air	1	2	3	4	5	
A specific place you want to visit (e.g. Killin)	1	2	3	4	5	
A specific heritage site you want to visit (e.g. Bannockburn)	1	2	3	4	5	
A specific natural site you want to see (e.g. Ben Nevis)	1	2	3	4	5	
A natural sight you want to see (e.g. mountains, trees in autumn)	1	2	3	4	5	
Getting away from 'civilisation'	1	2	3	4	5	
Proximity of amenities (toilets, café etc)	1	2	3	4	5	
Location of friends/family members	1	2	3	4	5	
A place connected to your family's past	1	2	3	4	5	
Location of specific wildlife (seal colony, birds etc)	1	2	3	4	5	
Location of a specific outdoor activity (e.g. pony trekking/kayaking)	1	2	3	4	5	
Other reason (please state below)	1	2	3	4	5	

Other reasons

4.5. There are many factual programmes about the British countryside broadcast on television and radio. Which of the following statements most accurately reflects your attitude towards these programmes? (tick appropriate statement)

I always make a special effort to watch/listen	
I watch/listen when I can	
I watch/listen if there is nothing better on	
I hardly ever watch/listen	
Don't know	

4.5.1 Please list any programmes about the countryside which you regularly watch/listen to.

4.6 There are many factual programmes about History and Archaeology broadcast on television and radio. Which of the following statements most accurately reflects your attitude towards these programmes (tick appropriate statement).

I always make a special effort to watch/listen	
I watch/listen when I can	
I watch/listen if there is nothing better on	
I hardly ever watch/listen	
Don't know	

4.6.1 Please list any programmes about history or archaeology which you regularly watch/listen to.

4.7 Do you read any of the following books: (Tick as appropriate)

	Regularly (1+ monthly)	Sometimes	Never	Don't Know
Books about the British Countryside				
Books about a specific area (please state which below)				
Books about history/Archaeology				
Books about a specific period of history				

4.8 Do you read any of the following magazines?: (Tick as appropriate)

	Regularly (1 + Monthly	Sometimes	Never	Don't Know
Current Archaeology				
Scotland in Trust				
British Archaeology				
BBC Wildlife				
National Geographic				
BBC History				
Any outdoor activity magazines (e.g. Trail) (please specify below)				
Other History/Natural History publications (please name below)				

Other Publications:

Thank you for your time. I may wish to contact you with some supplementary questions. If you agree to this, please enter your contact details below and indicate your preferred method of communication

Thanks,

Camilla Priede

Address:
Tel no:
Email address:

Bibliography

Adams, C 1994. The fish community of Loch Lomond, Scotland: its history and rapidly changing status *Hydrobiologica* **290**

Aldreed, H 1997. Existence value, moral commitments and in-kind valuation p155-169 in Foster (ed) *Valuing Nature? Economics, Ethics and Environment* London, Routledge

Alexandra, J & Riddington, C 2007. Redreaming the rural landscape *Futures* **39** 324-339

Allison, J 1999. Self determination in cultural resource management: indigenous people's interpretation of history of places and landscapes In Ucko, P. J & Layton, R *The Archaeology and Anthropology of Landscape* London, Routledge

Antorp, M 2005. Why landscapes of the past are important for the future *Landscape and Urban Planning* **70** 21-34

Armit, I 2003. *Towers in the North; the brochs of Scotland* Stroud, Tempus

Ashmore, P 1996. *Neolithic and Bronze Age Scotland* London, Batsford

Ashmore, W & Knapp A.B (eds) 1999. *Archaeologies of landscape.* Oxford, Berg

Atkinson, J , Lelong, O, McGregor, G McLellan, K 2003. *Ben Lawers Historic Landscape Project: Excavations at Kiltyrie and Meall Greigh* GUARD project report 1580

Azqueta, D & Delacámara, G 2006. Ethics and Environmental Management *Ecological Economics* **56** 524-533

Ballantyne, C & Dawson, A 1997. Geomorphology and Landscape Change p23-45 in Edwards, K and Ralston, I (eds) *Scotland Environment and Archaeology 8000BC-AD1000* Chichester, Wiley

Barker, J & Smith, F. Power, positionality & practicality; Carrying out fieldwork with children *Ethics, Place & Environment* **4(2)** 142-147

Barker, P 1993. *Techniques of Archaeological Investigation* London, Routledge

Barnard, A & Spencer, J 1996. *Encyclopaedia of Social and Cultural Anthropology* London, Routledge

Barnes, T.J 2001. Retheorising Economic Geography-from the Quantitative Revolution to the 'Cultural Turn' *Annals of the Association of American Geographers* **93(1)** 546-565

Bauer, M 2000. Classical Content Analysis: a review in Bauer, M & Gaskell, G ed. *Qualitative Researching with text image and Sound* London, Sage

Becker, C 2006. The human actor in ecological economics: Philosophical

approach and research perspectives *Ecological Economics* **60** 17-23

Bendall, S 1992. *Maps, Land and Society* Cambridge, Cambridge University Press

Bender, B 1993. Landscape: meaning and action. In Bender, B (ed.) *Landscape, politics and perspectives* Oxford, Berg

Bender, B 1998. Stonehenge, Making Space Oxford, Berg

Bender, B 1999. Subverting the Western Gaze: Mapping alternate worlds. In Ucko, P. J & Layton, R *The Archaeology and Anthropology of Landscape* London, Routledge

Bender, B 2006. Place and Landscape in Tilley, C, Keane, W, Kuchler, S, Rowlands, M, Spyer, P *The handbook of material culture* London, Sage

Berger, J 1980. Understanding a photograph. P 291-293 in Trachtenberg (ed) *Classic essays in photography* New Haven, Leete's Island Books

Berry B & Marble D 1968 (eds) *Spatial Analysis; a reader in Statistical Geography* New Jersey, Prentice Hall

Binford, S & Binford, L 1968. *New perspectives in Archaeology* Chicago, Aldine Press

Boss, J 2001 *Ethics for life: An Interdisciplinary and Multicultural Introduction* Mountain View, Mayfield

Bourdieu, P. 1984. *Distinction: a social critique of the judgement of taste.* London, Routledge.

Bowman 1986. *The Highlands and Islands: a Nineteenth century tour* Gloucester, Sutton

Bradley, R 1984. *The Social Foundations of Prehistoric Britain* New York, Longman

Bradley, I 1999. *Celtic Christianity* Edinburgh, Edinburgh University Press

Brannen, J 1992. *Mixing Methods: Qualitative and Quantitative Research* London, Gower

Brannen, J 2004. Working Qualitatively and Quantitatively p312-326 in Seale, C Godo, G Gubrium, J & Silverman (eds) *Qualitative Research Practice* London, Sage

Brassley, P 1998. On the unrecognised significance of the ephemeral landscape *Landscape Research* **23(2)** 119-132

Bray, W & Trump, D 1970. *The Penguin Dictionary of Archaeology* London, Penguin

Bray, A 2001. *An Archaeological survey in Glen Luss* Association of Certificated Field Archaeologists (University of Glasgow) Occasional Paper No 19

Brown, G 2006. Mapping Landscape Values and Development Preferences: a method for Tourism and Residential Development Planning *International Journal of Tourism Research* **8** 101-113

Brown, K. M, Taylor, L.O 2000. Do as you say: say as you do: evidence on gender differences in actual and stated contributions to public goods *Journal of Economic Behaviour and Organisation* **43** 127 – 139

Bryman, A 2001. *Social Research Methods* Oxford, Oxford University Press

Bunce, M 1994. *The Countryside ideal: Anglo American images of landscape* London, Routledge

Butler, R & Hall, C M 1999. Image and Re-imaging of Rural Areas p155-122 in Butler R, Hall C M & Jenkins J *Tourism and Recreation in Rural Areas* Chichester, Wiley

Campbell, R .D 1999. *Loch Lomond and the Trossachs* Edinburgh, Mainstream Press

Carman, J 2002. *Archaeology and Heritage* London, Continuum

Carman, J 2006. *Landscape Values as a 'Third Way': places as non utilitarian phenomena* Paper delivered at 'Exploring Landscape Values' workshop, Aberdeen 2/3/06

Carver, M 1996. On Archaeological Value *Antiquity* **73** 143-8

Cavill, P & Jackson, M 2000. From Rome to Augustine: Britain before 597 p 9-15 in Chadwick, H (ed.) *Not Angels but Anglicans: A History of Christianity in the British Isles* Norwich, Canterbury Press

Chadwick, A 1998 Archaeology at the edge of chaos, further towards reflexive excavation methodologies *Assemblage* **3** (internet journal -http://www.assemblage. group.shef.ac.uk/3/3chad.htm accessed 7/2/08)

Chatwin, B 1989. *The Songlines* London, Picador

Childe, V. 1929. *The Ayrans: a story of Indo-European origins* London, Routledge

Clark, J Darlington, J & Fairclough, G 2004 *Using Historic Landscape Characterisation* English Heritage and Lancashire County Council

Clark, J & Stein, T 2003. Incorporating the natural landscape within an assessment of community attachment *Forest Science* **49(6)** 867-876

Clarke, D. L 1968. *Analytical Archaeology* London, Methuen

Cloke, P & Little, J 1997 Introduction: Other countrysides. In Cloke, P & Little, J *Contested Countryside Cultures* London, Routledge

Cloke, P, Cook, I, Crang, P, Painter, J & Philo, C 2004 *Practicing Human Geography* London, Sage

Coles, G &Mills C 1998. *Life on the Edge, Human settlement and Marginality* Oxford, Oxbow books

Collis, J 1981. A theoretical study of hillforts In Guilbert, G 1981, *Hillfort studies: essays for A.H.A Hogg* p. 66-78 Leicester, Leicester University Press

Colombo, S Calatrava-Requena, J & Hanley, N 2006. Analysing the social benefits of soil conservation methods using stated preference techniques *Ecological Economics* **58(4)** 850-861

Cope, J 1998. *The Modern Antiquarian* London, Thorsons

Cosgrove, D 1985. Prospect, Perspective and Evolution of the landscape idea *Trans. I.B.G. new series* **10(1)** 45-62

Cosgrove, D 2006. Modernity, Community and the Landscape Idea *Journal of Material Culture* **11(1/2)** 49-66

Council of Europe *European Landscape Convention* http://www.coe.int accessed 27/2/2006

Crang, M 1998. *Cultural Geography* London, Routledge

Crofts, R 2001. Scotland's Cultural Landscape p 109-114 in Macinnes, L & Kelly, R (ed) *The Cultural Landscape* ICOMOS, UK

Darvill, T. 1995 Value systems in archaeology. p40-50 In Cooper, M.A., Firth, A., Carman, J. and Wheatley, D. (eds) *Managing Archaeology*. London, Routledge

Davidson Kinghorn, Diane 2002. *Luss and Arden Community Futures – Community Profile* Unpublished report for Loch Lomond and the Trossachs National Park

Defoe, D 1725. A Tour through the Whole Island of Great Britain

Dennet, T & Spence, J 1975. Photography, Ideology and Education, reprinted in Alvardo, M, Buscombe, E & Collins, R *Representation and Photography* London, Palgrave

Derby, W 2000. *Landscape and Identity; geographies of nations and class in England* Oxford, Berg

Devine, T 1994. *Clanship to the Crofters' War: The social transformation of the Scottish Highlands* Manchester, University Press

Devine-Wright, P 2005. Beyond Nimbyism: towards an integrated framework for understanding public perceptions of wind energy *Wind Energy* **8** 125-139

Dixon, T. N. D 2004. Underwater Survey and Sampling in *Ben Lawers Historic Landscape Project Annual Report 2003-2004* Glasgow, GUARD

Dower, M 2001. The variation in landscape policies across Europe p96-108 in Macinnes, L & Kelly, R (ed) *The Cultural Landscape* ICOMOS, UK

Duncan, I, Davis, L & Sorensen, J 2004. Introduction p1-20 in Davis, K, Duncan, I & Sorensen, J (eds.) *Scotland and the Borders of Romanticism* Cambridge, University Press

Durie, A.J 2003. *Scotland for the Holidays; Tourism in Scotland c. 1780-1939* East Linton, Tuckwell Press

Edensor, T 2002. *National Identity, Popular Culture and Everyday Life* Oxford, Berg

Edmonds, M Sheridan, A & Tipping, R 1992. Survey and Excavation at Creag na Caillich, Killin, Perthshire *Proc. Soc. Antiq. Scot* **122** 77-122

Edmonds, M 1999. *Ancestral Geographies of the Neolithic* London, Routledge

Edmonds, M 2006. Who Said Romance was Dead? *Journal of Material Culture* **11(2)** 167-188

Edwards, K & Whittington, G 1997. Vegetation Change pp63-82 in Edwards, K and Ralston, I (eds) *Scotland Environment and Archaeology 8000BC-AD1000* Chichester, Wiley

EFTEC 2005. *Valuation of the Historic Environment* Report for HLF, English Heritage, DCMS & Department for Transport

Eickhoff, M 2005. German Archaeology and National Socialism. Some historiographical remarks *Archaeological Dialogues* **12(1)** 73-90

Eliot, T.S 1948. *Notes Towards the Definition of Culture* London, Faber & Faber

Emmett, R 1948. *Saturday Slow* London, Faber

Ermischer, G 2004. Mental Landscape: as idea and concept *Landscape Research* **29(4)** 371-383

Faber 2008. How to be an Ecological Economist *Ecological Economics* (in press)

Fay, B 1996. *Contemporary philosophy of Social Sciences* Oxford, Blackwells

Fenyo, K 2000. *Contempt, Sympathy and Romance: Perceptions of the Highlands and the Clearances during the famine years* East Linton, Tuckwell Press

Finlayson, B & Edwards, K 1997. The Mesolithic p109-126 in Edwards, K & Ralston, I (ed.) *Scotland, Environment and Archaeology 8000 BC – AD 1000* Chichester, Wiley

Firsoff, V A 1954. *In the hills of Bredalbane* London, Robert Hale

Fjortoft, I & Sageie, J 2000. The Natural Environment as a playground for children: Landscape description and analyses of a natural playscape *Landscape and Urban Planning* **48** (2000) 83-97

Forestry Commission 2007. *History of the Forestry commission* (web resource)

Forsyth, R 1806. *The Beauties of Scotland,* Vol 3

Fowler, P 2001. Cultural Landscape: Great Concept, Pity About the Phrase p64-82 in Macinnes, L & Kelly, R (ed) *The Cultural Landscape* ICOMOS, UK

Fowler, P 2003. *World Heritage Cultural Landscapes* Paris UNESCO World Heritage Centre

Fowler, P 2004. *Landscapes for the world: conserving a global heritage* Macclesfield, Windgatherer Press

Fry, M 2005. *Wild Scots: Four Hundred Years of Highland History* London, John Murray

Garrod, G & Willis, K 1999. *Economic Valuation of the Environment* Cheltenham, Edward Elgar

Gell, A 1992. *The Anthropology of time* Oxford, Berg

Giddings, R & Yarwood, R 2005. Growing up, going out and growing out of the countryside: Childhood experiences in rural England *Children's Geographies* **3(1)** 101-114

Gilpin, W 1789. *Observations, relative chiefly to Picturesque Beauty made in the year 1776 of several parts of Great Britain particularly the High-Lands of Scotland* London, Blamire

Glendening, J 1997. *The High Road: Romantic Tourism, Scotland and Literature 1720-1820.* Macmillan, Basingstoke

Gobo, G 2004. Sampling, representativeness and

generalizability p435-456 in Seale, C Godo, G Gubrium, J & Silverman (eds) *Qualitative Research Practice* London, Sage

Gourlay, D & Slee, B 1998. Public preferences for landscape features: A case study of two Scottish Environmentally Sensitive Areas *Journal of Rural Studies* **14(2)** 249-263

Graber, D 2001. *Towards an Anthropological theory of Value* New York, Palgrave

Grasseni, C 2004. Skilled Landscapes: mapping practices of locality *Society and Space* **22** 699-717

Gregory, D 2000. Phenomenology p579-581 in Johnston, R.J Gregory, D Pratt,G & Watts M *The Encyclopaedia of Human Geography* 4ᵗʰ Edition Chichester, Wiley

Haartsen, T Groote, T & Huigen, P 2003. Measuring age differentials in representations of rurality in The Netherlands *Journal of Rural Studies* **19** 245-252

Halfacree, K 1994. The importance of 'the rural' in the constitution of counter urbanisation: evidence from England in the 1980s *Sociologica Ruralis* **34** 164-89

Halle, U 2005. Archaeology in the Third Reich. Academic scholarship and the rise of the 'luntic fringe' *Archaeological Dialogues* **12 (1)** 91-102

Hammersley, M 2000. Varieties of social research *International Journal of Social Research Methodology: Theory and Practice* **3(3)** 221-231

Harker, C 2005. Playing and affective time-spaces *Children's Geographies* **3(1)** 47-62

Hastings, G Stead, M & McDermott, C 2004 How food promotion influences children *Education* **(79)** 14-15

Harrison, J.G 2005. *People in a landscape: a report for the Ben Lawers Historic Landscape Project* Unpublished project report.

Hernando Gonzalo, A 1999. The perception of landscape amongst the Q'eqchi p254-263 in Ucko, P. J & Layton, R *The Archaeology and Anthropology of Landscape* London, Routledge

Herzog, T. R, Herbert, E. J, Kaplan, R. & Crooks, C. L. 2000. Cultural and Developmental comparisons of Landscape Perceptions and Preferences *Environment and Behaviour* **32(3)** 323-346

Hewison. R & Holden, J 2006. Public value as a framework for analysing the value of heritage: the ideas. p14-18 in Clark, K (ed) *Capturing the Public Value of Heritage* Swindon, English Heritage

Hirsch, E & O' Hanlon, M 1996. *The Anthropology of Landscape* Oxford, Berg

Hodder, I 1982. *The Present Past: an introduction to anthropology for archaeologists.* New York, Pica Press

Hoskins, W.G 1955. *The Making of the English Landscape* London, Hodder and Stoughton.

Hubbard, P 2006. Nimby by another name? A reply to Wolsink *Trans, Inst Br Geogr* **NS 31** 92-94

Hunt, M 1993. Racism, Imperialism, and the travellers gaze in Eighteenth-Century England *Journal of British Studies* **32(3)** 333-357

Ingold, T 2000. *The Perception of the Environment: essays in livelihood, dwelling and skill* London, Routledge

Ingold, T 2006. Rethinking the Animate, Re-animating thought *Ethnos* **71:1** 9-20

Jacobs, M 1997. Environmental Valuation, Deliberative democracy and Public Decision Making Institutions p211-231 in Foster (ed) *Valuing Nature? Economics, Ethics and Environment* London, Routledge

Jackson, S & Scott, S 2006. Childhood p216-232 p305-324 in Payne, G ed *Social Divisions* Baisingstoke, Palgrave Macmillan

Jay, S & Wood, C 2002 The emergence of local planning authority on high-voltage electricity pylons *Journal of Environmental Policy and Planning* **4** 261-274

J. Paul Getty Trust 1999. *Economics and Heritage conservation* unpublished meeting report.

Jedrej, C & Nutall, M 1996. *White Settlers: the impact of rural repopulation in Scotland* UK, Harwood Acadmic

John, D. R 1999. Consumer socialisation of children: a retrospective of twenty five years of research *Journal of Consumer Research* **26(3)** 183-213

Johnson, M 1999. *Archaeological Theory: An Introduction* Oxford, Blackwell

Johnson, M 2007. *Ideas of Landscape* Oxford, Blackwell

Johnson, J. L 2000. *Scotland's nature in trust: the National Trust for Scotland in its wild land and crafting management* London, Poyser Natural History

Johnston, R 1998. Approaches to the perception of Landscape: philosophy, theory, methodology. *Archaeological Dialogues,* **5** 56-68

Jones, A 2006 Animated Images: Images, Agency and Landscape in Kilmartin, Argyll, Scotland *Journal of Material Culture* **11(1/2)** 211-225

Jones, M 2003. The concept of Cultural Landscape: discourse and narratives p21-51 in Palang, H & Fry, G (ed) *Landscape Interfaces* Netherlands, Kluwer

Jones, O 2001. 'Before the dark of reason' some ethical and epistemological considerations on the otherness of children *Ethics, Place and Environment* **4(1)** 172 - 178

Jones, S 2005. 'That stone was born here and that's where it belongs': Hilton of Cadboll and the negotiation of identity, ownership and belonging. In S. Foster and M. Cross (eds) *Able Minds and Practiced Hands. Scotland's early medieval sculpture in the 21st century*, pp37-54. Edinburgh: Society for Medieval Archaeology.

Jauhiainen, J & Mönkkönen, M 2005. Seasonality: Nature, People's Preferences and Urban Planning in Oulunsalo, Finland *Landscape Research* **30(2)** 273-281

Kaltenborn, B. P 1998. Effects of sense of place on responses to environmental impacts *Applied Geography* **18(2)** 169-189

Kaltenborn, B & Bjerke, T 2002. Associations between Landscape Preferences and Place Attachment: a study in Røros, Southern Norway *Landscape Research* **27(4)** 381-396

Kay, B 1996. *The complete Odyssey: Voices from Scotland's recent Past*, Edinburgh, Polygon

Kelly, N 2006. Children's involvement in policy formation *Children's Geographies* **4(1)** 37-44

Kenny, J 2002. *Visual Repertoire, focussing activity and the 'Value of Heritage': Using the 'mental library of views' to evoke local place-identity, Britain and Europe* Unpublished PhD thesis, Lancaster University

Kilpatrick, A Dixon, P Maciness, L & Parkinson, S 2006 *The Historic Land-use Assessment Project* http://www.rcahms.gov.uk/pdfs/AR0506_14_21.pdf

Knight, P 2004 Glaciers: art and history, science and uncertainty *Interdisciplinary Science Reviews* **29(4)** 1-9

Krippendorff, K 2004. *Content Analysis; an introduction to its methodology* London, Sage

Lange, E & Schmid, W 2003. Ecological Planning With Virtual Landscapes: Three Examples From Switzerland *Landscape Journal* 156-165

Layton, R 1999. The Awala totemic landscape: ecology, religion, politics. in Ucko, P. J & Layton, R *The Archaeology and Anthropology of Landscape* London, Routledge

Lee, J 2007. Experiencing Landscape, Orkney land and farming *Journal of Rural Studies* **23(1)** 88-100

Loch Lomond and Trossachs National Park Authority 2005. *National Park Plan 2005 Consultative Draft* Balloch, LLTNP

Macdonald, A 2007 *The Visual Issue : an investigation into the techniques and methodology used in windfarm computer visualisations* http://www.thevisualissue.com

Mackay, J.W 1995. People, Perceptions and Moorland p102-111 in Thompson, D.B.A Hester, A.J& Usher, M.B *Heaths & Moorland: Cultural Landscapes* Edinburgh, HMSO

Maclennan 2002. Ben Lawers Historic Landscape Project: Interim report : Croftvellich (unpublished project report)

Macmillan, D Philip, L Hanley, N Alvarez-Farizo, B 2002. Valuing the non-market benefits of wild goose conservation: a comparison of interview and group based approaches *Ecological Economics* **43** (2002) 49-59

Macpherson, H 2005 Landscape's Ocular-centrism – and beyond? P 95-104 in Tress, B., Tress, G., Fry, G., Opdam, P. (eds.) *From landscape research to landscape planning: Aspects of integration, education and application.* Heidelberg, Springer

McClanahan, A 2004. *The Heart of Neolithic Orkney in its Contemporary Contexts* Unpublished project report for Historic Scotland

McCormack, J 2002. Children's Understandings of rurality *Journal of rural studies* **18** 193-207

McCrone, D Morris, A & Kiely, R 1995. *Scotland the Brand* Edinburgh, Edinburgh University Press

McKerrow, W Mac Niocaill, C & Dewey, J.F 2000. The Caledonian Orogeny Redefined *Journal of the Geological Society of London* **157** 1149-1154

McKirdy, A. and Crofts, R. (1999) Scotland: The Creation of Its Natural Landscape. Scottish Natural Heritage.

MacLennan, S 2002. Killin Community Profile Unpublished report for Loch Lomond and the Trossachs National Park

Makdisi, S 1998. *Romantic Imperialism* University Press, Cambridge

Marrs, R.H & Pakeham, R.J 1995. Bracken Invasion – Lessons from Past & Prospects for the Future p180-193 in Thompson, D.B.A Hester, A.J& Usher, M.B *Heaths & Moorland: Cultural Landscapes* Edinburgh, HMSO

Matless, D. 1998. *Landscape and Englishness.* London, Reaction Books

Matthews, H Taylor, M Sherwood, K Tucker, F & Limb, M 2000. Growing up in the Countryside, Children and the rural idyll *Journal of Rural Studies* **16** 141-153

Matthews 2003 Coming of Age for Children's Geographies *Children's Geographies* **1(1)** 3-5

Miller, J 2002. *The Dam Builders; Power from the Glens* Edinburgh, Birlinn

Milton, K 2002. *Loving Nature* London, Routledge

Mitchell, J 2000. *The Sheilings and Droveways of Lochlomondside* Stirling, Monument Press.

Mitchell, J 2001. *Loch Lomondside* London, Harper Collins

Mizoreff, N 1999. *An introduction to Visual Culture* London, Routledge

Moor-Colyer, R & Scott, A 2005. What kind of landscape do we want? Past, present and future Pespectives *Landscape Research* **30(4)** 501-523

Morton, H 1933. *In Scotland Again* London, Methuen & co.

Muir, E 1936. *Scott and Scotland* London, Routedge

National Trust for Scotland 2004. *Property Statement for Ben Lawers* Unpublished property statement

Oerlemans, O 2002. *Romanticism and the Materiality of Nature* Toronto, University of Toronto Press

Olivier, L 2004. The past of the present. Archaeological memory and time *Archaeological Dialogues* **10(2)** 204-213

Olwig, K.R 2005. Liminality, Seasonality and Landscape *Landscape Research* **30(2)** 259-271

Olwig, K.R 2002 *Landscape, Nature and the Body Politic* Wisconsin, University Press

Onwuegbuzie, W & Leech, L 2005. On becoming a pragmatic researcher: the importance of combining quantitative and qualitative research methodologies *International Journal of Social Research Methodology* **8(5)** 375-387

O'Rourke, E 2005. Landscape planning and community participation: Local lessons from Mullaghmore, the Burren National Park, Ireland *Landscape Research* **30(4)** 483-500

Palang, H, Fry ,G Jauhiainen, J Jones, M & Soovali, H 2005. Editorial: Landscape and Seasonality – Seasonal Landscapes *Landscape Research* **30 (2)** 165-172

Palmer, C 2005. An Ethnography of Englishness, Experiencing Identity through Tourism *Annals of Tourism Research* **32(1)** 7-27

Paterson, A 2002. *Scotland's Landscape: Endangered icon* Edinburgh, Edinburgh University Press

Perez, J 2002. Ascertaining Landscape Perceptions and Preferences with Pair-wise Photographs: planning rural tourism in Extremadura, Spain *Landscape Research,* **27(3)**, 297–308,

Philip, L.J 1998. Combining quantitative and qualitative approaches to social research in Human Geography – an impossible mix? *Environment and Planning A* **30** 261-76

Phillips, M 2001. Restructuring social imaginings in rural geography *Joural of Rural Studies* **14(2)** 121-153

Philo, C 1992. Neglected rural geographies: a review *Journal of Rural Studies* **8(2)** 193-207

Piore, R 2001. The Background to the European Landscape Convention p31-37 in Macinnes, L & Kelly, R (ed) *The Cultural Landscape* ICOMOS, UK

Pratt, A. C 1996. Discourses of Rurality: Loose Talk or Social Struggle? *Journal of Rural Studies* **12(1)** 69-78

Prebble, J 1971. *The Lion in the North* London, Secker and Walberg

Prentice, R & Guerin, S 1998. The Romantic Walker? A case study of users of iconic Scottish Landscape *Scottish Geographical Magazine* **114(3)** 180-191

Preucel, R & Hodder, I 1996. Representations and Antirepresentations, P 519-530 in Preucel, R & Hodder, I (eds) *Contemporary Archaeology in Theory: a reader* Oxford, Blackwells

Proshansky, H.M, Fabian, A.K and Kaminoff, R 1983. Place identity: Physical world socialisation of the self' *Journal of Environmental Psychology* **3** 57-83

Reed, 1980. *Sir Walter Scott: Landscape and Locality* London, The Athone Press

Reser, J. P & Bentrupperbäumer J. M 2005. What and where are environmental values? Assessing the impacts of current diversity of use of environment and World Heritage Values *Journal of Environmental Psychology* **25** 125-146

Robertson, Walford, R & Fox A 2003. Landscape meanings and personal identities: Some perspectives of East Anglian Schoolchildren *International research into Geographical and Environmental Education* **12(1)** 46-53

Robertson, M 2000. Young people speak about the landscape *Geography* **85(1)** 24-36

Rose, G 2000. *Visual Methodologies* London, Sage

Rye, J .F 2006. Rural youth's images of the rural *Journal of Rural Studies* **22** 409-421

Ryen, A 2004. Ethical issues p230-247 in Seale, C Godo, G Gubrium, J & Silverman (eds) *Qualitative Research Practice* London, Sage

Sang, N & Birnie, R 2007. Spatial Sampling and Public Opinion in Environmental Management: a case study of the Ythan catchment *Landuse Policy* in press

Sauer, C 1925. The Morphology of Landscape. In Leighly, J *Land and Life: a selection from the writings of Carl Sauer* Berkeley, University of California Press

Schama, S 1996. *Landscape and Memory* London, Fontana Press

Schlapfer 2008. Contingent Valuation; a New Perspective *Ecological Economics* **64** 729-740

Scott, A & Shannon, P 2007 Local landscape designations in Scotland: Opportunity or barrier to effective landscape management *Landscape and Urban Planning* in press

Scottish Executive 2005. *The Rural Stewardship Scheme* http://www.scotland.gov.uk/library5/rural/rss1.pdf accessed 31/3/06

Scottish Hydro Electric 2007 *Power from the Glens* Scottish and Southern Energy

Seamon, D & Mugerauer, R 1989. *Dwelling, Place and Environment towards a phenomenology of person and world* New York, Columbia University Press

Searle, C Godo, G Gubrium, J & Silverman, D 2004. Introduction: inside qualitative research pp1-14 in Seale, C Godo, G Gubrium, J & Silverman (eds) *Qualitative Research Practice* London, Sage

Semple, E 1911. *The Influences of Geographic Environment* London

Shaw, I & Jameson, R 2002. *A Dictionary of Archaeology* Oxford, Blackwell

Shaw-Taylor, L 2001. 'Parliamentary Enclosure and the Emergence of an English Agricultural Proletariat', *Journal of Economic History* **61(3)** 640-662

Simmons, I. G 1993. *Interpreting Nature: Cultural Constructions of the Environment*

Smout, T.C. 2005. Landseer's Highlands p 13-18 in Ormond, R (ed) *The Monarch of the Glen: Landseer in the Highlands* Edinburgh, National Galleries of Scotland.

SNH 1999. *National Parks for Scotland: Scottish Natural Heritage's advice to government* Perth, SNH

SNH 2000. *Policy Summary: National Scenic Areas* http://www.snh.org.uk accessed 16/3/06

SNH 2003. *Scotland's Future Landscapes? Encouraging a wider debate* a discussion paper from Scottish Natural Heritage

SNH & HS 2005. *Guidance on Local Landscape Designations* Perth: SNH

Soliva, R 2007. Landscape stories: using ideal type narratives as a heuristic device in rural studies *Journal of Rural Studies* **23** 62-74

Soulsby, J.A 1993. Rural geography and the Central Highlands in the 18th century: a singular view In Dawson, A, Jones, H, Small, A, Soulsby, J (eds) *Scottish Geographical Studies* Geography departments of St Andrews & Glasgow

Stedman, R 2002. Toward a social psychology of place *Environment and Behaviour* **34(5)** 561-581

Stedman, R 2003 Sense of place and forest science: toward a programme of quantitative research *Forest Science* **49(6)** 822-829

Stedman, R.C 2003 Is it really just a social construct? The contribution of the physical environment to sense of place *Society and Natural resources* **16** 671-685

Stephenson, J 2005. *A language for Landscape: a framework for understanding values in landscapes* Precirculated paper presented to the 10th UNESCO Universities Heritage Forum, Newcastle April 2005

Stewart, M 2000. *Loch Tay it's woods and it's people* Edinburgh, Scottish Native Woods

Strang, V 1999. Competing perceptions of landscape in Kowanyama, North Queensland. P206-217 in Ucko, P. J & Layton, R *The Archaeology and Anthropology of Landscape* London, Routledge

Tarnas, R 1991. *The Passion of the Western Mind* London, Pilmco

Těšitel, J Kušovà, D & Bartoš, M 2003. Tourists' Reasons for Visiting Mountain Areas: a case study of the Šumava Mountains *Landscape Research* **28(3)** 317-322

Thompson, M 1979. *Rubbish Theory: The creation and destruction of value* Oxford: OUP

Tilley, C 1994. *A Phenomenology of Landscape* Berg, Oxford

Tilley, C 2002. Metaphor, Materiality & Interpretation p23-55 in Buchli, V (ed) *The Material Culture Reader* Oxford, Berg

Tilley, C 2006. Identity, Place, Landscape and Heritage *Journal of Material Culture* **11(1/2)** 7-32

Tipping, R, Edmonds, M and Sheridan, I 1993. Paleoenvironmental investigations directly associated with the Neolithic axe 'quarry' on Beinn Lawers, near Killin, Perthshire *New Phytologist* **123** 585-597

Thomas, J 1999. *Time, Culture and Identity* London, Routledge

Thomas, J 1999. *Understanding the Neolithic* London, Routledge

Thompson, M. 1979. *Rubbish Theory: the creation and destruction of value.* Oxford, Clarendon Press.

Treagus, J.E 2003. The Loch Tay Fault: type section geometry and kinematics *Scottish Journal of Geology* **39(2)** pp. 135-144

Tress, B Tress, G & Fry G Researchers' Experiences, Positive and Negative, in Integrative Landscape Projects *Environmental Management* **36(6)** 792-807

Trevor-Roper, H 1983. The invention of tradition: the highland tradition of Scotland p15 – 41 in Hobsbaum, E & Ranger, T 1983. *The Invention of Tradition* Cambridge, Cambridge University Press

Trigger, B 1990. *A History of Archaeological Thought* Cambridge, Cambridge University Press

Tuan, Y. F 1977. *Space and Place: The perspective of experience* Minneapolis: University of Minnesota Press.

Ucko, P.J 1999 Introduction: gazing on the landscape and encountering the environment. In Ucko, P. J & Layton, R *The Archaeology and Anthropology of Landscape* London, Routledge

UNESCO 2006. World Heritage List http://whc.unesco.org/en/list/ accessed 20/3/06

University of Newcastle (2002) Visual Assessment of Wind farms Best Practice. *Scottish Natural Heritage Commissioned Report* F01AA303A.

Venkatachalam, L 2004. The Contingent Valuation Method: a Review *Environmental Impact Assessment Review* **24(1)** 89-124

Ward Thompson, C Aspinall, P, Bell, S & Findlay, C 2005. "It gets away from Everyday Life": Local Woodlands and Community Use – What makes a difference? *Landscape Research* **30(1)** 109-146

Wallwork, J & Dixon, J. A 2004. Foxes, green fields & Britishness: on the rhetorical consumption of place and national identity *British J. Soc. Psych.* **43** 21-39

Whyte, I & K 1991. *The changing Scottish Landscape 1500-1800.* London, Routledge

Williams, D. R. & Vaske, J. J 2003. The measurement of place attachment: Validity and generalisability of a psychometric approach *Journal of Forest Sciences* **49(6)** 830-840

Williamson, T 1995. *Polite Landscapes* London, Sutton

Williamson, T 2002. *The transformation of Rural England* Exeter, University Press

Willis, K.G. & Garrod G. D. 1993. Valuing Landscape: a contingent valuation approach *J. Env. Management* **4** 1-22

Willis, K G, Garrod, G.D, Benson, J.F & Carter, M 1996. Benefits and costs of the wildlife enhancement scheme: A case study of the Pevensey levels *Journal of Environmental Planning and Management* 39(3) 387-401

Winchester, H Kong, L & Dunn, K 2003. *Landscapes: ways of imagining the world* Harlow, Pearson Prentice Hall

Withers, C 1983. Geography of Language: Gaelic-Speaking in Perthshire, 1698-1879 *Transactions of the Institute of British Geographers* New Series 8(2) 125-142

Withers, C. W. J 1993. Picturing Highland Landscapes: George Washington Wilson and the photography of the Scottish Highlands in the 19th century. In Dawson, A, Jones, H, Small, A, Soulsby, J (eds) *Scottish Geographical Studies* Geography departments of St Andrews & Glasgow

Wolsink, M 2006. Invalid theory impedes our understanding: a critique on the persistence of the NIMBY *Trans, Inst Br Geogr* **NS 31** 85-91

Womack, P 1989. From Improvement to Romance: Construction of the myth of the Highlands Macmillan Press, Basingstoke.

Wooley, H 2006. Freedom of the City: Contemporary Issues and Policy Influences on Children and Young People's Use of Public Open Space in England *Children's geographies* **4(1) 45-59**

Yarwood, R 2005. Beyond the Rural Idyll: images, countryside change and geography *Geography* **90(1)** 19-31

Yamashita, S 2002. Perception of water in the Landscape: use of photo-projective method to compare child and adult residents' perceptions of a Japanese river environment *Landscape and Urban Planning* **62** 3-17

Young, L & Barrett, H 2001. Adapting visual methods: action research with Kampala street children *Area* **33.2** 141-152

Internet References

Royal Commission on the Ancient and Historic Monuments of Scotland – pastmap service http://www.rcahms.gov.uk

Loch Lomond and the Trossachs National Park 2005 National Park Plan 2005 Consultative report http://www.lochlomond-trossachs.org/park/

Beauly Denny Public Enquiry http://www.beaulydenny.co.uk

Scottish Tourism Statistics 2006 http://www.scotexchange.net/tourism_in_scotland_2006_national.pdf

Scottish Executive 2000. Rural Scotland A New Approach http://www.scotland.gov.uk/library2/doc15/rsna-11.asp

Scottish Executive 2006 Planning etc (Scotland) act

http://www.opsi.gov.uk/legislation/scotland/acts2006/pdf/asp_20060017_en.pdf

www.ingramcontent.com/pod-product-compliance
Lightning Source LLC
Chambersburg PA
CBHW061006030426

42334CB00033B/3376

9 781407 306285